WHITE HOUSE ETHICS

WHITE HOUSE ETHICS

The History of the Politics of Conflict of Interest Regulation

Robert N. Roberts

Contributions in Political Science,
Number 204

GREENWOOD PRESS
New York • Westport, Connecticut • London

Library of Congress Cataloging-in-Publication Data

Roberts, Robert North.
  White House ethics : the history of the politics of conflict of
interest regulation / Robert N. Roberts.
      p.   cm. — (Contributions in political science, ISSN 0147–1066;
no. 204)
    Bibliography: p.
    Includes index.
    ISBN 0-313-25934-8 (lib. bdg. : alk. paper)
    1. Conflict of interests—United States—History.   2. United
States—Officials and employees—Selection and appointment—History.
3. Government executives—United States—Selection and appointment—
History.   4. Cabinet Officers—United States—Selection and
appointment—History.   I. Title.   II. Series.
KF4568.R63 1988
342.73'088—dc19
[347.30288]   87–24962

British Library Cataloguing in Publication Data is available.

Library of Congress Catalog Card Number: 87–24962
ISBN: 0–313–25934–8
ISSN: 0147–1066

First published in 1988

Greenwood Press, Inc.
88 Post Road West, Westport, Connecticut 06881

Printed in the United States of America

The paper used in this book complies with the
Permanent Paper Standard issued by the National
Information Standards Organization (Z39.48–1984).

10 9 8 7 6 5 4 3 2 1

Contents

Preface

This book presents a chronological history of the evolution of the system for regulating conflicts of interest involving employees and officials of the executive branch and the role played by the White House in developing and implementing conflict of interest policy. It is the main theme of this book that efforts to deal with the conflict of interest problem have failed because of a general lack of understanding of how the system developed and as the result of continuing disagreement over what constitutes a prohibited conflict of interest under current rules and regulations.

Besides the debate over sanctions, the recent experience of the Reagan Administration has again demonstrated the serious problem of applying broad restrictions on various types of conflicts of interest without further hampering the ability of a president and agencies and departments to recruit and retain individuals for high-level government positions. Congress and President Carter believed that the Ethics in Government Act with its provisions for the appointment of special prosecutors, public financial disclosure for top officials, tighter restrictions on lobbying by former officials, and the establishment of the Office of Government Ethics would help to assure swift action against high-level officials who broke the law. But nearly ten years after the passage of the Ethics Act, the constitutionality of the independent counsel provision remains in doubt and critics of the Office of Government Ethics argue that it often refuses to vigorously pursue allegations of wrongdoing leveled against high-level officials.

It is hoped that this history of the evolution of the system for dealing with conflicts of interest at the federal level will increase general understanding of the subject of conflict of interest regulation and of some of the reasons why conflict of interest problems recur from administration to administration.

Acknowledgments

I would like to express my sincere appreciation to a number of individuals and organizations who supported the research and writing of this book, especially Dr. James D. Carroll of the Brookings Institution and Professor David Rosenbloom of Syracuse University who provided early support for this research.

The United States Office of Government Ethics funded the early research for this book during 1979 and 1980. This book would not have been possible without the cooperation of J. Jackson Walter and David H. Martin who both served as Directors of the Office of Government Ethics. I would like to express thanks to the staff of the Office of Government Ethics who helped this author understand the complexities of modern conflict of interest regulation. Robert Flyn, Gary Davis, Jack Covaleski, Norman Smith, Lawrence Garrett III, and Jane Ley deserve particular thanks for the assistance they rendered from 1979 to the present.

I dedicate this book to my wife, Deborah, and to my children, William and Caitlin.

WHITE HOUSE ETHICS

Introduction

PROTECTING THE PUBLIC TRUST: THE POLITICS OF CONFLICT OF INTEREST REGULATION

The Reagan presidency began with more than cautious optimism. Ronald Reagan's 1980 landslide brought the Republican Party control of the Senate for the first time in nearly thirty years. The president quickly converted his electoral and popular mandate into ideological control of the Democratic House of Representatives. Masterful use of the media and effective congressional lobbying belied the prediction that a political victory could not be transformed into workable programs. With surprising ease the president mobilized the necessary forces to pass a budget with sharp reductions in the growth of domestic spending, a massive increase in defense spending, and a three-year tax cut. The 1984 landslide affirmed Ronald Reagan's place as the most popular president to serve a second term since Franklin Roosevelt. Not until the controversy over the shipment of arms to Iran and the use of profits from that sale to fund the operations of the Nicaraguan rebels did the popularity of the president wane.

The Reagan presidency has not escaped accusations concerning appearances of impropriety by members and former members of the Reagan team.[1] The majority of these misconduct cases have ended with the official being cleared of possible violations of criminal law and executive branch standards-of-conduct regulations. Nevertheless, critics of the Reagan administration's ethics record maintain that the president and his associates have done little to assure that top appointees adhere to the highest standards of official integrity in order to avoid even the appearance of impropriety with respect to their official duties. These critics maintain that many Reagan appointees have had difficulty separating their private from their public lives.[2]

Laws against bribery of public officials and the misuse of government property can be traced back to the beginning of the nation's history. However, as the power of the national government grew during the nineteenth century, so did concern that these restrictions were not enough to protect the public purse strings from individuals within and outside the government who were intent on obtaining favorable treatment for themselves or their private clients.

The effort to tighten controls has continued well into the twentieth century. Recent years have seen the proliferation of public financial disclosure requirements, tighter restrictions on the acceptance of gifts by public employees, and increased efforts to stop the "revolving door"—a practice allowing former government employees to work for organizations competing for government contracts or subject to heavy government regulation and allowing the government to hire individuals coming from heavily regulated industries.[3]

Our increased preoccupation with appearances of impropriety by public officials is, in large measure, the result of the massive growth of government. With a national budget approaching one trillion dollars and a national debt exceeding two trillion, no system of audits and checks can assure that officials will not use their public positions to further their own financial interests, assist members of their families or friends, enhance their career opportunities after they leave government, or push for the public acceptance of ideological agendas. Since the scale of the national government is unlikely to change in future decades, conflict of interest problems are bound to plague future presidential administrations as they have plagued the Reagan White House.

The controversial nature of modern efforts to manage official propriety has created the present sharp difference of opinion on whether attempts over the last four decades to legislate ethics in government have worked to protect the public trust or to deter talented citizens from public service.[4]

THE EVOLUTION OF A SYSTEM

Most misconduct cases involving presidential appointees since the end of the Second World War, it should be noted, have involved allegations of conflicts of interests and appearances of using public positions to further private interest. They have not involved instances of outright theft, graft, or bribery. Therefore, before addressing the question of how a president and Congress might improve the program for preventing and dealing with conflicts of interest, we need to understand the history of the program we now have.

The formal executive-branch system for regulating conflicts of interest and the appearance of conflicts has evolved over a period of 130 years. Originally it consisted of a few Civil War Era statutes related to procurement. Now it consists of a complex set of statutory and administrative prohibitions and procedures applicable to all levels of federal personnel, and particularly to high-level presidential appointees.

The unparalleled growth of the national government with its greatly increased economic responsibilities affected the evolution of our conflict of interest integrity problem. Within generations, the young republic had pushed across a treacherous wilderness, threaded through impassable mountains, and survived burning deserts to establish the territorial boundaries of the new country and to seize the immeasurable riches of an open frontier. Within decades, it had crisscrossed the continent with railways, spawned teeming cities, fired belching steel mills, and most of all, discovered ways to accumulate wealth that would have been unimaginable to Benjamin Franklin. Within a short time, the wealth of this nation was funneled into multimillion dollar corporations, forced inevitably into a symbiotic partnership with government by the fear that excessive private power could threaten the fabric of the republic.

Government needed "big business"—its financial wizardry, its managerial experience, and its technical skill—to transform an agrarian country into the greatest industrial nation of the world. Two World Wars convinced the nation that its survival depended on maintaining a strong industrial and technical base. Big business needed Government as well—its power was required to mobilize the nation's resources and to undertake projects impossible for a single corporation to pursue.

As the industrial revolution led to the growth of great private power centers, however, scandals of wartime profiteering, allegations of preferential treatment for private business, and concern over the lobbying activities of special-interest groups led to demands for greater regulation and supervision of the private sector to protect the public interest. Congresses and presidents found it increasingly difficult to counter the logic that additional measures were necessary to prevent private economic interests from exercising too much influence over government decision makers.

Prompted by the crisis politics of the Depression Era, government moved into every segment of domestic life. Agencies multiplied; entitlements and social programs proliferated. Federal offices came alive with a myriad of lawyers, consultants, accountants, project directors, and policy analysts, for enormous funds had to be dispensed and numberless benefit programs administered. After the Second World War, the United States found itself in the position of indefinitely maintaining a large standing army, spending billions of dollars annually to protect not only this country but also its allies around the world. In a word, a bureaucracy became a behemoth that needed watching.

Because battles over public policy would be fought increasingly in the halls of federal agencies and departments, it would become much more important to find ways to influence key decision makers in order to get them to accept a particular point of view or perspective. The growth of big business and big government presented problems for those concerned with protecting public confidence in the fairness and objectivity of government decision making. The motives of those vested with vast discretionary authority will always be subject to doubt; the temptation to use such authority for personal gain will always seem irresistible. With so much at stake, private interests might always use their influence with government decision makers to gain preferential treatment.

A final factor, the double-edged impact of the mass media on politics, helps to explain the post-Watergate preoccupation with official ethics. News stories on allegations of official misconduct, on suspicious self-dealing, and on appearances of conflicts of interest reinforce the public's skepticism about the ethics of public officials. The media observe the old adage that where there is smoke, there is fire in conflict of interest allegations involving government personnel. Furthermore, the eagerness of both political parties to use any suggestion of scandal to discredit their opponents and attract voter support compounds the problem.

If a moral stance gives ammunition to political parties and helps to win elections, persistent media exposure has made it more difficult to recruit competent and experienced citizens for government service, particularly for top appointive positions. It is not the relatively low executive salaries and the disruption to career and family alone that make qualified executives reluctant to serve the government; it is the unwillingness to subject themselves and their families to the glass-house atmosphere of national politics.

A study of the evolution of the present executive-branch system for preventing conflicts of interest will reveal the role played by these factors. More important, it may also show that the current system of propriety management has done little to assure long-term public confidence in the integrity of public officials.

A Problem of Definition

A problem of definition has long hampered legislative efforts to control conflicts of interests and appearances of impropriety. The phrase "conflict of interest regulation" has come to mean many things to many people, groups, and special interests. As a result, the objectives of conflict of interest regulation remain unclear.[5]

In a broad sense, conflict of interest regulation in the federal service rests on the concept that a public employee should not engage in any activity that might give the appearance of using an official position for personal advantage. Conflict of interest regulation is the "regulation of evil before the event; it is regulation against potential harm."[6] It assumes that the appearance of a conflicting interest poses a serious enough threat to objective decision making and public confidence in that objectivity to warrant a prohibition on conduct that might create a conflict of interest or the appearance thereof.[7] In other words, public employees and officials must be above suspicion with respect to the motives for actions they take in their positions as public servants.

Conflicts of Interest and Presidential Government

Although Congress enacted the first substantive conflict of interest prohibitions during the mid-nineteenth century, it was not until the close of the Second World War that conflict of interest matters dramatically affected the American presidency. Since that time, the White House has had to pay much closer attention to the private affairs of nominees and to their conduct in office in order to guard against appearances that the actions of these top decision makers might be shaped by factors other than the public interest. It is this focus on top political appointees that has shaped conflict of interest management since the Second World War. Although relatively few of the close to three million federal employees are implicated in misconduct scandals, charges of official impropriety against any high-level presidential appointee are certain to discredit the president. As long as the national government dominates domestic and international affairs, this situation is likely to continue.

When Congress enacted the Ethics in Government Act of 1978 (largely in response to Watergate), supporters believed that the reforms would solve the problems of public integrity and conflict of interest once and for all. These reforms clearly have not done so. They have significantly increased the chances that allegations of misconduct will become subjects of formal investigations. Before Congress rushes into a new round of reforms brought about by the scandals of the Reagan presidency, however, it might be well to review how the United States got to the present state of conflict of interest control.

NOTES

1. Thomas Riehle, "Scandals, Etc. from A to Z," *National Journal,* January 14, 1984, pp. 92–93. For critical profiles of 100 key political appointees of Ronald Reagan's first term, *see* Ronald Brownstein and Nina Easton, *Reagan's Top 100 Officials* (Washington, D.C.: Presidential Accountability Project, 1982).

2. David Wise, "Why the President's Men Stumble," *New York Times Magazine* (July 18, 1982): 14–17, 44, 46.

3. Common Cause, *Serving Two Masters: A Common Cause Study of Conflicts of Interest in the Executive Branch* (Washington, D.C.: October, 1976); William J. Lanouttee, "The Revolving Door—It's Tricky to Stop It," *National Journal* 9 (November 9, 1977): 1796–1803.

4. *See* Bayless Manning, "The Purity Potlatch: An Essay on Conflicts of Interest, American Government, and Moral Escalation," in *The Federal Bar Journal* 24 (Summer 1964): 243.

5. Report of the Association of the Bar of the City of New York, *Conflict of Interest and Federal Service* (Cambridge, Mass.: Harvard University Press, 1960), p. 19.

6. Manning, "The Purity Potlatch," p. 243.

7. Lloyd N. J. Cutler, "Conflicts of Interest," *Emory Law Journal* v. 30 (Fall, 1981): 1015–34.

I

The Antecedents

Modern executive-branch conflict of interest regulation has two primary goals: to prevent the use of public office for personal gain and to maintain public confidence in the integrity and objectivity of decision making in executive-branch agencies and departments. The roots of this regulatory system were firmly planted in early American history and shaped by American attitudes toward public service.[1]

THE EARLY YEARS, 1789–1861

The history of American public service in the early nineteenth century gives little indication that government officials considered conflicts of interest a significant management problem. In fact, up to the election of Andrew Jackson in 1828, the federal service was notably free from scandals.[2] For one thing, "fitness of character," the primary qualification for appointment to George Washington's administration, was tied closely to social status.[3] The elitist background of early federal employees seemed to reduce the temptation to use public office for personal gain. For another thing, over the terms of the first six presidents, most federal employees enjoyed a good deal of job security.[4]

An additional reason is the fact that during the first three or four decades of presidential history, the federal bureaucracy consisted mainly of clerks performing routine tasks like collecting taxes, supervising customs, and operating the postal system.[5] Such tasks might have presented some opportunity for employee theft, but they did not place most employees in a position to influence any decision making that might enhance an outside financial interest or improve the employee's chances of obtaining lucrative employment outside government. In other words, since "citizens had little to ask of the federal government, and the White House had few favors to distribute," the smallness of the federal bureaucracy reduced incentives for official misconduct.[6]

The Spoils System and the Decline of Public Service Ethics

The election of Andrew Jackson in 1828 led to the increased use of political affiliation as a criterion for federal employment. If the spoils system, as this practice was termed, arguably created a more democratic federal service, it also contributed to a decline in public service ethics. Many national figures blamed the spoils system for the erosion of standards of conduct. In 1829, for example, Henry Clay wrote:

Incumbents, feeling the instability of their situation and knowing their liability to periodic removals, at short terms, without regard to the manner in which they have executed their trust, will be disposed to make the most of their uncertain offices while they have them, and hence we may expect immediate cases of fraud, predation and corruption.[7]

Appointments came to be regarded as proper payment for partisan service, not as long-term career opportunities, and as attitudes about public service changed, prospects for public graft multiplied. These included increased federal funding for public works, transportation projects, and the sale of public lands. Significant amounts of money could be made by officials putting their private interests before the responsibilities of their office.

In 1835, for example, the Senate Committee on Public Land reported instances of unlawful collusion between land speculators and federal land agents in field offices.[8] Probably the most sensational case of unethical conduct by a federal official involved Samuel Swartwout, the chief customs officer for the Port of New York from 1829 to 1838. After he fled to England, an audit determined that during his eight years in office he had stolen $1,225,705.67.[9]

This deterioration of traditional standards did not go unnoticed. For example, Amos Kendall, postmaster general from 1829 to 1840, issued a strict code of conduct for postal employees. Kendall admonished his clerks that "the practice of rigid morality by those engaged in public business" is essential to protect the reputation of the government. Kendall's Code of Official Ethics included a long list of rules governing work habits, office conduct, the use of government property, and personal morals. For instance, the code specifically prohibited postal clerks and members of their family from accepting "any present or gratuity . . . from any person who has business with the office."[10]

Claims Agents and Official Misconduct

At the close of the Revolutionary War, Congress established itself as the branch of government responsible for hearing and resolving claims against the federal government. After 1830, those who had suffered damage to property during the Revolutionary War or the Mexican War of 1846, or who believed they were entitled to pensions because of the military service, flooded Congress with claims for monetary relief.[11] Although Congress delegated some jurisdiction over claims to the Treasury Department and other federal agencies, not until the creation of the court of claims in 1865 did Congress attempt to bring some order to the system.[12]

Because of the time and distances involved in traveling to the nation's capital, few claimants could go to Washington to prosecute their own claims. Instead, they typically obtained the assistance of an influential friend or hired an agent to press their claims "with supporting affidavits and whatever additional documentation was available."[13] Members of Congress and former government officials set up offices to prosecute claims before Congress, the Treasury, and other departments, openly advertising that they had the contacts to help expedite claims.[14] Congressional committees were not judicial bodies, however, and more often than not they lacked the time or expertise to conduct thorough investigations of the merits of claims.

This practice, it was argued by critics, clearly permitted "fraudulent, exorbitant, or unjust claims to be presented."[15] By the early 1850s, enough pressure had grown to require that something be done about the fraudulent prosecutions of claims and particularly about the involvement of government officers and employees.

The controversy over the prosecution of claims intensified in 1850, when conflict of interest charges were made against members of the administration of Zachary Taylor. The main scandal involved a pre-Revolutionary claim of George Galphin, a former Georgia Indian trader, who argued that the British government owed him some $43,000 which was uncollectable because of the war. After years of lobbying, the Galphin family got Congress to pass a bill ordering the secretary of the Treasury to settle the claim. Although Secretary of the Treasury William Morris Meredith agreed to pay the principal, he refused to pay the interest, a sum in the hundreds of thousands of dollars. Attorney General Reverdy Johnson disagreed with Meredith's decision, however, and ordered the payment of both principal and interest, which amounted to $235,000.[16]

The ruling of the attorney general did not end the controversy. Critics of the decision learned that President Taylor's secretary of war, George W. Crawford, had received $95,000 for representing the Galphin claim before he took office. They wondered whether Crawford might have influenced the decisions of Meredith and Johnson. A subsequent House investigation determined that the entire claim was unjust, that the law compelled the payment of principal, and that Meredith's payment of the interest was unauthorized.[17] At the same time, the House investigation found no evidence that Crawford had used his position to influence Johnson and Meredith, and that all evidence indicated that they had no knowledge of Crawford's interest in the prosecution of the claim. As one author wrote, however, "This was merely the smoke of a fire which was to flare up in the 1850's."[18]

It was public reaction to a claim brought before the Mexican War Claims Commission that forced legislative action in 1853. The treaty of Guadalupe Hidalgo, which was signed at the close of the Mexican War, authorized the expenditure of $3,250,000 to compensate parties who suffered damages from the war.[19] A Dr. Gardiner submitted a claim for losses resulting from the destruction of his silver mine. Senator Thomas Corwin of Ohio served as the claimant's attorney before the commission.

By the time the claim was found fraudulent, Senator Corwin had resigned from the Senate to become secretary of the Treasury in the Administration of Millard Fillmore. A subsequent investigation cleared Secretary Corwin of charges that he had knowingly prosecuted the fraudulent claim and also determined that he had sold his interest in the claim prior to becoming secretary of Treasury.[20]

Nevertheless, disclosure of the fraudulent nature of the claim and of Senator Corwin's involvement caused an uproar in Congress and the press. Shortly after completing its investigation, the committee appointed to inquire into the Gardiner claim reported (passed) out a bill to prevent frauds upon the Treasury of the United States. In a January 6, 1853, speech before the House, Congressman Preston King of New York explained that the legislation was aimed to prevent frauds against the Treasury and to stop what he believed to be groundless imputations against Congress.[21] During the January 1853 debate over the enactment of the reform legislation, Congressman King argued that such conduct raised serious questions regarding the integrity of public officials:

Some cases which have attracted the public attention by the large amount of the fee paid by the claimant have excited—perhaps I should say justly excited—suspicion that the official and personal influence of the officer, as well as the legal skill of counsel, was sought by the claimant. This certainly no person would justify. The integrity of our public men should be free from suspicion and imputations that cannot fail to grow out of such a practice.[22]

During the same debate, while arguing for passage of the legislation, Congressman Andrew Johnson labelled the practices of members of Congress prosecuting claims before Congress a clear conflict of interest. Johnson recognized that lawyer members of Congress did not give up their right to practice their craft merely because they had been elected to Congress, yet he saw an inherent conflict between serving as a representative or senator and acting as the spokesperson for private citizens seeking payments from the Treasury. Representatives would find it very difficult to be "guardians of the Treasury," while representing the interests of private parties.

Congressman Johnson drove home this point:

We find that interest and prejudice are so closely blended that they cannot be separated in matters of this sort.... Then we immediately see the impropriety of members of Congress acting as agents.... They cannot protect the interests of the people in their capacity of Representatives, and at the same time prosecute a claim against this Government. It is a conflict of interest and duty which cannot be reconciled. [Italics mine][23]

The object of the bill, as Johnson summed it up, was "to prohibit what is considered in one sense politically wrong, and to carry out what is morally right."[24]

As enacted on February 26, 1853, the law prohibited members of Congress and federal government employees from receiving anything of value for assisting private parties to prosecute claims against the United States or aiding in the prosecution of a claim. Moreover, it prohibited government employees from assisting in the prosecution of claims even though the employee received no compensation for the assistance. By limiting the second provision only to government officers and employees, Congress, it seems, did not want to prevent members of Congress from assisting constituents without compensation.[25] (For reasons impossible to determine, in its 1874 revision of the laws of the United States, Congress deleted the provision of the 1853 statute that applied to members of Congress.)

Congress enacted this claims representation prohibition primarily to prevent the reputation of Congress and federal agencies from being damaged by their members and employees who received government salaries and at the same time earned money to prosecute claims against the United States. As a later review of the legislation concluded, the statute reflected a belief that a conflict of interest exists when a member of Congress or a government employee tries at the same time to "faithfully protect the interests of the Government" and "represent adequately the interests of a client demanding some action by the Government."[26] The legislation also reflected the belief that government insiders could use their positions to obtain payment on claims without merit.

The 1853 statute was more a symbolic than a serious effort to control paid lobbying by members of Congress and government employees because it covered only the very narrow area of government claims. However, as federal expenditures increased over succeeding decades, so would concern that government employees and former officials were using their positions and knowledge of government to further their own financial interests.

Two years after the passage of the first conflict of interest statute, Congress passed the Court of Claims Act. Because the act gave the three-judge court only advisory power, Congress remained deeply involved in the resolution of claims against the United States. If a claimant lost in the Court of Claims, he could appeal the decision to Congress. If he won, he still had to get Congress to appropriate money to pay the award. With the advent of the Civil War, a whole new round of claims again directed national attention to conflict of interest problems.[27]

THE CIVIL WAR AND CONFLICTS OF INTEREST

Between 1861 and 1865, Congress enacted other conflict-of-interest-related statutes to reassure a skeptical public that government officials and individuals with special access to government officials were not reaping windfall profits by supplying the Union Army or by having fraudulent or improper war-related claims paid by the Treasury.

Civil War historians have well documented the large-scale corruption associated with the provisioning of the Union Army.[28] "Whether it was a matter of uniforms, food, horses, guns, or munitions," writes one historian, "the services were made to suffer while ill-gotten wealth was gathered by shameless profiteers."[29] High-level military personnel profited from arranging procurement contracts for private suppliers, and unscrupulous agents made fortunes on the sale of war supplies to the War Department. Historians have deservedly placed much of the blame on the "horde of government-paid officials who, either through criminal negligence or criminal collusion, permitted or encouraged this robbing of the government treasury and cruelty to the American soldiers."[30]

Although it is difficult to point to a single case as causing renewed calls for further conflict of interest regulations, the Hall-Carbine Affair had much to do with mobilizing support for legislative action. In a confusing series of events beginning in early 1861, the War Department ended up buying back for $22.50 each thousands of weapons that Secretary of War Simon Cameron had approved to be sold to private dealers for $3.50 a piece because they were defective. Charges were made that government officials might have profited from these transactions.[31]

The Hall-Carbine Affair and other reports of corrupt purchasing practices led to the appointment of the Van Wyck Special Congressional Committee to investigate the scope of the problem. The committee's 2,500-page final report condemned the procurement practices of the Department of War and forced President Lincoln to dismiss Cameron and to appoint Edwin M. Stanton, as the new Secretary.[32]

In July 1862, Congress took a number of steps to deal with increasingly sharp public criticism of the procurement system. First, it prohibited the subletting of contracts, required notification of the letting of all contracts, and declared that cases of procurement fraud would be tried by court martial under military law.[33] Second, Congress required that all contracts let by the War, Navy, and Interior Departments be accompanied by an affidavit attesting that the contract was let "fairly without benefit or advantage [to the person issuing the contract], or allowing any such benefit or advantage corruptly to the other party."[34] A short time after its passage, however, the affidavit requirement was repealed because of administrative problems.

In addition to these procurement reforms, Congress passed the second major conflict of interest law, "An Act to Prevent Members of Congress and Officers of the Government of the United States from Taking Consideration for Procuring Contracts, Office or Place from the United States."[35] The law made it a criminal violation for a government official or a member of Congress to accept any compensation for aiding another party in obtaining a contract.[36] Because the 1853 statute had dealt only with the prosecution of claims against the United States, members of Congress and federal employees could legally solicit contracts on a fee for service basis. This second statute thus closed a major loophole.

The 1853 and 1862 in-service with- and without-compensation representation statutes, however, did not deal with the conflict of interest created by government employees making decisions that had a direct impact on their financial well-being. Such conduct, despite the merits of a particular decision, was bound to raise suspicion that the decision was made to benefit the employee.

Apparently intending to solve this self-dealing problem, in February 1863, Congress prohibited federal employees and officials from transacting business with "any bank or other commercial corporation" on behalf of the United States if the transaction might bring pecuniary benefit to the government employee.[37] The law provided for criminal penalties consisting of a fine of not more than two thousand dollars and imprisonment for a term not exceeding two years. Added at the last minute to legislation directed at fraudulent contractors, "the amendment was agreed to without a single word of debate."[38] A 1909 revision of the Federal Penal Code made it clear that Congress intended to apply the provision to any corporation, and not only to "banking or other commercial" institutions.[39]

Despite the fact that few government employees would ever be prosecuted under the 1863 self-dealing measure, it put a reluctant Congress on record as finding something inherently wrong about federal officials participating in negotiations that might bring financial benefits to the employee either directly or indirectly. Even if the official acted without regard to his or her private interests, the appearance of impropriety and self-dealing would still exist. However, not until the Second World War was the definition of self-dealing extended beyond the narrow limitations of government contracts. At that time, Congress passed another conflict of interest measure as part of a much broader effort to head off criticism of self-dealing.

The last of the Civil War Era conflict of interest statutes, passed in June 1864, established a new in-service paid representation prohibition that covered all types of departmental proceedings, not only those proceedings involving claims.[40] Again, congressional debate provides little reason why Congress wanted to extend the in-service paid representation bar beyond claims. Supporters of the statute, it appears, wanted to stop members of Congress and other government officials from representing citizens at court-martial proceedings.

Studies of the Civil War have documented that "military officers, acting under orders from the State and War Departments... [arrested] persons suspected of disloyalty or espionage, and [confined] them without trial in military prisons, for indefinite terms."[41] This practice continued throughout most of the Civil War. In the 1866 case of *ex parte Milligan,* the Supreme Court finally placed severe limitations on this use of military law when it held that the Constitution unmistakably prohibited the trial of civilians in military courts while civilian courts remained open.

Union loyalists apparently pushed the statute through the Congress as a means of checking perceived disloyalty of members of Congress and government officials in defending those arrested for their disloyalty to the Union. The statute, however, did not apply to civilian judicial proceedings. In a subsequent recodification of the representation bar, Congress extended it to all federal judicial proceedings. Public outrage over profiteering and other procurement abuses clearly motivated Congress to enact more conflict of interest statutes.

THE MORAL SLUMP CONTINUES

The decline in national public service ethics did not stop with the end of the Civil War. During the presidency of Ulysses S. Grant (1869–1876), widespread and deep corruption "pervaded every executive department and involved Cabinet members, White House staff, members of the Grant families, and many thought the President himself."[42] Surprisingly, however, the period saw few legislative or administrative efforts to curb the self-aggrandizement of government officials and their associates operating inside and outside the government. One scandal just before the Gold Panic of 1869 involved the apparent attempt by gold speculators to influence federal monetary policy for their own speculative purposes. The scandal raised serious questions about the ethics of President Grant, members of his family, and other high-level officials. The scandal also demonstrated the increasing impact of government policy on the nation's financial markets.

In an attempt to corner the gold market and drive up its price, a group of speculators, including Jay Gould, James Fisk, and one of their associates,

Abel Corbin (who happened to be the husband of President Grant's sister) began making large purchases of gold early in 1869.[43] At a dinner party which included the president and his sister, Mr. Gould tried to find out what the policy of the federal government would be on future gold sales. Large sales of gold by the government would quickly drive down the price of gold and would cost the speculators dearly. Abel Corbin, who had not informed the president of his involvement in the speculative activities of Gould and Fisk, tried to convince President Grant that it would not be in the best interest of the country for the federal government to make large gold sales. However, after a series of events which led to the president learning of Corbin's involvement and caused Grant to write his sister advising that her husband withdraw from the speculative enterprise, the government put four million dollars worth of gold on the market on September 24, 1869. The action drove down the inflated price of gold and ruined many speculators.[44]

A subsequent congressional investigation, arguably biased in favor of President Grant and his administration, found no evidence of misconduct on the part of the president. The investigation, however, revealed that the assistant treasurer of the United States, General David Butterfield, had borrowed $1,500,000 to speculate in gold. He made a small profit of $25,000 for all his efforts. Grant removed Butterfield from office in October of 1869.[45]

The practice of former members of Congress and former government officials going into the business of prosecuting claims against the government also became more pronounced during the 1860s. Congress, however, had steered clear of attempting to limit the activities of former government officials before federal agencies and departments. A series of scandals involving former Grant appointees, however, brought pressure on Congress to consider limitations on the representational activities of former federal officials with respect to federal proceedings.

Early in 1872, James Garfield, congressman from Ohio, proposed an amendment to the Post Office Appropriations Bill making it a misdemeanor for a former government employee to assist in the prosecution of claims before offices in any executive department for two years after leaving the government. Violators of this post–government-service representation prohibition would face a maximum of a year in jail and/or a fine up to $5000.[46]

When the Garfield amendment reached the floor of the Senate in May 1872, opponents of the restriction used the same arguments that critics of postemployment restrictions use today. Senator Mathew Hale Carpenter of Wisconsin attacked the provision as palpably unjust and glaringly unconstitutional.[47] He argued that employees hired prior to the passage of the provision had assumed they could go into such enterprises, and that to apply the law to those currently employed by the government would constitute an unconstitutional, ex post facto law. The majority of those who opposed the amendment simply believed that there was no need to regulate the conduct of former government officials before the government.

Senator George Edmunds of Vermont, in contrast, argued that no greater abuse in government existed than "having people who are employed in the Government give up their employment and turn around and become the agents and attorneys of those who wish to get money out of the Treasury through the Department."[48] These former departmental employees could use their influence with their friends in the departments to obtain favorable treatment on claims. Although Edmunds agreed that the help of the vast majority of departmental clerks could not be bought by a former official, there was still a natural tendency for a departmental clerk to help a former associate in private practice. As he explained:

That man retires from his three or four thousand dollar position and comes up the next day as the attorney, having a contingent fee of $10,000, if you please; he goes right back into the Department, hunts up the proper clerk in that bureau, and uses his influence upon him; I do not say always corruptly in the sense of using money, but uses the influence which naturally could be exercised by a man of capacity upon people with whom he had been associated, and the first you know a claim which never ought to have been paid has taken its money out of the Treasury.[49]

Besides the problem of former officials exercising undue influence on former associates, other supporters of the postemployment bar argued it was wrong for individuals to leave government with confidential inside information and turn around and use it against the government in claims cases.[50]

Opponents of the statute unsuccessfully attempted to reduce its impact by amending it to permit a former official to work on claims before a bureau within his former department if he had not previously worked for that particular bureau. Senator Oliver Morton of Indiana doubted that there was any sense "in saying that a man who has been employed in the Patent Office shall not be allowed to practice before the Commissioner of the General Land Office or the Commissioner of Pensions, or any other bureau or any officer in that Department not connected with that class of duties upon which he was employed."[51] Interestingly, Congress would include such a provision when it strengthened postemployment prohibitions as part of the Ethics in Government Act of 1978.

Opponents also failed to convince Congress to limit the legislation to claims to recover money. Senator Edmunds supported the broader language of the bill on the grounds that

it is just as much against just policy, and against the protection of the people, who have some rights as well as claimants, to allow a member of Congress, or a member of a Department, to undertake the land-grant business before the Commissioner of the Land Office as it would be to undertake the money business in the Treasury Department.[52]

Despite these defeats, critics of the legislation won a major victory when, without any debate or explanation, Congress voted to drop all criminal penalties for violating the law.[53] This action left it up to each agency or department to find ways to punish violators. Critics also convinced Congress to limit the no-contact period to two years after termination of government service and to limit the bar to assisting in the prosecution of claims that were pending in the former employee's department during the period in which the former employee worked for the department. These changes effectively gutted the legislation, but Congress had gone on record as finding something wrong with former government officials engaging in certain types of representational activities with respect to their former government employers.[54] On the one hand, Congress realized that such conduct by former officials had the potential of exploding into a national political issue. On the other hand, few members of Congress really wanted to strictly regulate the conduct of former officials before Congress and government agencies.

Between the passage of the 1872 law and the 1962 revision of all of the major conflict of interest statutes, no federal case on the subject of postemployment representations was reported. Congress appears to have enacted the prohibitions solely as a means of deflecting public criticism of government claims and procurement practices.

A FORGOTTEN LEGACY

These early conflict of interest statutes reflected a consensus that government employees and former government employees should not assist private citizens in the prosecution of claims against the United States. Moreover, they reflected a belief that it was disloyal for government employees to go into business representing private parties in actions against the United States. Finally, they recognized that the potential for abuse or the appearance of abuse of a public position for personal gain was enormous if government employees took action with respect to matters in which they had a direct or indirect financial interest.

These early efforts, however, were more symbolic than substantive. They did not reflect a ground swell of congressional support to enforce standards of conduct on members of Congress and government employees and officials. However, for obvious political reasons, future Congresses and presidents could not propose or even suggest their repeal without facing the risk of being labelled supporters of unethical government. Equally significant, even symbolic attempts to establish higher standards of conduct for elected and nonelected personnel raised public expectations for more honest public servants. When new scandals occurred, pressure would increase for new laws and regulations.

These early efforts to regulate conflicts of interests in Congress and the executive branch foreshadowed much more serious problems as the role of the national government in the economic affairs of the country expanded. The early conflict of interest controversies also showed that while bribery, kickbacks, and employee theft still constituted major abuses by public servants, as much damage to public confidence in public institutions could be done by more obscure actual or apparent conflicts of interest.

THE GILDED AGE AND HONEST GRAFTERS

The decline in public service ethics would continue well into the latter half of the nineteenth century. While the scandals of this period more often than not involved the traditional forms of official graft and corruption, they provided additional evidence of how fortunes could be made by having the right government officials in a company's employ. The Credit Mobilier scandal, involving a corporation established to funnel congressional subsidies to the Union Pacific Railroad Company for the construction of its section of the transcontinental railroad, showed how low standards of official conduct could sink.[55]

On September 4, 1872, the headline of the *New York Sun* read, "The King of Frauds: How the Credit Mobilier Bought Its Way into Congress." Congressman Oakes Ames of Massachusetts, it was disclosed, had established the corporation, but when his relationship to the venture was made known, he had distributed his share of stock to a number of members of Congress for a price far below the actual value. The Credit Mobilier investigation ruined many political careers. It even implicated Vice President Schuyler Colfax, who admitted to having received Credit Mobilier stock while he was serving as Speaker of the House of Representatives. Impeachment proceedings against Colfax were dropped, however, on grounds that his involvement took place prior to his assuming the office of vice president.[56]

Further scandals implicated other high Grant administration officials. The Whiskey Ring affair resulted in the loss of millions of dollars in tax revenue from distillers who failed to pay national alcohol taxes. Equally embarrassing, during Grant's second term, Secretary of War William W. Belknap was forced to resign because of corruption in the management of Indian Affairs.[57]

The scandal coming closest to a twentieth-century conflict of interest controversy involved the private financial dealings of Secretary of the Navy George Robeson. In 1876, a congressional investigation revealed that Robeson had deposited some $320,000 in his bank accounts between 1872 and 1976.[58] Some members of the House Committee on Naval Affairs believed he had received this money from A. G. Cattell and Company, a Philadelphia grain and feed firm that supplied the Navy with various goods. The books of Cattell and Company, however, showed no record of direct payments to Robeson.[59] The Democratic majority of the committee found strong evidence that "a system of corruption had grown up in the administration of revenues entrusted to the control and direction of the Secretary of the Navy." They referred to this form of official misconduct as "Cattellism."[60] On the other hand, the three Republicans on the committee vigorously disagreed with the conclusions of the majority. They concluded that there was no evidence that Robeson's relationship with the Cattell Company involved Navy business.

These investigations of official misconduct received a great deal of publicity, but produced very little congressional action. Congress refused to outlaw gifts to members of Congress or even to consider the idea of public financial disclosure.[61] Republicans generally took the position that the charges were politically motivated, yet corruption became the primary issue of the disputed election of 1876.

As historian David Loth noted in his 1938 work, *Public Plunder: A History of Graft in America,* the "neat distinction between honest and dishonest graft was drawn a great deal in the eighties and nineties."[62] According to Loth,

The honest grafters were lawyers who habitually drew fees from private interests seeking government aid, contractors who consistently won bids for public works, executives of big corporations sent into public office to represent their companies rather than their constituencies, machine bosses who recognized the short-sightedness of double crossing their industrial allies.[63]

Gradually the issue of conflicts of interest, or honest graft, took on definite ideological and class overtones directly related to the rise of large corporations and monopolies in the United States. Critics such as Loth viewed these "honest grafters" as being worse than "dishonest grafters" because of their effort to control government through the secretive use of their economic power and through the ability to prevent regulation of such conduct. Another historian of the Gilded Age scandals argues that when "one . . . observe[s] that twentieth-century conflicts of interest more than match nineteenth-century graft, the Gilded Age has lost some of its dubious distinction."[64]

CIVIL SERVICE REFORM AND PUBLIC SERVICE ETHICS

Despite the failure of reformers to control honest graft, the 1880s saw the success of the civil service reform movement with the similar goal of restoring public trust in the integrity of the national public service. Much of the support for civil service reform came from those who blamed the decline in public service ethics on the spoils system. An 1877 congressional investigation of the New York Customhouse, for example, attacked spoils appointments for encouraging and perpetuating "official ignorance, inefficiency and corruption which . . . have burdened the country with debt and taxes, and assisted to prostrate the trade and industry of the nation."[65]

Writing about the civil service reform movement, Frederick Mosher commented, "Few reform movements in American history could draw so clear a distinction between right and wrong, between 'good guys' and 'bad guys.' "[66] Civil service reformers set out "to make active politics once more attractive to men of self-respect and high aspirations." Civil service reform was to be the ultimate solution for the government integrity problem.[67]

On January 16, 1883, President Chester Arthur signed the Civil Service Act, which was known as the Pendleton Act. The legislation would provide merit system protection for only ten percent of the federal work force, but over subsequent decades the vast majority of employees obtained coverage.[68] Nevertheless, Congress would refuse to follow the English model of a career administrative class or permanent undersecretaries. Congress wanted to protect the power of Presidents to make patronage appointments, particularly at the policy-making level, and to protect its power of confirmation for top executive-branch positions. Equally important, the Pendleton Act required entry at all levels. This feature, noted civil service historian Paul Van Riper, "is unique among modern public service."[69] Congress believed that free entry would protect the democratic charter of the federal service and provide for more lucrative patronage appointments.

Despite strong political resistance and little help from presidents Grover Cleveland and Benjamin Harrison,[70] the new Civil Service Commission worked diligently to require appointments on the basis of merit and to stop the practice of requiring classified employees to contribute money to political parties. As chairman of the Civil Service Commission during the administrations of Benjamin Harrison and Grover Cleveland, Theodore Roosevelt successfully pushed for higher standards of conduct in federal agencies and departments. Later, as president, Roosevelt moved quickly to prosecute those guilty of misconduct when scandals erupted over corruption in the Indian Service, the Land Office, and the Post Office Department.[71]

The Dream and the Reality

Nineteenth-century civil service reformers believed that civil service reform would attract good and honest people to government service. These good people would develop a high sense of loyalty to their government and to the public, and would thus be able to resist temptations to violate the public trust for personal profit and gain. However, late nineteenth-century civil-service reformers could not have envisioned the rise of a national government with 2.9 million employees and budgets over a trillion

dollars. They could not have foreseen the magnitude of the tasks of regulating huge segments of the American economy, distributing benefits to
millions of citizens, and awarding contracts to thousands of companies.
They could not have anticipated the blurring of boundaries between the
private and public sectors, and they misjudged the ability of civil service
reform to end honest graft or conflicts of interest.

PUBLIC POLICY, POLITICS, AND CONFLICTS OF INTEREST

Throughout his presidency, Theodore Roosevelt supported strong federal
intervention to protect the environment; for example, he called for the
removal of millions of acres of land from private development, and for the
removal of large tracts of Alaskan coal land from private mining interests.
When William Taft became president in March of 1909, however, Progressive Republicans feared that the new president would dismantle Roosevelt's policies, including his environmental program.[72] Their fears proved
justified when Taft's secretary of the interior, R. A. Ballinger, removed the
Roosevelt ban on the mining of Alaskan coal lands owned by the Guggenheim family.

The Ballinger decision overturned the prior decision of Roosevelt's secretary of the interior, James Garfield, who had ruled that the Guggenheim
coal mining was illegal. As commissioner of the General Land Office in the
Interior Department during the Roosevelt Administration, Ballinger left
after losing the fight to allow development. Chief Forester Gifford Pinchot
had led the effort to block development and to protect the Alaskan wilderness.[73]

Soon after the Ballinger decision to permit development, Pinchot and a
Ballinger subordinate, Louis R. Glavis, alleged that during the time Ballinger was out of government (in private law practice during 1908) he had
violated the federal law by aiding private citizens in prosecuting claims
against the Interior Department. Ballinger admitted to having acted as a
lobbyist, but denied any violation of federal law. President Taft found that
Ballinger had done nothing improper and dismissed Pinchot and Glavis for
insubordination.[74]

This action failed to end the controversy, however. At the request of
President Taft, a House committee investigated the charges against Secretary
Ballinger. After forty-five days of hearings, the Republican majority cleared
Ballinger of all charges of official misconduct. The four minority members,
however, condemned the Secretary's actions.

The Ballinger-Pinchot controversy badly damaged the Taft Administration, and for a short period of time became a major national issue. It signified
the reemergence of conflict of interest reform as an issue with obvious
partisan and ideological overtones. The Progressive Movement, with its

sharp dislike for big business, looked for ways to rein in private power and influence. New conflict of interest statutes were seen as a means to accomplish this objective.

Salary Supplementation and Divided Loyalties

By the early twentieth century, a number of large foundations began to offer their financial assistance to federal agencies that were short of funds and manpower. For instance, between 1906 and 1913, the Rockefeller Foundation's General Education Board spent approximately $250,000 to support Southern education and agricultural projects that the Interior Department lacked the funds to support.[75] The Foundation gave the Interior Department full control of these demonstration projects.

Despite strong Southern support, in 1914 Progressive Republican Senator William Kenyon of Iowa began a vigorous campaign to stop private foundations from providing funding, including the General Education Board.[76] Kenyon argued that government employees paid by the the Rockefeller family would be indebted to the Education Board and not to their department. In other words, they could not serve two masters at the same time. However, strong opposition from Southern Democrats in the House blocked passage of a Senate bill prohibiting the Interior Department from taking money from the General Education Board. During 1915, a proposal by the Rockefeller Foundation to fund a government study of labor problems in the United States focused new attention on the supplementation issue.

In 1915, President Woodrow Wilson's Commission on Industrial Relations began a broad inquiry into the activities of philanthropic trusts. It would subsequently accuse many of them of trying to extend their control over the nation's educational system. Commission members and union leaders John Lennon and James O'Connell urged Congress to take the funds of these foundations "for the creation and maintenance of public works that will minimize the deplorable evil of unemployment . . . for other legitimate purposes of a social nature, directly beneficial to the laborers who really contributed the funds."[77]

Then, in 1917, Senator George Chamberlain of Oregon sharply criticized the Interior Department's Bureau of Education for allowing the Rockefeller and Carnegie Foundations to pay the salaries of some bureau employees.[78]

Despite a forceful defense of the program by P. P. Claxton, Commissioner of the Bureau of Education,[79] on January 26, 1917, Senator Chamberlain introduced an appropriations amendment "specifically prohibiting the Bureau of Education from using the services of anyone whose salary was paid by sources outside the Government."[80] The legislation provided for a fine of not less than $1000 or imprisonment of not less than six months, or both.

Speaking in support of the amendment, Senator Miles Poindexter of Washington argued that Congress should pass the prohibition in order to

safeguard the nation's educational system from the "cult of Rockefeller" and the "cult of Carnegie," and the viewpoint which they represent in politics and in government [which] is just as much to be guarded against in the educational system of the country as a particular religious sect.[81]

On March 3, 1917, Congress passed the supplementation prohibition amendment. Surprisingly, it applied to all executive-branch employees instead of being limited solely to the Bureau of Education.[82]

The supplementation prohibition was a minor victory for the Progressive Movement, which was bent on checking the power of foundations in American society. Many Progressives believed that those with strong ties to large corporations and their foundations would always put their interests ahead of the interests of the common citizen.[83] Only extreme vigilance would prevent private powers from dictating the national agenda.

MOBILIZATION AND CONFLICTS OF INTEREST

The mobilization for the First World War turned into an experiment in government-business cooperation. Despite the general success of bringing high-level corporate executives to work on wartime boards and agencies, the practice would come in for strong criticism throughout the duration of the war from a vocal minority who believed these barons of business and industry used their public positions to further the interests of their companies, which profited from the war. The critics reserved their harshest attacks for the government's practice of paying these officials one dollar a year while they received full compensation and benefits from their private employers.

Prior to the war, it had become common practice for agencies to use their dollar-a-year scientists, educators, and technical specialists to provide expert assistance not otherwise available within the organization.[84] The practice of paying emergency or temporary employees a dollar a year resulted from the passage of a 1905 statute that "forbade the employment of personnel by the federal government without compensation."[85] According to one explanation, Congress passed the statute to control Theodore Roosevelt's practice of staffing commissions with unpaid members to provide presidential advice for setting public policy. According to another explanation, Congress sought to prevent volunteers from "establishing a basis for future claims against the Government for services not intended or agreed to be gratuitous."[86] The statute created so much confusion, however, that in 1913 the Attorney General issued an advisory opinion distinguishing between gratuitous services and voluntary services that had been contracted for. Regardless of the reason, however, agencies turned to the use of dollar-a-year personnel to avoid any appearance of violating the 1905 legislation.

In contrast to the pre-War, dollar-a-year personnel, wartime agencies brought into government "leaders and captains of industry and finance, highly capable, highly paid in private business, and in some quarters, highly suspect."[87] These generalists tended to fill key policy making positions essential to the success of war mobilization. The National Defense Act of 1916 authorized the employment of personnel without federal compensation.

President Wilson strongly supported the use of high-powered, dollar-a-year and without-compensation men with strong business backgrounds. Wilson's initial appointments to the Advisory Commission of the Council on National Defense included men like Julius Rosenwald, president of Sears Roebuck and Co.; Daniel Willard, president of the Baltimore and Ohio Railroad; Howard E. Coffin, vice president of Hudson Motor Car Company; Dr. Franklin H. Martin, Regent of the American College of Surgeons; Samuel Gompers, president of the American Federation of Labor; and Bernard Baruch, a financial specialist.[88]

Responding to criticism of the predominance of business executives, Wilson maintained that "the time of some members of the Advisory Board could not be purchased. They serve the Government without remuneration, efficiency being their sole object and Americanism their only motive."[89] Nevertheless, President Wilson's strong support for the use of private-sector executive talent did not quell persistent criticism of the practice. As the *New York Times* commented on June 17, 1918:

Out of Congress, as well as in it, however, there has been a feeling, first, that the law forbidding the Government to accept free services from anybody is a good one, and that $1 a year is not a salary or wage, but a mere evasion of the law's letter. . . . A solvent nation does not expect or want its private citizens to make financial sacrifices in its favor; it can and should pay its way.[90]

Critics particularly attacked the involvement of cooperative committees of the Council on National Defense in the setting of prices for commodities. At one point, Speaker of the House Champ Clark declared that "the Attorney-General should put every one of those fellows in jail between now and Saturday night who keep prices up."[91]

The criticism had some effect. In August of 1917, Congress passed an amendment to the Food and Fuel Bill making it illegal for any federal employee, whether serving in a full-time or an advisory capacity, to solicit or attempt to "induce any person or officer authorized to execute or to direct the United States to make any contract" it the agent or employee had "any pecuniary interest in such contract or order."[92] Although the law did not prohibit an employee from holding a financial interest in a company holding contracts with the government, it prohibited all full-time or advisory employees from actively advocating new financial arrangements with these private enterprises.

When Congress gave the War Industries Board full responsibility for mobilizing war production, President Wilson appointed Bernard Baruch as chairman. As chairman, Baruch proceeded to rapidly expand recruitment of businessmen for mobilization positions.[93] Of the 740 individuals listed as having served on the board, the majority came from backgrounds in commercial, financial, and industrial organizations. The remainder came from universities, private legal practice, and government.[94]

The First World War produced little evidence that dollar-a-year executives used their positions for personal financial gain or to benefit their private-sector employers. Moreover, strong evidence exists that the alternative would have been "to raise government salaries to astronomical heights, draft labor and management, or put the experts in uniform."[95] Nevertheless, the role of businessmen in government would become a major force in shaping the future evolution of conflict of interest regulation.[96]

EFFICIENCY AND ECONOMY, AND THE ERA OF NORMALCY

In a January 1925 address before the Society of Newspaper Editors, Calvin Coolidge made his famous remark, "The business of America is business."[97] In accord with that premise, post–war Republican administrations retreated from Progressive prewar efforts to break up large private trusts, and resisted efforts to regulate the nation's economic system. Business-oriented concepts of scientific management replaced morality as the cornerstone of civil-service reform. Expansion of merit systems was advocated as the way to promote "efficiency and economy in terms of dollars and cents."[98] To improve government, government needed to become more like business. Few in America believed that a close working relationship between business and government presented any ethical problems. The strength of this widely held belief is best demonstrated by the reaction to the Teapot Dome scandal. The story has been fully told, and only the magnitude of the scandal need be recalled.

The setting for the scandal was created in 1912, when at the urging of conservationists and scientists who feared that "unrestricted tapping of petroleum could lead to critical shortages in the future," President Taft set aside two naval oil reserves in California, one at Elk Hills and the other at Buena Vista Hills.[99] In time, however, Westerners who saw the reserves as an infringement upon their right to develop the natural resources of the West persuaded Congress to pass the Land Leasing Act of 1920, permitting limited drilling on public lands. As historians Samuel Eliot Morison and Henry Steele Commager recounted, there followed a conspiracy that saw

Secretary of the Interior Albert Fall "with the connivance of Secretary of the Navy Edwin Denby enter into a corrupt alliance with the Doheny and Sinclair oil interests to give them control of the immensely valuable naval oil reserves."[100]

One congressional investigation determined that Fall had received $100,000 from Edward Doheny in November 1921, and another $300,000 from Sinclair before the Interior Department issued drilling permits. Although Fall was convicted of accepting a bribe, Harry Sinclair and Edward Doheny were found not guilty of bribery.[101] The Supreme Court ultimately upheld the annulment of the oil leases.

The Teapot Dome scandal produced little public or congressional pressure for reform. The August 2, 1923, death of President Warren Harding provided an excuse to put the Teapot Dome scandal aside and removed corruption as a national political issue. On the other hand, the confirmation problems of Charles Beecher Warren for attorney general demonstrated that not everyone had lost interest in conflict of interest matters. The battle over his confirmation was even more surprising in the light of the fact that the Senate had rarely investigated the backgrounds of presidential nominees for actual or potential conflict of interest problems.[102]

Warren seemed perfect for the position of attorney general. A former businessman and an attorney, he had headed a large corporation up to the time of his nomination, and had served as a national committeeman of the Republican Party and as an ambassador to Japan and Mexico.[103] On February 9, 1925, however, the *New York Times* reported that between 1902 and 1906 Mr. Warren had represented the interests of the American Sugar Refining Company and that during this period he had managed the takeover of a number of smaller refining companies and created the Michigan Sugar Company, of which he became president.[104]

Senator James Reed of Missouri fought to block Warren's confirmation on the grounds that if confirmed, Mr. Warren would "paralyze every prosecution of every trust and grant immunity to every scoundrel who engaged in a conspiracy against the people of the United States."[105] Simply stated, he felt that Warren's background indicated he would not vigorously enforce the antitrust laws. On March 10, 1925, the Senate rejected the nomination of Mr. Warren by a vote of 41 to 39. Although President Coolidge threatened to appoint Warren by way of a recess appointment, on March 18 the Senate again refused to confirm him, one of the few times that the Senate had ever refused to confirm a presidential nominee for a high-level executive position.

As had been the case in Teapot Dome, however, the rejection of Warren did not signal a new interest on the part of the Senate to closely scrutinize the backgrounds of presidential nominees. Not until after the Second World War did background checks for ideological and financial conflicts of interest become a common part of confirmation proceedings.[106]

The Era of Normalcy, 1919–1929, only postponed the debate over whether additional measures were needed to guard against conflict of interest situations created by businessmen going into government and shortly thereafter returning to their private sector careers. The Great Depression, attributed by many Americans to the excesses of corporate America, made the fear of private power a majority view.

THE NEW DEAL AND APPEARANCES OF IMPROPRIETY

In spite of close scrutiny by its critics, the administration of Franklin Roosevelt avoided major scandals during its twelve years. One explanation for this is that the administration had turned to a new type of "ideological patronage" and recruited young lawyers and intellectuals who approached their jobs with a religious zeal.[107] This religious zeal, it was argued, made it unthinkable for these recruits to use their public positions for personal gain. Another explanation is that government outlays offered "limited opportunities for windfalls," since most of the increased expenditures took the form of relatively "small scale aid to individuals."[108] Still another theory is that federal agencies and departments were able to resolve the most serious conduct problems internally and thus avoid any embarrassing and damaging public disclosures.

The best evidence that Franklin Roosevelt recognized the serious damage that could be done to the credibility of his administration by appearances of impropriety involving government personnel comes from Roosevelt's attempt to regulate stock speculation by federal employees and officials.

In June of 1935, President Roosevelt asked Harry B. Mitchell, director of the Civil Service Commission, to issue a policy against speculation in stocks by federal officers and employees. Roosevelt explained:

I have given much consideration to the general problem of speculation in stocks and commodities in the Government service. . . . It is my thought that if I could prescribe regulations for all of the officers and employees of all branches of the Executive Branch of the Government, the Congress might follow the good example with legislation relating to the Judiciary and the Legislature.[109]

The letter sparked a two-year debate within the administration over the need for such a statement. Strong opposition to such a prohibition came from the Civil Service Commission, which took the position that federal employees should have the same right to speculate as any private citizen, and from the Justice Department, which doubted that such a restriction was legal and that it could be enforced. In 1937, as part of a compromise, Roosevelt issued a letter to the Civil Service Commission admonishing employees to avoid speculation, but not defining speculation or providing a mechanism for the enforcement of the policy. The letter read as follows:

I believe it to be sound policy of the Government that no officer or employee shall participate directly or indirectly in any transaction concerning the purchase or sale of corporate stocks or bonds or commodities for speculative purposes. Engagement in such speculative activities by any officer or employee, whether under the competitive civil service or not, should be among the matters considered by the heads of departments and establishments and by the Commission in passing upon questions concerning his qualifications or retention or advancement. . . . I would appreciate it if you would take steps to make this known throughout the Government service.[110]

The Civil Service Commission and federal agencies made no effort to implement the Roosevelt letter. In time, World War II produced real conflict of interest problems for the Roosevelt White House.

THE BUSINESSMEN RETURN: WORLD WAR II MOBILIZATION

Highly suspicious of the intentions of leaders in the business and financial communities, organized labor and many Roosevelt administration officials questioned whether war mobilization required the hiring of large numbers of private-sector executives to direct the transformation of the country from a peacetime to a wartime economy. Regardless of this attitude, without-compensation executives played a major role in wartime mobilization.

Although wartime planning continued between the two wars, World War II mobilization began seriously in the spring of 1939 with the revision of the War Department's Industrial Mobilization Plan.[111] The plan proposed to give a War Resources Board overall policy control over the mobilization program, and called for the recruitment of businessmen to fill the most important management positions. Shortly thereafter, President Roosevelt established a new War Resources Board. The Board proceeded to compile a long list of volunteer business executives in the event of a national emergency.[112] Organized labor and many congressional New Deal Democrats responded angrily to the War Resources Board mobilization plan, particularly to the proposed use of large numbers of private executives. As a result of this strong pressure, in October of 1939 Roosevelt abolished the Board.[113]

Later, after considerable debate, President Roosevelt reactivated the National Defense Advisory Board, but made sure that businessmen did not dominate the Board. Members included William S. Knudsen, a Danish immigrant who had become president of General Motors Corporation; Sidney Hillman, a Lithuanian tailor who had became president of the Amalgamated Clothing Workers Union; Edward Stettinius, Jr., president of United States Steel; and Chester C. Davis, a South Dakota farm boy who had become a member of the Board of Governors of the Federal Reserve System.[114]

Because of uncertainty surrounding the authority of the federal government to appoint dollar-a-year and without-compensation personnel, President Roosevelt obtained authorization from Congress in 1940 to appoint an indefinite number of such personnel to expedite defense mobilization.[115] Within a short time, President Roosevelt appointed one hundred dollar-a-year and without-compensation employees to the National Defense Advisory Council.[116]

In January 1941, Congress replaced the National Advisory Council with a formal mobilization agency, the Office of Production Administration (OPA). In February 1941, a more comprehensive nominating procedure for dollar-a-year personnel went into effect, requiring White House clearance and nomination before such appointees could go to work for the OPA.[117] The White House required the clearance process primarily to guard against national security risks, but also, in part, to calm critics who feared that enemies of the president would work their way into key mobilization positions. This clearance requirement made it extremely difficult for the OPA to move rapidly to increase the number of dollar-a-year and without-compensation employees.

Delays in White House clearance led William S. Knudsen, director general of OPA, to urgently request President Roosevelt to grant OPA the authority to make appointments without White House and presidential approval.[118] Presidential Assistant James Rowe advised the president to support the director's request on the grounds that "such delegation would remove criticism of you personally for the appointment of many men antagonistic to the Administration's domestic policies, and therefore anathema to most of your consistent supporters during the past eight years."[119] Late in October 1941, President Roosevelt granted OPA the authority to make dollar-a-year and without-compensation appointments without White House approval. The delegation, however, required that the OPA continue background investigations and that appointments be limited to men of "outstanding experience and ability."[120] The White House had major concerns regarding the ideological loyalty of many of the dollar-a-year appointees. Appointment authority placed the conflict of interest problem squarely in the hands of Knudsen and OPA. If any of the dollar-a-year and without-compensation employees were found using their positions to further their own interests or the interests of their former employers, critics of the policy would have a field day.

Throughout the war, congressional committees closely scrutinized OPA and its on-loan executives. For instance, a Special Committee Investigating the National Defense Program, established in March 1941, and chaired by Senator Harry S Truman, focused its efforts on rooting out fraud and waste associated with war mobilization and production. A committee report released in January 1942 condemned the whole nonsalaried system and concluded that these employees brought "definite advantage to their companies through contracts and inside information and generally favored big business as against small business."[121] The committee insisted that dollar-a-year personnel were in a much better position than the ordinary man in the street to know what types of contracts the government was about to let and how their companies should proceed to get consideration.[122]

Besides intentional favoritism, the Truman Committee most feared a subconscious tendency of these on-loan executives "to judge all matters before them in the light of their past experiences and convictions."[123] To guard against unintentional bias, the committee recommended that all dollar-a-year personnel be placed on government salaries and be required to "divorce themselves from their private positions" because their companies had such a "large stake in the defense program."[124]

Shortly after the appearance of the committee's first report, President Roosevelt issued Executive Order 9024, placing the responsibilities of the OPA under the jurisdiction of a new War Production Board (WPB). The new chairman of the board, Donald M. Nelson, rebutted the charges concerning the bias of dollar-a-year and without-compensation employees. In January 1942 testimony before the Truman Committee, Chairman Nelson warned that continued criticism would deter needed people from accepting positions with the board. As Nelson testified:

You make men afraid to come down here. I mean honest, straight-forward men who can help this picture, and companies that are willing to sacrifice and make sacrifices to have men come down here are afraid for them to come for fear your committee expresses the attitude of the Government toward men that have been called in at our request to help in this emergency.[125]

Nelson criticized the committee for suggesting that regular government salaries could attract the specialists needed for the war effort. Family financial obligations, Nelson argued, made it very difficult for these experts to accept large pay cuts, especially since they came to Washington to fill temporary positions rather than to build careers.

Finally, Nelson assured the senators that the WPB had taken adequate steps to screen dollar-a-year and without-compensation employees (WOCs) for conflicts of interest and to prevent them from using their positions for personal financial gain or to aid their private-sector employers. First, Nelson argued, the WPB appointed only individuals of "unimpeachable integrity" and of "outstanding business or technical ability." Second, the board made every effort to fill positions with individuals on regular government salaries before turning to dollar-a-year personnel. Third, dollar-a-year and WOC employees were not placed in positions where their decisions might directly affect the affairs of their own companies. Finally, an investigative agency of the federal government in each case conducted a comprehensive background check of each nominee prior to formal appointment.[126]

Although the 1872 prohibition on former government officials assisting in the prosecution against claims against the United States included no criminal sanctions,[127] the statute deterred some private executives from taking wartime positions for fear that once they returned to their private employers, any contacts with government departments might be interpreted as violations of the law and thus subject them or their employers to administrative sanctions or public notoriety.

To remove confusion surrounding the application of Section 99 to dollar-a-year personnel, Congress attached a rider to the Renegotiation Act of 1942 "exempting from the post-employment restrictions . . . employees appointed by the Secretaries of War, Navy, and Treasury and by the Maritime Commission." The rider, however, included a provision that "no such employee should ever prosecute a claim against the United States arising from any matter with which he was directly involved while in office."[128] The replacement of the 1872 postemployment restriction with a lifetime bar narrowed the scope of the postemployment prohibition from claims pending in a department at the time the employee was employed to claims with which the former official had been directly involved. This made "the post-employment prohibition turn on a nexus between the officer and the claim."[129]

Congress wanted to permanently prevent dollar-a-year executives from switching sides before the claim was settled or resolved, but to permit them to contact government agencies with respect to claims which the former officials had not been involved with while in government. However, Congress made no effort to regulate non-claims-related, postservice contacts. In 1948, Congress incorporated the proviso in the federal criminal code as Section 284 of the United States Code.

Almost all studies of World War Two mobilization recognize the contributions made by nonsalaried employees. For example, a 1947 review of war mobilization by the Brookings Institution found that the "tremendous tasks of civilian government could not have been performed without the help of the administrative talents of industry, the labor organizations, the foundations and officials of the universities and colleges."[130]

Nevertheless, concern over possible conflicts of interest forced wartime agencies to take unprecedented steps to guard against appearances of impropriety. The rules of the game regarding conflicts of interest had changed. After the war, growing animosity between the parties, media hunger for a good story, and sharp differences of opinion over the direction of public policy, all contributed to a "moral escalation" generally unrecognized by observers of the period. The absence of any major scandals since 1932 helped to convince many that the New Deal had restored integrity in government.

By 1945, then, the conflict of interest issue had gone far beyond concern with the prosecution of fraudulent claims. It now involved the issue of how to assure that decision making in government was not influenced by personal economic interests or interests of outsiders who wanted something from the government.

NOTES

1. These themes are highlighted in the Association of the Bar of the City of New York, *Conflict of Interest and Federal Services,* (Cambridge, Mass.: Harvard University Press, 1960), p. 7.

2. *See* Leonard D. White, *The Federalists* (New York: Free Press, 1965), p. 514.

3. David H. Rosenbloom, *Federal Service and the Constitution* (Ithaca, N.Y.: Cornell University Press, 1970), pp. 33–35.

4. Leonard D. White, *The Jeffersonians,* (New York: Free Press, 1965), pp. 347–85.

5. Emmette S. Redford, *American Government and Economy* (New York: Macmillan Co., 1968), p. 8.

6. C. Van Woodward, ed. *Responses of the Presidents to Charges of Misconduct* (New York: Delacorte Press, 1974), p. xv.

7. Leonard D. White, *The Jacksonians* (New York, Free Press, 1965), p. 435.

8. Senate Doc. 151, 23d Cong., 2d Sess, March 3, 1835.

9. White, *The Jacksonians* (New York: Free Press, 1965), p. 420.

10. Ibid., p. 435.

11. *See* Report of the House Committee on Revolutionary War Pensions, No. 378, 22d Cong., 1st Sess (1832). *Also see* William M. Wiecek, "The Origin of the United States Court of Claims," *Admin. Law Review* v. 20 (1967), p. 390.

12. Wilson Cowen, Philip Nichols, Jr., and Marion T. Bennett, *The United States Court of Claims: A History, Part II* (Washington, D.C.: The Committee on the Bicentennial of the Independence and the Constitution of the Judicial Conference of the United States, 1978) p. 8.

13. Ibid., p. 9.

14. Ibid.

15. White, *The Jacksonians,* p. 418.

16. The discussion of the Galphin claim is based on the account in Van Woodward's *Responses of the Presidents to Charges of Misconduct,* pp. 87–90.

17. *Congressional Globe,* 31st Cong., 1st Sess., p. 1340.

18. Wiecek, p. 395.

19. Association of the Bar, p. 32. The claim was filed for $500,000.

20. Frederick W. Ford, acting assistant attorney general, Office of Legal Counsel, unpublished memorandum for the Attorney General, re *Conflict of Interest Statutes,* December 10, 1856, p. 34.

21. *Congressional Globe,* 2d Sess. 32d Cong. January 6, 1853, p. 242.

22. *Congressional Globe,* Appendix, 32d Cong., 2d Sess., January 13, 1853, p. 295.

23. *Congressional Globe,* Appendix, 32d. Cong., 1st Sess., Jan. 12, 1853, p. 64.

24. Ibid.

25. Frederick W. Ford, unpublished memorandum for the Attorney General, re *Conflict of Interest Statutes,* December 10, 1856, pp. 41–42.

26. Ibid., p. 42.

27. Wiecek, pp. 396–97.

28. *See* James Garfield Randall, *The Civil War and Reconstruction* (Lexington, Mass.: D.C. Heath and Company, 1969), pp. 319–24, 486–89, and Fred Albert Shannon, *The Organization and Administration of the Union Army, 1861–1865* (Gloucester, Mass.: Peter Smith, 1965), pp. 54–76 and 120–24, for a detailed description of the abuses occurring during the period.

29. Randall, p. 319.

30. Shannon, pp. 56–57.

31. The story of the Hall Carbine Affair is reported in Gustavus Myers, *History of the Great American Fortunes,* vol. 3 (Chicago, Ill.: Charles H. Kerr and Company, 1910), pp. 170–76. A more detailed analysis of the controversey can be found in R. Gordon Wasson, *The Hall Carbine Affair: An Essay in Historiography* (Danbury, Conn: private printing, 1971).

32. Shannon, p. 58; Wasson, p. 49. *See also* Government Contracts in *House Reports,* 37th Cong., 2d Sess., Report No. 2.

33. Shannon, p. 74.

34. *See* 12 Stat. 412 (1862), cited in Association of the Bar, p. 41.

35. *See* Stat. 577 (1862). *See also Cong. Globe,* 37th Cong., 2d Sess., p. 3378 (1862).

36. The 1962 revision of the conflict of interest statutes incorporated the substantive elements of Section 216, Title 18 of the United States Code into Section 201 of Title 18, bribery of public officials and witnesses.

37. Frederick Ford, Memorandum for the Attorney General, p. 101.

38. Ibid.

39. *Cong. Rec.* 777 (January 16, 1908).

40. *Cong. Globe,* February 10, 1864, pp. 555, 561.

41. Samuel Eliot Morison and Henry Steele Commager, *The Growth of the American Republic,* vol. 1 (New York: Oxford University Press, 1962) pp. 739, 741. *See also* Van Woodward, *Responses of the Presidents,* pp. 120–21.

42. Van Woodward, p. xvi.

43. Van Woodward, p. 134. See also *Gold Panic Investigations,* 41st Cong., 2d Sess., House Report 31, March 1, 1870, p. 2.

44. Van Woodward, p. 134.

45. Ibid.

46. *Cong. Globe,* 42d Cong., 2d Sess., March 20, 1872, pp. 1846–47.

47. *Cong. Globe,* 42d Cong., 2d Sess., p. 3108.

48. Ibid., p. 3109.

49. Ibid., p. 3109.

50. Frederick Ford, memorandum, p. 65.

51. *Cong. Globe,* 42d Cong., p. 3110.

52. Ibid.

53. Ibid., p. 3113.

54. Association of the Bar, p. 48.

55. *See also* William B. Hesseltine, *Ulysses S. Grant* (New York: Dodd, Mead, 1935), pp. 309–12.; Allan Nevins and Hamilton Fish: *The Inner History of the Grant Administration,* 2 vols. (New York: F. Unger and Company, 1957); Jay Boyd Crawford, *The Credit Mobilier of America: Its Origin and History, Its Work of Constructing the Union Pacific Railroad and the Relation to Members of Congress* (Boston: C. W.

Calkins, 1888, and New York, 1971); *Credit Mobilier Investigation,* 42d Cong., 3rd Sess., House Report 77, February 18, 1873.

56. Van Woodward, p. 146.

57. White, *The Republican Era: 1869–1901* (New York: Free Press, 1965), pp. 368–72.

58. *See Investigations of the Navy Department,* 44th Cong., 1st Sess., House Report, 784, July 25, 1876, pp. 1–198; Van Woodward, p. 153.

59. Van Woodward, p. 153.

60. *Investigations of the Navy Department,* p. 159.

61. Ari Hoogenboom, "Did Gilded Age Scandals Bring Reform?" in *Before Watergate,* ed. Ari Hoogenboom (New York, Columbia Univ. Press, 1978), p. 129.

62. David Loth, *Public Plunder: A History of Graft in America* Westport, Conn.: Greenwood Press, 1966, p. 215.

63. Ibid, p. 208.

64. Ari Hoogenboom, "Civil Service Reform and Public Morality," in the *Gilded Age,* ed. Howard Wayne Morgan (Syracuse, N.Y.: Syracuse University Press, 1970), p. 78.

65. U.S. Congress, House, Executive Document 8, 45th Cong., 1st Sess., (October 25, 1877), p. 15.

66. Frederick Mosher, *Democracy and the Public Service,* (New York: Oxford Univ. Press, 1968), 1sed. p. 65.

67. Carl Schurz, editorial, *Harper's Weekly,* 37 (July 1, 1893), cited in David H. Rosenbloom, *Federal Service and the Constitution* (Ithaca, Cornell University Press, 1971) p. 72.

68. Mosher, p. 65.

69. Van Riper, p. 101.

70. John D. Hicks, George E. Mowry, and Robert E. Burke, *The American Nation* (Boston: Houghton Mifflin, 1955), p. 65.

71. C. Van Woodward, pp. 208–9.

72. Morison and Commager, *The Growth of the American Republic,* vol. 2 (New York: Oxford University Press, 1962) p. 506.

73. *See* Elmo R. Richardson, *The Politics of Conservation: Crusades and Controversies, 1897–1913* (Berkeley: University of California Press, 1962).

74. C. Van Woodward, p. 242.

75. John Lankford, *Congress and the Foundations in the Twentieth Century* (River, Wisc.: Wisconsin State University Press, 1964), pp. 20–27.

76. One year earlier, the Rockefeller Foundation failed to obtain a national charter because of strong opposition from Progressive Senators. The Rockefeller Foundation then obtained a New York State charter.

77. Lankford, p. 39.

78. *See* 54 *Cong. Rec.,* 2039–47, January 26, 1917.

79. *See* 54 *Cong. Rec.,* 2045, Letter of January 13, 1917.

80. 54 *Cong. Rec.,* pp. 2039–40.

81. Ibid., p. 2043.

82. In the 1948 recodification of Title 18, Section 66 became 18 U.S.C. 1914. The 1962 revision of the conflict of interest statutes made a number of other changes. *See* Section 209 of Title 18 for the 1962 revision.

83. *See* Arthur S. Link, *Woodrow Wilson and the Progressive Era, 1910–1917,* (New York: Harper, 1963).

84. See Stoddard, "Exit the Dollar-a-Year Man," *The Independent,* July 6, 1928, p. 16, cited by Paul G. Dembling and Herbert F. Forest, "Government Service and Private Compensation," Pt. 1, *George Washington Law Review* 20 (December 1951): 182.

85. Paul P. Van Riper, *History of the United States Civil Service,* (Evanston, Ill.: Row Peterson, 1958) p. 263; 31 U.S.C. 665(b).

86. Paul G. Dembling and Herbert F. Forest, "Government Service and Private Compensation," part 1, p. 177. *See also* Van Riper, p. 264.

87. Dembling and Forest, p. 117.

88. Michael D. Reagan, "Serving Two Masters: Problems in the Employment of Dollar-a-Year and Without Compensation Men," (Ph.D. dissertation, Princeton, 1959) p. 3.

89. Quoted in Grosvenor B. Clarkson, *Industrial America in the World War* (Boston: Houghton Mifflin Co., 1929), pp. 21–22.

90. *New York Times,* June 17, 1918, p. 12, as cited in Reagan, p. 14.

91. *New York Times,* May 25, 1917, p. 13.

92. Reagan, p. 17.

93. For a detailed discussion of World War I mobilization, *see* Robert D. Cuff, *The War Industries Board: Business-Government Relations during World War I* (Baltimore, Maryland: Johns Hopkins, 1973).

94. Bernard M. Baruch, *American Industry in the War: A Report of the War Industries Board* (Washington, D.C.: Government Printing Office, 1921), pp. 290–315.

95. Van Riper, p. 264.

96. James P. Johnson, "Co-option, Conflict of Interest or Cooperation: The U.S. Fuel Administration of World War I," in Hoogenboom, ed., *Before Watergate,* pp. 179–80.

97. William Allen White, *A Puritan in Babylon* (New York: Macmillan Co., 1938) pp. 264–65.

98. Van Riper, p. 312.

99. Morison and Commager, p. 621; for complete discussions of the scandal, *see* Burl Noggle, *Teapot Dome: Oil and Politics in the 1920's* (Baton Rouge, La.: Louisiana State University, 1967); Robert K. Murry, *The Politics of Normalcy: Government Theory and Practice in the Harding Administration* (New York: Norton, 1977).

100. Morison and Commager, p. 621.

101. Ibid.

102. *See,* in general, Joseph P. Harris, *The Advice and Consent of the Senate* (Berkeley: University of California, 1953).

103. Ibid.

104. Ibid., p. 121.

105. Ibid., p. 122.

106. For recent discussions of the role of conflicts of interest in Senate confirmations, *see* Bruce Adams, *The Senate Rubberstamp Machine* (Washington, D.C.: Common Cause, 1977); Bruce Adams, *Promise and Performance* (Lexington, Mass.: Lexington, 1979); Calvin G. Mackenzie, *The Politics of Presidential Appointment* (New York: Collier Macmillan, 1980).

107. Van Riper, pp. 324–25.

108. Van Woodward, p. 305.

109. Memorandum, Franklin D. Roosevelt for the United States Civil Service Commission, June 11, 1935, Official File, Franklin D. Roosevelt Library.

110. *The Public Papers and Addresses of Franklin D. Roosevelt* (New York: Macmillan Company, 1941), p. 170.

111. Michael Reagan, "Serving Two Masters, pp. 24–29.

112. James A. McAleer, *Dollar-a-Year Compensation Personnel Policies: Historical Reports on War Administration* (Special Study, no. 27: Civilian Production Administration, April 20, 1947), p. 2.

113. Reagan, p. 28.

114. Ibid., pp. 29–30.

115. 54 Stat. 430 (June 26, 1940); 54 Stat. 78 (October 9, 1940).

116. McAleer, p. 8.

117. Reagan, p. 54. The new clearance form required a statement of experience, proposed duties, an indication of citizenship, a statement of previous salary, and the signature of the nominee. The FBI also was required to conduct a background check for national security reasons.

118. Letter, William S. Knudsen for President Roosevelt, September 24, 1941, Official File 4000, Franklin D. Roosevelt Library, p. 1, about the need to staff the OPA rapidly to meet the emergency.

119. Memorandum, James Rowe, Jr., to President Roosevelt, September 30, 1941, Official File 4000, Franklin D. Roosevelt Library.

120. Memorandum, Franklin D. Roosevelt for director of the Office of Production Management Administration, October 30, 1941, Official File 4000, Franklin D. Roosevelt Library.

121. Senate Report No. 480, 77th Cong., 2d. Sess., Pt. 5 (1942).

122. Ibid., pp. 8–9.

123. Ibid.

124. Reagan, p. 208.

125. United States Senate, 77th Cong., 1st Sess., Special Committee Investigating the National Defense Program, *Hearing,* part 10: War Production Policy Regarding Dollar-a-Year Men, p. 4027.

126. Ibid., p. 4028.

127. Association Report of the Bar, p. 50.

128. Ibid.

129. Francis T. Cain, *Federal Employees in War and Peace: Selection, Placement, and Removal* (Washington, D.C.: The Brookings Institution, 1949), pp. 40–41.

130. Ibid., p. 41.

II

Conflict of Interest and the Truman Administration

During the First World War, President Wilson ignored criticism of the role of dollar-a-year men in wartime agencies. Subsequently, President Franklin Roosevelt backed away from the issuance of strict regulations governing stock speculation by federal employees. During the Second World War, the Roosevelt White House had serious reservations about the political loyalty of many nonsalaried executives, but steered clear of the sensitive issue of how to guard against conflicts of interest by delegating the responsibility for the appointment and supervision of dollar-a-year and without-compensation men.

THE MORAL SLUMP

Between 1947 and 1952, however, a series of revelations about the questionable conduct of several officials close to President Harry Truman rocked the White House. Congressional investigations uncovered corruption, gross official misconduct, and abuse of office in several federal agencies. Republicans pointed to these scandals as evidence of poor leadership by Truman and the Democrats. New Deal and Fair Deal Democrats viewed these scandals as a betrayal of the Roosevelt legacy. The media and experts in government and public administration wrung their hands over how such a "moral slump" could have occurred. The Truman White House tried but failed to put the "moral slump" issue behind it.

Historians generally attribute the scandals disclosed between 1947 and 1951 to the failure of the Truman Administration to enforce high standards of conduct and to the poor judgment of the president regarding the character of his top appointees.[1] While serious, the scandals for the most part involved allegations of financial conflicts of interest, improper acceptance of gifts and gratuities from private interests having substantial dealings with the government, and charges of influence peddling, but did not involve bribery, kickbacks, or theft. Despite this situation, critics attacked the Truman Administration as if another Teapot Dome scandal had taken place.

Financial Speculation and Public Morality

In October 1947, Dr. Wallace H. Graham, the president's White House physician, admitted that he had made substantial profits from grain speculation. Graham denied that he had used inside government information but resigned nevertheless.[2] Edwin Pauley, special assistant to the secretary of the army, acknowledged that he had made a profit of $932,703 through stock market speculation during the preceding three years.[3] Pauley vigorously denied that he had used inside government information. Regardless of his denial, Pauley resigned from the Department of the Army in January 1948.

Subsequent congressional investigations revealed that many government officials had regularly speculated in stocks and commodities, but found little evidence they had illegally used inside government information.[4] Neither the lack of evidence nor the fact that no law or regulation prohibited speculation by government personnel helped to mitigate public criticism of such conduct. As Franklin Roosevelt had warned in his 1937 letter on stock speculation, the public would assume that a government employee making large amounts from stock and commodities speculation had used inside government information. However, the Civil Service Commission and the majority of federal agencies and departments had done very little to make officials and employees aware of the Roosevelt letter on speculation.

General Vaughn and the Five-Percenters

The second major scandal of the Truman administration involved charges of influence peddling. Known as the five-percenters, these self-appointed ombudsmen sold their services to private citizens and small businesses, claiming that they could help get contracts, legislative favors, and other benefits "out of the vast and forbidding cornucopia of government."[5] They convinced prospective clients that to get a favorable hearing, the average citizen or small company must know someone who had contacts with the appropriate federal agencies and officials. According to Truman scholar Cabell Phillips, the five-percenters used the pitch "that they '[knew] the ropes' in Washington, [had] 'drag' in the important departments and bureaus, and [could] bypass all the tedious bureaucratic channels by getting a sympathetic hearing directly with the man at the top.'"[6]

Some government officials tried to persuade the public that they need not hire a lobbyist to get fair treatment from federal agencies and departments. Secretary of Defense Louis Johnson, for example, publicly attacked the five-percenters and urged the public to ignore their sales pitch. He argued emphatically that "there is no need for anyone to intervene between small business and the Government to procure Government contracts."[7]

The secretary of defense, however, faced considerable embarrassment when the *New York Herald Tribune* disclosed that while serving as a consultant to the War Assets Administration, James V. Hunt operated a management consulting firm to help small businesses get government contracts. This information led Senator Clyde R. Hoey, Democrat from North Carolina, to hold hearings on the activities of five-percenters within defense agencies.

The hearings implicated President Truman's close friend and military aide, Brigadier General Harry H. Vaughan, in the consulting activities of Mr. Hunt. The investigation determined that General Vaughn had attended cocktail parties where Mr. Hunt entertained clients and prospective clients, and that on one occasion Vaughn had accepted a freezer from one of Hunt's clients. No evidence turned up to prove that General Vaughn had personally profited from the transaction or that he had done anything in return for the deep freeze. Nevertheless, the appearance of impropriety forced Vaughn to resign.[8]

One Senate subcommittee investigation placed much of the blame for the five-percenter scandal on the shoulders of government officials. "The influence peddler," the report read, "would find it difficult, it not impossible, to continue his activities without the assistance or tacit approval of friendly Government officials."[9] Besides recommending technical changes in contracting procedures to guard against conflicts of interest, the subcommittee recommended establishing formal standards of conduct for all government officials and employees. At the same time, it recognized that the effectiveness of codes of conduct would depend on whether agencies vigorously enforced them.[10]

Of all the conduct problems considered by the subcommittee, the acceptance of gifts by government employees received the most criticism. "Any public official who accepts a gratuity" made a serious mistake, the subcommittee argued, for "if he gets something for nothing from persons doing business with the Government, it is because they hope he may reciprocate in some way." The only practical solution for a public official, therefore, was "to refuse to accept any gratuities from businessmen or others who may do business with the Government."[11]

Official Misconduct in the Reconstruction Finance Corporation

Disclosures of gross mismanagement in the Reconstruction Finance Corporation further strengthened the public perception that favoritism and influence peddling were undermining public service ethics. In 1932, at the urging of Herbert Hoover, Congress had established the Reconstruction Finance Corporation (RFC) to provide loans to businesses facing bankruptcy during the Great Depression.[12] During the Second World War, the RFC helped to finance the conversion of plants to meet defense needs. The corporation had an excellent record until the close of the war, when it began making highly speculative loans for such enterprises as "oil-drilling operations, prefabricated housing manufacture and resort hotels," and dealing with individuals and corporations of questionable financial soundness.[13]

Early in February 1950, the Lustron Corporation defaulted on $37,000,000 worth of RFC loans. Unable to recover much of the loan, the RFC suffered a huge loss. This loan and a number of other defaults led the Senate to give the junior Democratic Senator from Arkansas, J. William Fulbright, the task of investigating the allegations of wrongdoing.

Before releasing its highly critical report on the RFC, Senator Fulbright and the subcommittee tried unsuccessfully to convince President Truman that the situation needed immediate White House action to stop "favoritism and influence" in the corporation's loan decisions. The president refused to reorganize the RFC, and consequently the committee made its report public in early February 1951.

Besides finding strong evidence of mismanagement and political favoritism in the corporation's loan programs, the preliminary report implicated a number of people in attempts to influence the decisions of the RFC board. Among those identified was the special assistant to President Truman, Donald Dawson, who, the report claimed, had used his influence with the RFC Board to obtain special consideration for some of his friends.[14] This report and continued press criticism forced President Truman to ask Congress to reorganize the RFC. Congress approved the reorganization plan by April 1951, and a short time later President Truman nominated the highly respected Stuart A. Symington as the board's single administrator. The final report of the Fulbright subcommittee diplomatically found no evidence that the "offices of the President were officially used in influencing the lending policies of the Corporation."[15]

Throughout the RFC scandal, President Truman had strongly objected to the insinuation that his administration lacked concern about ethics in government. He deeply resented the role played by members of his own party in pressing investigations that he believed only provided ammunition for Republican critics.

Crisis and the Bureau of Internal Revenue

Without question, "the most odorous ingredient of the 'mess in Washington,'" as one critic put it, involved serious irregularities in the management of the Bureau of Internal Revenue and the Tax Division of the

Department of Justice.[16] Investigations uncovered instances of bureau employees extorting "large sums from delinquent tax-payers," of other employees avoiding payment of their own personal income taxes, and of gross mismanagement at all levels of the bureau.[17] These disclosures touched off a firestorm of criticism and turned the moral slump into a national political issue.

The organizational structure of the Bureau of Internal Revenue explains in part how this vital federal bureau got caught in a scandal. The bureau's highly decentralized system of tax collection involved sixty-four regional offices and a collector of internal revenue for each office. These regional collectors decided whether to forward suspected tax fraud cases to bureau headquarters in Washington. The bureau, in turn, decided whether to forward cases to the Justice Department's Tax Division for possible prosecution. Finally, the law gave the president authority to appoint "all the top officials in the sub-bureaucracy, from the Commissioner down to the Deputy Collector."[18] It is not surprising that over time the position of collector became "particularly choice as a means of rewarding local party strong men, who were in unique positions to reward their friends and to punish their enemies. It had been that way since the tax service was created."[19]

The Truman White House expected Republicans to use the allegations of official misconduct to discredit the president and his policies. However, the administration was totally unprepared for the much broader outpouring of public concern over the "mess in Washington."[20] Criticism by liberals troubled the Truman White House the most.

A March 1951 article entitled "Ethics in Government," for instance, summarized questionable practices uncovered by ongoing congressional investigations. The most serious problems involved someone in a career or political position:

1. accepting gifts and entertainment from interests attempting "to win special consideration for the giver's interests";
2. holding a financial interest "in a business which sells to firms subject to his official judgement or discretion";
3. and using a position to further his future financial or employment opportunities.

In addition, the article criticized "the acceptance by a resigned office holder of a post or retainer from a firm whose interests he recently considered in an official capacity, and the offering of such a post."[21] This list dramatically demonstrates how conflict of interest problems had become as damaging as traditional forms of official misconduct.

The "politics as usual" explanation does not account for the indignant reaction to the scandals from members of President Truman's own party. "As the stories of malfeasance came out," wrote Alonzo Hamby, "liberals almost without exception reacted with anger and indignation," and in a fashion almost identical to the nineteenth-century critics of honest graft, they struck out at the president.

They still adhered to the value of nineteenth century Mugwumps who had fought for the merit system, applauded the maxim that public service was a public trust, and idealized the honest nonpartisan government administrator. The federal bureaucracy belonged to all the people and was designed to serve their interests impartially. Any special influence was reprehensible and, if it involved outright dishonesty, was doubly so.[22]

The impressive record of the Roosevelt Administration in directing an unprecedented growth in the federal bureaucracy without a corresponding increase in acts of official misconduct only increased the indignation of liberals. That record, they were convinced, proved that the modern administrative state was manageable and that government could distribute economic benefits and regulate the economy on the basis of need and merit rather than friendship, contacts, and the self-interest of government personnel.

When the guardian of the public interest—the public servant—seemed all too willing to put his own interests before those of the public, it knocked one of the cornerstones of the New Deal off its foundation. If, after all, morality and the liberal state did not go hand in hand, the future looked bleak. Private wealth and power combined with personal greed seemed capable of destroying the credibility of government programs designed to protect the general public and help the less fortunate.

The Liberal Response: Ethical Reform in Government

In March 1951, Senator Fulbright introduced a resolution proposing the establishment of a bipartisan commission on ethics in government. Although Congress failed to establish such a commission, Paul H. Douglas, political scientist and senator from Illinois, used a subcommittee of the Senate Committee on Labor and Public Welfare to conduct a far-reaching investigation of the "mess in Washington."[23]

The Douglas subcommittee hearings on the Fulbright resolution, held in June and July 1951, soon became a forum on the state of public service ethics and ethics in society at large.[24] Educators, religious leaders, political figures, and others concerned about a perceived decline of moral standards in the country testified. Some witnesses criticized the federal agencies for failing to provide employees with clear ethical guidelines regarding acceptable conduct. Other witnesses argued that the entire country, and not only the federal government, was suffering a crisis in morality.

On October 17, 1951, the Douglas subcommittee issued its report, *Proposals for Improvement of Ethical Standards in the Federal Government, including*

Establishment of a Commission on Ethics.[25] The subcommittee placed much of the blame for the apparent decline in public service ethics on an ethics double standard widely practiced by the American people. "The clever man who makes a 'fast buck' gets a certain amount of acclaim, provided he makes enough of them," stated the report. "There is a tolerance in American life for unscrupulous methods, which, if they should become universal, would destroy the very society in which they are tolerated."[26]

In proposing steps to prevent the occurrence of improprieties, the sub-committee recognized the "dangerous area" that gave certain forces the opportunity to drive public servants "from the straight and narrow path of virtue." The dangerous area was the exercise of administrative discretion vital to the growth of the administrative state. The report reads:

The abuses of discretion or the exploitation of power are most serious chiefly where the Government is dispensing valuable rights and privileges, constructing extensive public works, spending vast sums for military supplies and equipment, making loans, granting direct or indirect subsidies, levying taxes, and regulating the activities of privileged monopolies or economic practices in which there is a public interest.[27]

The report assumed that that government would remain heavily "action-laden." The subcommittee rejected calls for a smaller government, and prepared a liberal blueprint for ethics reform to protect the public trust. First, a National Commission on Ethics in Government, appointed by the president, would conduct an exhaustive review of the state of government ethics and propose necessary reforms.[28] Second, Congress would amend the Administrative Procedure Act to supplement the rarely invoked criminal statutes with strong administrative sanctions.

Under the second recommendation, the law would require the summary dismissal of federal officials and employees for

1. engaging "in any personal business transaction or private arrangement for per-sonal profit which accrues from or is based upon official position, authority, or confidential information of the official or employee,"
2. accepting "any valuable gift, favor, or service directly from any person or or-ganization with which the official or employee transacts business with the gov-ernment";
3. discussing "future employment outside the government with a person or an organization with which there is pending official business";
4. divulging "valuable commercial or economic information of a confidential char-acter to unauthorized persons or releasing such information in advance of its authorized release date"; or
5. becoming "unduly involved, for example, through frequent luncheons, dinners, parties, or other expense social engagement with persons outside the Government with whom they do official business."[29]

The subcommittee took the position that mandatory dismissal would send a clear message that even appearances of bias on the part of federal personnel would not be tolerated. These practices, the subcommittee stated,

tend to make public officials consciously or unconsciously partial in handling issues which come before them; they create a suspicion of bias even where it may not exist; they tempt public officials to put personal interests ahead or in conflict with the public interests; or they are damaging or unfair to members of the public.[30]

The third major reform issue concerned the activities of former officials before federal agencies and departments. The temptation of lucrative post-government-service employment, the subcommittee believed, created a strong incentive for government employees to look the other way to make themselves more attractive to potential private employers. In addition, as their nineteenth-century counterparts had argued, former officials could exercise too much influence on their friends in key policy-making positions.

In order to deal with the "revolving-door" problem, the Douglas subcommittee proposed to broaden restrictions on former government personnel representing private clients before government agencies. Specifically, it proposed that Congress should impose a lifetime bar on former government officials representing private clients with respect to a matter which they previously handled or of which they had some direct knowledge while employed by government.[31] This lifetime bar went considerably beyond the restriction involving the prosecution of claims.

Even more important, the subcommittee proposed a new general lobbying restriction unrelated to the government work previously done by the former employee. Former federal officials who left with a rank of GS–15 or above could not for two years after leaving the federal government "appear before the federal agency in which they were formerly employed as the representative of a person or organization doing business with the Government."[32] This proposal represented an effort to curtail general lobbying activities by former officials. This blanket no-contact rule, the subcommittee believed, would help to insulate vulnerable government officials from undue outside pressure and reduce the opportunity for former government officials to make a living lobbying their former agencies. However, not until thirty years later, in the aftermath of Watergate, did Congress enact a criminal conflict of interest statute that paralleled the two-year, no-contact bar proposed in 1951.[33] Significantly, the subcommittee did not propose to prohibit former officials from taking jobs with private organizations holding government contracts or subject to heavy government regulation.

In proposing these new revolving-door restrictions, the subcommittee recognized but discounted their impact on the ability of federal government to recruit and retain scientific, technical, and professional manpower. Many of those entering public service after the Second World War did not have the same religious zeal for the public service as their New Deal counterparts. The subcommittee felt that this "new breed" would have few reservations about leaving the federal government for higher pay or career advancement.

The Douglas subcommittee also tended to downplay the relationship between the revolving door and the presidential appointments process. In the postwar years, it had become much more difficult to attract and keep the best and brightest individuals for policy-making positions. New restrictions, it could be argued, would make it even more difficult for presidents to staff key positions.

The revolving-door issue, the subcommittee believed, also included hiring individuals with close ties to organizations that held a vested interest in government programs. Individuals with backgrounds in business and industry could not be expected to put the public interest above their private interests. The subcommittee reported that

the most difficult problem would seem to be that of an industry background which makes it difficult for a man who has grown up in a particular industry to make governmental decisions which touch that industry and yet give due weight to the public interest.[34]

In particular, top positions in defense agencies "should not be filled by persons drawn from the industries they regulate."[35]

In brief, the Douglas subcommittee report reflected the position that general lobbying as well as switching sides on particular matters threatened the credibility of public decision making. Even if government employees resisted lobbying, the contacts would give the public the perception that favoritism was the key to getting something from Washington. The liberal state could not operate under such a cloud.

The fourth and most dramatic reform proposed by the Douglas subcommittee was mandatory public financial disclosure for all members of Congress, all federal officials receiving a salary of $10,000 or more or holding positions of GS–15 and above, and the principal officials of national political parties. The proposal would have required disclosure of "their incomes, assets, and all dealings in securities and commodities."[36]

The subcommittee argued that public disclosure would help to "protect from innuendo" honest public servants while making it a great deal easier to detect and deter wrongdoing.[37] It would, in a word, allay public suspicion about questionable financial dealings of high-level public servants and force private interests to think twice about using their financial resources to influence key government policy makers. Although the subcommittee recognized that public disclosure would impinge on the privacy rights of public officials, this sacrifice was necessary to restore public confidence in government ethics and end the moral slump.

The remaining items on the reform agenda focused on strengthening existing conflict of interest statutes, establishing a more effective mechanism for resolving allegations of misconduct leveled against high-level federal officials, and instituting general reforms of the political system in an effort to reduce the reliance of public officials on special interests. For instance, the subcommittee recommended:

1. the creation of a court of ethics "to hear complaints regarding improper practices of public officials";
2. the revision of "legislation governing corrupt practices in elections and lobbying";
3. public financial assistance for candidates in election campaigns;
4. "the formulation and adoption of ethical codes by professional groups"; and
5. the general strengthening of "the Federal personnel policy and personnel system."[38]

In brief, the central theme of the Douglas subcommittee report was its focus on how private power and influence threatened the integrity of government. Therefore, every effort must be made to reduce the influence of private power. The problem was not big government but rather special interests that refused to let the policy-making process operate without attempting to obtain preferential treatment.

Congress would not enact any of the reforms recommended by the Douglas subcommittee. Nevertheless, by 1980 almost all its recommendations had found their way into law or regulation.

DAMAGE CONTROL AND THE WHITE HOUSE

The scandals of the late 1940s and early 1950s clearly struck a sensitive nerve in the public consciousness. Historians have almost uniformly criticized President Truman for his handling of the controversies. According to one writer, "Whatever his achievements in other fields, President Truman was unable to enforce high standards of conduct throughout his administration, nor did he invariably select appointees capable of observing high standards."[39] According to another, "Truman's erratic response raised disturbing doubts about his leadership and his concept of government."[40] Still another wrote, "Truman may himself have contributed unwittingly to creating the climate in which a handful of cheats, frauds, and simple fourflushers in the government managed to spray the taint of corruption across his second administration."[41] One close associate of the the president attributed this situation to Truman's 1948 election victory, which forced those who wanted something "to deal with him or not at all." If they could not influence the president directly, they could attempt to influence those friends of the president "who could get his ear."[42]

President Truman, who had led the charge against dollar-a-year men during the Second World War, was genuinely puzzled by the public reaction to what he believed were relatively minor instances of official impropriety in the context of a vast federal bureaucracy. In time, however, the White House staff came to grasp the implications of the new morality for the presidency as an institution.

Congressional investigations of the five-percenters and the RFC left the Truman White House apprehensive about the Douglas subcommittee's investigation of the "moral slump." For example, on June 9, 1951, Charles Murphy, special counsel to the president, received a memorandum about the upcoming hearing with information about the witnesses from a confidential source. Possible witnesses included Chester Barnard, Senator Benton, Robert M. Hutchins, Harold Ickes, Paul Appleby (Syracuse University), Philip Neibuhr, Ralph Bunch, Professor V. O. Key (Yale), Rabbi Philip Bernstein, Peter Odagrad, Everett Clinchy, former senator Robert Lafollette, James B. Conant, John L. Lewis, Irving Dillard, David Lilienthal, Harold Dodds (Princeton), Roscoe Pound, Senator Fulbright, Bishop Scarlett, William Green, Dr. Jasper Shannon, Bishop Hass, Dorothy Shaver, Judge Learned Hand, Archbishop Shell, Paul Hoffman, Rabbi Silver, and Mildred McAfree Horton.[43]

Besides the Douglas subcommittee hearings, other Democrats put pressure on President Truman to get out in front on the ethics issue. Congressman Charles Bennett of Florida urged Truman to support a code of ethics for all federal employees, which had been introduced as H. Con. Res. 128. Under the code federal officers and employees were given the following instructions:

1. put loyalty to God and country above loyalty to persons, party, or government department;

2. uphold the Constitution, laws, and legal regulations of the United States and of all governments therein and never be a party to their evasion;

3. give a full day's labor for a full day's pay;

4. seek to find and employ more efficient and economical ways of getting tasks accomplished;

5. never discriminate unfairly by the dispensing of special favors or privileges to anyone, whether for remuneration or not, and never accept favors or benefits from persons doing business with the government;

6. make no private promises of any kind binding on the duties of office (a government employee has no private word which can be binding on public duty);

7. engage in no business with the government either directly or indirectly;

8. never use any information coming to him in public functions as a means of making private profit;

9. expose corruption whenever discovered; and

10. never seek to influence another to violate these principles.[44]

In a letter responding to Congressman Bennett's request for presidential support of the "ten golden rules" of government ethics, President Truman left little doubt that at this time he put no stock in the idea of a code. In the president's words:

Unless a man is fundamentally sound ethically, you can't teach him what to do as a public servant. There is only one code that is fundamental in the lives of the people who make up the free countries and the code is found in the twentieth chapter of Exodus and in the fifth, sixth, and seventh chapters of the Gospel according to St. Matthew.[45]

The president's letter to Congressman Bennett concluded, "All of the hearings and all of the conversation will not produce a code of ethics. It has to be in a man's heart to start with."[46]

Besides not supporting Congressman Bennett's code of ethics, President Truman let Senator Douglas know that he objected to the subcommittee's circulating an executive branch questionnaire on government ethics without prior White House approval. The questionnaire asked for views on a number of conflict-of-interest-related questions. Specifically, it asked whether:

1. government employees should receive gifts or favors from private interests having dealings with federal agencies and departments;
2. the federal government should employ persons with strong industry backgrounds;
3. there should be restrictions on government employees taking jobs with firms doing business with the employees' former government agency;
4. government business should be discussed outside of office hours at social gathering; and
5. there should be stricter regulation of financial conflicts of interests.[47]

In a lengthy answer to the president's criticism, Senator Douglas argued that "spiritual injunctions cannot of themselves produce the basic integrity and good judgment that will help to lift the moral standards of man" because "as each age develops new situations and problems, we are required to make new and more difficult decisions as to what is the proper application of basic ethical principles to which we all subscribe." Douglas was sure that President Truman supported "the continuing search for truth and justice and methods of fair dealing among men, particularly as these are affected by the action of government."[48] Aware of Truman's record of disclosing procurement abuses during the Second World War, Douglas took special note of the president's prior "keen interest in steps to raise standards in government and in the national government."[49]

Defending both the subcommittee's use of a questionnaire and its hearings, Douglas stressed the positive tone of the proceedings and his effort to break away from the "necessarily negative tone of many of the valuable

Congressional investigations recently made.... We emphasized to witnesses that we were not interested in exposing individual derelictions," he said, "but in trying to find remedies and grow new and healthy tissue."[50] Besides, Douglas pointed out, testimony had not been limited to problems in the executive branch. Much of the testimony dealt with congressional ethics. The Douglas letter apparently did not convince Truman of a need for further investigations.

In August 1951, President Truman responded with an angry note to a proposed questionnaire that another congressional committee wanted to distribute to the Bureau of Internal Revenue enforcement personnel. He wrote, "Attached documents are totalitarian. If one was sent to me for an answer, I'd tell the sender to go to Hell."[51]

President Truman's Message to Congress on Ethical Standards in the Executive Branch and the Cleanup Campaign

Throughout the summer of 1951, the pressure to take presidential action mounted. The White House had been informed that the Douglas subcommittee would issue its report in the fall. Consequently, on September 27, 1951, a reluctant President Truman sent a message to Congress on the subject of ethical standards in the federal government.

The message asked Congress to enact a law requiring all presidential appointees, elected federal officials, military aides, and certain other federal officials earning more than $10,000 a year to file a disclosure statement, revealing income and such other income sources as investments in real estate, securities, gifts, and loans. His message to Congress, however, was accompanied by a strong attack against individuals and groups he believed were using the conduct cases for political purposes:

To my mind the most disturbing feature of the charges and rumors stirred up by these attempts is their effect on the confidence of the American people in their Government.... This is a terrible distortion of the true facts about our Government. It would be tragic if our citizens came to believe it.[52]

Congress was not enthusiastic about public financial disclosure for its members and did not act on Truman's message. After the 1952 election, the idea of public financial disclosure died.

In November 1951, Francis Biddle, attorney general of the United States from 1941 to 1945, wrote President Truman about a recent decision of the Board of the Americans for Democratic Action, which called for a team of special prosecutors to investigate the Bureau of Internal Revenue scandal.

In his view, these scandals threatened the presidency and, therefore, swift and forceful action was vital.

The seriousness of the situation cannot be exaggerated. We have been back from Europe only ten days and I find the chief topic of conversation on all sides is the alleged dishonesty in the Bureau of Internal Revenue, and, I regret to say, in the Department of Justice. It is inconceivable that the matter will blow over as some optimistic Democrats occasionally suggest. The enemies of your administration will keep it stirred up, and the public are outraged, uncertain, and almost ready to believe anything. In view of these circumstances, leaving action in the ordinary administrative channels will not stem the tide of rising indignation.[53]

The White House assured the former attorney general that the president understood the seriousness of the Bureau of Internal Revenue scandal and intended to create a Committee on the Conduct of Official Business. Between October and December 1951, Charles Murphy and his staff worked on a reform plan that would be acceptable to the president and to Democratic members of the House and Senate.

The letter to Biddle provides ample evidence that President Truman had given Charles Murphy, special counsel to the president, responsibility for dealing with the ever-increasing official misconduct scandal. Murphy and his staff acted as White House troubleshooters responsible for crucial ad hoc assignments for the White House. Murphy was "the cleaner-upper of nasty operational crises." In addition, he was responsible for preparing the president's speeches, major public statements, and messages to Congress, and he was in charge of the staff work for developing the president's own legislative program.[54]

Murphy and his staff proposed an executive order establishing a three-member investigatory panel consisting of Robert Ramspeck, chairman of the Civil Service Commission, J. Edgar Hoover, director of the Federal Bureau of Investigation, and a third member to be appointed to a new post as a special assistant to the attorney general. The panel was to have overall responsibility for uncovering cases of improper conduct and the authority to take action to punish those responsible. However, the Justice Department was to hold overall responsibility for prosecuting any wrongdoing.

The committee was needed, the draft explained, because "as the operations of government have become more important to the financial interests of our citizens, efforts by the unscrupulous to influence Government officials to act for private gain have become more prevalent and more serious." The executive branch needed more effective tools to control individuals hoping for special favors, influence peddlers, and those interests that had "become parasites on the business community and a threat to the reputation of honest government."[55]

In December 1951, the White House asked Federal Judge Thomas Murphy to fill the third position on the committee. However, once word of the forthcoming appointment appeared in the press, critics of the Truman Administration argued that Judge Murphy could not "conduct a thorough investigation of an administration headed by the President who appointed him to the bench."[56] Judge Murphy decided that under such circumstances he could not be very effective.

From the time J. Howard McGrath became attorney general in August of 1949 until his resignation in April 1952, he resisted all efforts for an independent probe of official misconduct allegations. Such a step, McGrath insisted, would give the impression that the Justice Department could not be trusted. Largely because of McGrath's resistance, Truman postponed plans to establish a committee on the conduct of official business.

Back to the Drawing Board

Despite the continuing strong opposition of the attorney general to any type of independent investigation, Charles Murphy and his staff continued to work on a cleanup campaign outside the Justice Department. Donald Hansen, one of Murphy's assistants, drafted a new proposal for presidential action that included provisions for:

1. the establishment of a three-man cleanup committee responsible to the attorney general;[57]

2. the creation of a permanent inspection service with overall responsibility for investigating and prosecuting misconduct on the part of government employees and those doing business with the government;[58]

3. a new code of ethics for federal employees and officials that would create uniform standards of conduct for all executive branch personnel;[59]

4. the appointment of a bipartisan commission on government ethics;

5. comprehensive financial reporting by private interests doing business with the government;[60]

6. a requirement that federal employees and officials occupying sensitive positions file financial disclosure statements; and

7. new legislation authorizing the cancellation of government contracts where unethical conduct in procuring the contract was determined.

A short time later, Charles Murphy asked President Truman to implement most of the reforms outlined in the Hansen memorandum, and he urged Truman to appoint a special assistant to the attorney general with independent power to conduct investigations despite the attorney general's continuing opposition. Furthermore, Mr. Murphy urged the president to order the preparation of uniform employee standards of conduct to deal with issues such as acceptance of gifts, outside employment, and mandatory disclosure of outside income. "While cleaning up past misconduct is important," he wrote in a memorandum, "It is much more important to take constructive steps for keeping things straight in the future."[61] Only preventive measures, he was convinced, could achieve the long-term goal of protecting the impartiality of decision-making processes from the pressures of special interests.

Finally, Murphy argued for the creation of a new inspection service whose primary mission would be "to make sure that the Government maintains adequate facilities for policing itself and discovering wrongdoing on the part of its employees and those who do business with its employees."[62]

In late January 1952, President Truman decided for the time being to go ahead with only a small part of the reform recommendations.[63] Truman agreed to appoint a special assistant to the attorney general to conduct a quasi-independent investigation of allegations of official misconduct.

Newbold Morris and His House of Cards Come Tumbling Down

Early in February 1952, the White House announced the appointment of Newbold Morris, a New York Republican lawyer and a strong advocate of government reform, to the position of special assistant to the attorney general. Under the arrangement, Attorney General McGrath would have general control of the cleanup campaign, but Newbold Morris would have considerable independence to conduct the necessary investigations. It soon became clear that the attorney general and Morris disagreed sharply on how broad an investigation Morris should conduct.

When Morris could not get substantial financial support from the Justice Department, he complained to the White House that he had requested funding for two hundred positions but that the Justice Department requested only $50,000 from the Bureau of the Budget for the investigation.[64] The Justice Department made it clear that it did not intend Morris "to make much of a splash."

Closely following the fight over the funding of the investigation, Special Assistant Morris announced, without the approval of the attorney general or the White House, his intention to require key personnel in the Justice Department to submit financial questionnaires listing outside sources of income.[65] Morris also asked the president to establish boards of inquiry within federal departments and agencies to sift out charges of misconduct.[66] Furthermore, Morris disclosed that he intended to send out 25,000 financial questionnaires to high-level federal officers.[67]

The friction was too great, however, and the investigation made little progress. More important, the White House began to have serious doubts about the competency of Morris as an investigator. According to an internal White House memorandum:

In the two months that Morris has been Special Assistant to the Attorney General, no investigation efforts have been instituted other than the delivery of the questionnaire to the Department of Justice. Morris apparently is miscast in his role, as he is not an investigator by personality, is not a good administrator, talks too much and obtains more publicity than is necessary or desirable. . . . If there is continued inaction on Morris' part, the press and congressional committees will soon learn of that and the whole operation very well may blow up. It is highly possible that there well may be a blow up anyway, unless Morris obtains full cooperation from the Attorney General.[68]

On April 4, 1952, Attorney General McGrath dismissed Newbold Morris. On the same day, President Truman announced the resignation of Attorney General McGrath and the nomination of Federal Judge James P. McGranery as attorney general. Shortly after taking his position, Judge McGranery announced the end of the cleanup campaign and declared that all official misconduct cases would henceforth be handled through routine Justice Department channels.[69] The cleanup campaign fiasco greatly embarrassed the Truman Administration. No further effort was made to implement ethics-related reforms.

A QUIET REVOLUTION

President Truman clearly underestimated the impact of the "mess in Washington on his administration. On the other hand, one can make a strong argument that nothing could have prepared Truman and his White House for the reaction.

The Truman Administration scandals thus have an importance far beyond serving as an example of a president who failed to keep his own house in order. The country had become much more sensitive to the appearance of impropriety and expected the president to play a more direct role. However, as the Truman White House found out, an effective system for preventing conflicts of interests and other forms of official misconduct did not exist. Few agencies had clear standards of conduct, and most of the criminal conflict of interest statutes had little applicability to the operations of modern government.

The "mess in Washington" thus marks the beginning of a new era in government ethics, symbolized by a preoccupation with appearances of impropriety and conflicts of interest. The rules of the game had changed.

THE CRUSADE STUBS A TOE

It is ironic that while President Truman could not shake off the accusation that he showed no concern for integrity, the Eisenhower campaign easily weathered an admission that, while senator, vice presidential candidate Richard Nixon had accepted $18,235 from political supporters in California to help him defray the cost of going to Washington. The disclosures put candidate Eisenhower in a difficult position. Running against the "mess in Washington," Eisenhower had to reconcile the picture of a vice presidential candidate taking thousands of dollars for personal expenditures from private sources. Nixon saved his place on the ticket by making the now famous "Checkers Speech" and convincing Eisenhower and the party faithful that the fund was used to permit him to serve the nation and not to enrich himself or his family.

Despite the Nixon affair, the American people believed that General Eisenhower would clean up the "mess in Washington." Eisenhower came to Washington pledging not to tolerate any kind of impropriety on the part of his appointees or of anyone working for the federal government, but he would learn that such a pledge was easier to make than to keep.

NOTES

1. *See* Comer Van Woodward, ed., *Responses of the Presidents to Charges of Misconduct* (New York: Delacorte, 1974), pp. 325–347.

2. Ibid., p. 328.

3. Ibid.

4. Ibid.

5. Cabell Phillips, *The Truman Presidency* (New York: The Macmillan Company, 1966), p. 405.

6. Ibid.

7. U.S. Senate Subcommittee on the Committee on Expenditures in the Executive Departments, *The Five-Percenter Investigation*, 81st Cong, 2nd Sess., January 1950, p. 2.

8. Phillips, *The Truman Presidency*, p. 405.

9. U.S. Congress, Senate, *The Five-Percenter Investigation*, pp. 8–9.

10. Ibid., p. 20.

11. Ibid., p. 22.

12. Phillips, p. 306.

13. Ibid.

14. Phillips, p. 407.

15. U.S. Senate, Committee on Banking and Currency, *Study of the Reconstruction Finance Corporation and Proposed Amendment of the RFC Act,* Senate Report 649, 82d Cong., 1st Sess., August 20, 1951, p. 1.

16. Phillips, p. 411.

17. See U.S. House, Committee on Ways and Means, *Internal Revenue Investigation,* House Report 2518, 82d Cong., 1st Sess., January 3, 1953, pp. 26–27.

18. Phillips, p. 20.

19. Ibid.

20. Van Woodward, *Responses of Presidents to Charges of Misconduct*, p. 325.

21. Michael March, "Ethics in Government," Editorial Research Reports, vol. 2, 1951, pp. 827–46.

22. Alonzo L. Hamby, *Beyond the New Deal: Harry S Truman and American Liberalism* (New York: Columbia University Press, 1973), pp. 460–61.

23. Senators Humphrey (Minn.), Neely (W. Va.), Aiken (Vt.) and Morse (Oreg.) also served on the subcommittee with Senator Douglas, who held a doctorate in political science.

24. U.S. Senate, Subcommittee of the Committee on Labor and Public Welfare, *Hearing to Study Senate Concurrent Resolution 21,* 82d Cong., 1st Sess., 1951.

25. U.S. Senate, Committee on Labor and Public Welfare, Report of the Subcommittee on Labor and Public Welfare on *Ethical Standards in Government,* 82d Cong., 1st Sess., 1951.

26. Ibid., p. 9.

27. Ibid., p. 11.

28. The fifteen-member panel would have consisted of five members appointed by the vice president, five appointed by the Speaker of the House, and two career civil servants appointed by the president.

29. Douglas Subcommittee Report, p. 2.

30. Ibid., p. 11.

31. Douglas Subcommittee Report, p. 3.

32. Ibid.

33. See Section 207(c) of Title 18 of the United States Code, Title V of the Ethics in Government Act of 1978.

34. Douglas Committee Report, p. 20.

35. Ibid.

36. Ibid., p. 3.

37. Ibid., p. 39.

38. Ibid., pp. 4–6.

39. Van Woodward, p. 305.

40. Hamby, p. 361.

41. Phillips, p. 404.

42. Ibid.

43. Memorandum, Kenneth W. Hechler for Mr. Murphy, June 9, 1951, Official File, Harry S Truman Library. This was not the complete list as presented in the memorandum.

44. H. Con. Res. 128, June 26, 1951, 82d Cong., 1st Sess.

45. Letter, Harry S Truman to Congressman Charles Bennett, July 27, 1951, Official File, Harry S Truman Library.

46. Ibid.

47. Douglas Committee Questionnaire, July 1951, Official File, Harry S Truman Library.

48. Letter, Senator Paul Douglas to the president, August 4, 1951, Papers of Harry S Truman, Official File, Harry S Truman Library.

49. Ibid.

50. Ibid.

51. Hamby, p. 465.

52. U.S. President Harry Truman, Message to Congress, September 27, 1951.

53. Letter, Francis Biddle to the president, November 30, 1951, Papers of Harry S Truman, Official File, Harry S Truman Library. Francis Biddle served as the national chairman of the Americans for Democratic Action.

54. Richard E. Newstadt in Francis H. Heller, ed, *The Truman White House: The Administration of the Presidency: 1945–1953* (Lawrence, Kans.: The Regents Press of Kansas, 1980), pp. 93–104.

55. Memorandum, Charles S. Murphy for Mr. Short, December 8, 1951, Papers of Harry S Truman, President's Secretary File, Harry S Truman Library.

56. Hamby, p. 463. *See also* Proposed Statement by the President on the Establishment of a Committee on the Conduct of Official Business, Draft, December 10, 1951, Papers of Harry S Truman, President's Secretary File, Harry S Truman Library.

57. Outline of Possible Presidential Action on Integrity in Government, Draft by Donald Hansen, January 18, 1952. Papers of Harry S Truman, President's Secretary File, Harry S Truman Library.

58. Ibid., p. 2.

59. Ibid., pp. 3–4.

60. Ibid., p. 6.

61. Memorandum, Charles S. Murphy for the president, January 23, 1952, Papers of Harry S Truman, President's Secretary File, Harry S Truman Library.

62. Ibid., pp. 2–3.

63. Much of the following discussion of the January 24, 1952, White House meeting comes from a memorandum prepared for the director of the Bureau of the Budget. Memorandum, Bill Finan for the director (Bureau of the Budget), January 29, 1952, Papers of Charles S. Murphy, President's Secretary File, Harry S Truman Library.

64. Memorandum, Donald A. Hansen for Mr. Murphy, February 7, 1952, Papers of Charles A. Murphy, Harry S Truman Library.

65. *New York Times,* February 28, 1952.

66. Memorandum, Newbold Morris for the president, March 12, 1952, Papers of Harry S Truman, Official File, Harry S Truman Library.

67. *New York Times,* March 17, 1952.

68. Memorandum, Donald Hansen for Mr. Murphy, March 28, 1952, Papers of Charles Murphy, Harry S Truman Library.

69. Van Woodward, p. 340.

III

The Appearance of Impropriety: Conflicts of Interest and the Eisenhower Years

Although the Republicans used the "moral slump" issue successfully to discredit the Democratic Party during the 1952 campaign, the Eisenhower Administration slowly learned that conflict of interest problems were not the exclusive property of Democrats. Most of the problems involved the conduct of high-level officials recruited by the Eisenhower Administration from business and industry. Critics of the Eisenhower Administration's integrity argued that many recruits put their private interests above that of the public. Thus, by the end of Eisenhower's second term, conflict of interest had again became a national political issue. Even after eight years of Republican rule, the "mess in Washington" was a long way from being cleaned up.

CHANGING OF THE GUARD

Even before the November 1952 election, the groundwork for staffing an Eisenhower Administration had been laid. Soon after the 1952 Republican Convention, Harold E. Talbott, a New York businessman, asked the consulting firm of Mckinsey and Company to make a study of executive recruiting in the event of an Eisenhower victory.[1] The firm compiled a list of names of several thousand potential appointees to fill 915 top appointive positions.[2] The Republican Party had talked for years about "displacing so-called fuzzy-thinking Democratic bureau chiefs with hard-headed businessmen."[3]

The president and his staff sought to appoint political executives who would prevent a career staff from obstructing the president's program. As described by Civil Service historian Paul Van Riper, "Many incoming Republicans felt that the agencies had been staffed in large measure with loyal Democrats who for the most part had been blanketed into their jobs." Furthermore, many "Republicans seriously questioned whether the bulk of the career staff would be sympathetic with the new administration's policies."[4] On the other hand, many of those "blanketed-in" Democrats believed that Republican appointees intended to dismantle the government and use their positions to help already powerful special interests.

Out of the White House since 1952, the Republicans found it considerably easier to announce their goal of recruiting business executives than to find people willing to take positions. Many candidates rejected appointments because of low pay, disruption to their careers, or the dislocation of their families.[5] In spite of these problems, the Eisenhower Administration filled numerous positions with business recruits.[6] However, many of the appointees left companies that had substantial business with the federal government or a strong financial interest in the direction of government policy.[7] Critics argued that these appointees would be predisposed to favor special interests.

However, if President Eisenhower wanted appointees with strong business backgrounds, he also wanted to make sure that nothing in a nominee's background would raise questions of national security. To this end, the Eisenhower White House required the Federal Bureau of Investigation to conduct extensive background checks of prospective nominees.[8] These more formalized clearance procedures, however, failed to head off a number of nasty conflict of interest controversies over the confirmation of Eisenhower nominees.

Conflicts of Interest and Confirmation

In addition to winning the presidency, the 1952 election saw the Republicans take control of the Senate. The shift in party control did not stop the United States Senate from greatly increasing its review of the financial affairs of nominees for actual or potential conflicts of interest.

Prior to this period, the Senate had rarely looked into the financial affairs of a nominee as part of the confirmation process. When the Sentate refused to confirm Charles Beecher Warren, President Coolidge's nominee for attorney general, it did so because of fear that he would not aggressively enforce the antitrust laws, not because of his financial holdings.[9] During 1949 Carl Ilgenfritz, Truman's nominee to head the Munitions Board, was sharply criticized for his intention to continue to receive his salary from the United States Steel Corporation, an arrangement that would probably have violated the existing statutory prohibition on the private supplementation of the salaries of government employees.[10] The Senate refused to exempt Mr. Ilgenfritz from the prohibition, and subsequently voted 28 to 40 to reject his nomination.[11]

One month after his election, President-elect Eisenhower nominated Charles E. Wilson as secretary of defense, Roger Kyes as the deputy secretary of defense, Robert T. B. Stevens as secretary of the army, and Harold Talbott as secretary of the navy.[12] The disclosure that each of the nominees held substantial blocks of stock in companies with substantial dealings or contracts with the Department of Defense became a major obstacle to their confirmation.[13]

It should be noted that federal law at that time did not, and still does not prohibit Defense Department officials and employees from holding financial interests, such as stocks and bonds, in companies having substantial dealings with the Defense Department. The law required only that federal personnel refrain from taking action on specific matters that might affect their financial interests.[14] Nonetheless, members of the Armed Services Committee pressed Eisenhower's Defense Department nominees to divest themselves of such holdings because of the appearance of a financial conflict of interest and because of the general rule of the Committee on Armed Services that presidential appointees to the Defense Department divest themselves of stocks valued at $10,000 or more in defense-related companies.[15]

On January 15, 1953, Wilson appeared before a closed session of the Senate Armed Services Committee and announced that he "had severed all ties with General Motors Corporation, but retained ownership of 39,470 shares of General Motors stock and was a recipient of the company's pension plan and insurance benefits."[16] Wilson's refusal to divest clearly annoyed a number of the senators on the committee. When asked by Senator Hendrickson of New Jersey what he would do in a situation where he might have to make a decision adversely affecting General Motors Corporation, Mr. Wilson replied with words that have found a place in American history: "I cannot conceive of one because for years I thought what was good for our country was good for General Motors, and vice versa.[17]

Mr. Wilson also informed the committee that he would disqualify himself from personal participation in any Defense Department dealings with General Motors, a step, he said, that the White House agreed would eliminate any concern over possible conflicts of interest.

Realizing that he had little chance of being confirmed unless he complied with the Armed Services Committee rule regarding divestiture, on January 23, 1953, Wilson agreed to divest. On January 27, 1953, by a vote of 27 to 6, the Senate confirmed Wilson as secretary of defense.[18] Shortly thereafter, the Senate confirmed nominees Kyes, Stevens, and Talbott, after all three had agreed to divest themselves of stocks in companies having business with the Department of Defense.[19] In sharp contrast to the divestiture position of the Senate Armed Services Committee, almost all the other committees expressed only "passing concern for the outside financial interests of Presidential nominees."[20]

However, even the relatively limited confirmation problems of Eisenhower nominees led the White House to believe that its liberal critics were intent on using conflict of interest allegations to discredit administration appointees and to block the programs of the president.

CLEANING UP THE MESS IN WASHINGTON

Immediately on taking the reins of government, the Eisenhower Administration announced an aggressive campaign to root out corruption and inefficiency in what it viewed as a bloated federal bureaucracy. On February 7, 1953, President Eisenhower authorized the release of confidential tax returns of government employees to the Senate Government Operations Committee to aid the committee's efforts to detect unethical conduct by government employees.[21] Then, in September 1953, Attorney General Herbert Brownell announced a new program intended to vigorously enforce the criminal conflict of interest statutes.[22] The postemployment activities of former federal employees were to receive particularly close scrutiny.[23]

On November 17, 1953, a federal grand jury indicted former Assistant Attorney General Herbert Bergson for unlawfully representing two companies before the Antitrust Division of Justice, a division he had headed.[24] After resuming private law practice, Bergson began representing Minnesota Mining and Manufacturing Company, the Carborundum Company, and the U.S. Pipeline Company on antitrust matters. Specifically, Bergson applied to the Antitrust Division for a clearance letter regarding proposed mergers. Clearance letters gave companies some assurance that the Department of Justice would not test the legality of a proposed merger should it be attempted.[25] As head of the Antitrust Division, Bergson had handled two antitrust cases involving these three firms. After entering private practice, he represented the same companies with respect to their requests for clearance letters.

Section 284 of Title 18 of the United States Code prohibited former government employees from representing private parties involving any contract or claim that the former employee had worked on while employed in the government. A request for a clearance letter, Justice maintained, fell within the scope of the statutory prohibition on postemployment representational activities.

Bergson quickly accused the attorney general of a politically motivated indictment against a former high-level Democrat. At any rate, on January 20, 1954, Federal District Judge McLaughlin ruled that the application for a clearance letter did not constitute the prosecution of a "claim against the United States" under the provisions of Section 284. Only actions to recover money or property from the United States, the court ruled, came within the scope of the statutory meaning of "claim against the United States."[26]

The Bergson decision led Attorney General Brownell to ask Congress to put a lifetime prohibition against former government officials representing private parties before the government with respect to any matters in which they had participated while in government service and to make it clear that the prohibition applied to all forms of representational activities, and not only to the prosecution of claims against the government.[27] The attorney general's bill did not make it out of committee.

Between July 1, 1952, and June 30, 1953, the Department of Justice "brought only eleven prosecutions of matters involving possible violations of conflict of interest laws, and most of these dealt with alleged violation of the bribery statutes."[28] In a word, the publicity surrounding the cleanup campaign was not followed by large-scale prosecutions of government personnel.

After the initial flurry of activity, the Eisenhower White House quickly lost interest in making conflict of interest reform a top priority, even though the Justice Department wanted the narrow conflict of interest statutes updated.[29] Subsequent conflict of interest problems of high-level officials led the White House to steer clear of the conflict of interest problem. New legislation, it was thought, would give the public the impression that there was a problem needing attention.

Organizational Reform and Administrative Ethics

With the failure of the Justice Department's efforts to obtain passage of statutory conflict of interest reforms, a handful of federal agencies and departments instituted their own ethics reform programs. For example, on February 4, 1953, the Securities and Exchange Commission (SEC) announced the adoption of a new standards of conduct code for all commission personnel. The commission believed that these standards would reduce the likelihood of its employees being accused of giving preferential treatment to individuals and organizations regulated by the SEC. These landmark standards of conduct received the full support of Senator Douglas, who commented on the importance of the action:

As one who has been frankly critical of some practices that had developed there in the past, I want to take this opportunity to acknowledge and commend the step the SEC has thus taken to improve the standards of Government service.[30]

The commission recognized that internal SEC information relating to investigations and other securities industry activities could be worth millions of dollars to stock securities speculators. This group included SEC employees. At the same time, if SEC personnel accepted gifts or gratuities from individuals or organizations subject to SEC regulation or negotiated for jobs in the securities industry while employed by the SEC, the public might come to believe that the SEC favored the interests of those they regulated.

The commission's new standards of conduct applied to all SEC personnel, and strictly prohibited employees from using an SEC position or confidential information in private profit-making activities. The code also prohibited the acceptance of any valuable, gift, favor, or service from any person transacting business with the United States. The code, furthermore, prohibited an employee from discussing future employment opportunities with any person outside the government having official dealings with the SEC official. Finally, the code dealt with the unauthorized release of commercial or economic information and with social relationships with those having business pending before SEC personnel.[31]

In addition to the general standards of conduct, the SEC prohibited former SEC employees from representing private clients in SEC proceedings with respect to matters for which they had personal responsibility or knowledge while an employee of the commission. In contrast to the statutory prohibition, Section 434, the SEC postemployment bar was a lifetime prohibition and not limited to only two years.

On the postemployment issue, Senator Douglas believed the SEC's standards of conduct did not go far enough because they did not restrict the general lobbying activities of former SEC personnel. Douglas argued on the floor of the Senate that the commission should have adopted the recommendation of his subcommittee which prohibited former government employees from contacting their former government employers on any matter for two years after leaving government service. Douglas noted that the SEC regulation allowed former commission members and other employees to practice before the SEC "immediately after termination of their Commission services on matters which they themselves did not directly handle."[32]

The Bureau of Internal Revenue scandal was the motivating factor in strengthening SEC standards of conduct regulations. The SEC recognized that the existing criminal conflict of interest statutes failed to deal with the commission's most serious day-to-day conflict of interest problems. Appearance problems could be prevented only by internal enforcement of high standards of conduct.

Through the remainder of the 1950s, neither the White House nor the Civil Service Commission attempted to implement uniform standards of conduct for executive-branch employees and officials. A number of federal agencies, however, did follow the example of the SEC and tighten their internal codes to deal with actual and apparent conflict of interest problems. However, the momentum for conflict of interest reform died as conflict of interest became a partisan political issue.

As noted, the Eisenhower Administration made its cleanup campaign an early priority. However, a series of disclosures between 1955 and 1960 put Republicans and the White House on the receiving end of criticism that an administration did not care about ethics in government and looked the other way when high-level officials attempted to use their public offices for personal gain. These revelations would rekindle the debate over the effectiveness of existing regulations.

A common theme ran through these Eisenhower-era conflict of interest controversies: government officials had failed to separate their private financial dealings from their responsibilities as public servants. Because of this failure, they left the impression that they had used public positions for personal financial gain, whether they had intended to do so or not.

It is unnecessary to review all the complexities of conflicts of interest during the Eisenhower Administration, for although they received considerable public attention, they had little impact upon the popularity of President Eisenhower.[33] Some of the scandals merit study, however, because they demonstrate how political the debate over conflicts of interest had become, and because they provided the impetus for reforms that would come during the administration of John Kennedy.

POLITICS AND CONFLICTS OF INTEREST: THE SAGA OF DIXON-YATES

Of all the conflict-of-interest scandals that plagued the Eisenhower Presidency, the Dixon-Yates scandal demonstrated how easily conflict of interest controversies became entangled with partisan politics and public policy disputes.[34]

During the 1952 campaign, Eisenhower had argued that private enterprise should be responsible for meeting the future power needs of the country.[35] On the other hand, as a candidate, Eisenhower had pledged not to abolish the Tennessee Valley Authority (TVA). However, when Eisenhower submitted a revised budget to Congress on May 13, 1953, it did not contain thirty million dollars towards the construction of a new TVA power plant, an allocation which had been included in Truman's final budget which was sent to Congress shortly before Eisenhower took office.[36]

To aid the new administration in making its case against building public power capacity, Joseph M. Dodge, Director of the Bureau of the Budget, acted on the recommendation of George D. Woods, chairman of First Boston Corporation, and obtained the services of Adolphe Wenzell, vice president and director of First Boston, as an unpaid consultant on the issue of public or private control.[37] Reimbursed for expenses at ten dollars a day, Wenzell was asked to determine the "source and amount of the subsidies in TVA rates."[38] First Boston Corporation was one of the largest underwriters of power projects in the country.

The Wenzell report, submitted in September 1953, made several recommendations on how TVA's power generation and distribution program might be restructured to reduce costs. More important to the ensuing controversy, Wenzell expressed his strong opposition to any further increase in government-generated power, and recommended the sale of the TVA system to a private company.[39] The federal government, he advised, should get out of the business of producing power.

The decision not to fund the construction of another TVA power plant gave the administration the opportunity to show that private power could economically replace public-generated power. The problem was to present the case without enraging the powerful supporters of the Tennessee Valley Authority.

Early in 1954, the Atomic Energy Commission (AEC) entered into an agreement with Edward H. Dixon, president of Middle South Utilities, and Eugene A. Yates, chairman of the Board of the Southern Company, "to construct and operate a coal-fueled steam-generating plant at West Memphis, Arkansas," to supply the Atomic Energy Commission with supplemental electric power.[40] These two companies set up the Mississippi Valley Generating Company to operate the new plant.

The seeds of the controversy grew out of a new agreement between the Bureau of the Budget, the Atomic Energy Commission, the TVA, and Dixon-Yates. Mississippi Valley would still sell power from the new plant to the AEC, but the AEC would sell this power to the TVA, who would then have enough capacity in the area to serve the city of Memphis. In addition, the TVA could supply the additional power needed by the AEC. Through this complex arrangement, the Eisenhower Administration would demonstrate that there was no need for the federal government to directly produce any more power.[41]

Congressional critics saw the contract as the first step in the destruction of the TVA. The contract made national headlines on June 17, 1954, when Democratic National Chairman Stephen Michael implied that favoritism might have been involved in awarding the contract to the Dixon-Yates group because Bobby Jones, a close friend of President Eisenhower, was on the board of directors of the Southern Company.[42] This entirely unsubstantiated charge produced immediate denial from the White House and turned public opinion against the Democratic Party. In the wake of the backlash, First Boston Corporation quickly obtained approval to raise funds for the project.

Between the time of the initial announcement of the Dixon-Yates contract in June 1954 and early February 1955, opponents of Dixon-Yates searched hard for "some taint of immoral or illegal conduct associated with the contract, which would give them the issue they needed to dramatize it effectively as a corrupt deal."[43] They found an issue in the dual role of Adolphe Wenzell as government consultant and as a high official of First Boston Corporation.

On February 18, 1955, Senator Lester Hill, Democrat from Alabama, announced that his investigation revealed that while acting as a consultant to the Bureau of the Budget on the Dixon-Yates contract, First Boston was arranging the financing for the project. Senator Hill loudly protested the propriety of allowing someone serving as a government consultant on the public power issue to serve as a major officer in a private corporation responsible for financing such a project.[44] Hill wondered out loud why the administration had not disclosed Wenzell's role when the controversy over the contract first developed in June 1954.

In an effort to determine whether Wenzell or other officials had violated federal law during Dixon-Yates negotiations, the Antitrust Subcommittee of the Senate Judiciary Committee held public hearings during the summer of 1956.[45] On July 8, 1955, in testimony before the subcommittee, Wenzell declared that he had not tried to conceal his involvement in the negotiations, that his role as a government consultant was in no way related to his role in negotiating the Dixon-Yates contract, and that he had done nothing illegal or improper.[46]

Nevertheless, the disclosure of Wenzell's involvement effectively doomed the project. The city of Memphis announced it no longer needed TVA power because it intended to build its own power plant. Because of the decision in Memphis, the TVA announced that it no longer needed AEC power. Without the planned TVA purchase of power, the AEC would have to pay the full cost of the power. Critics urged the government to cancel the contract on the grounds that Wenzell had used his role as a government consultant to get business for his company.[47] In turn, the Dixon-Yates group made it clear that it would go to court to hold the government to the terms of the contract or to force the government to pay a considerable cancellation fee.

On July 11, 1955, Attorney General Brownell announced that President Eisenhower had decided to cancel the Dixon-Yates contract with the AEC because of the decision of the city of Memphis to build its own power plant, not because of the involvement of Wenzell and First Boston. Public pressure made it politically impossible for the Eisenhower Administration to voluntarily pay the more than million-dollar cancellation fee.[48] Critics argued that the contract was void because Wenzell violated federal law in participating in negotiations over the financing of the project.

In June of 1959, the United States Court of Claims held that the government had to pay Dixon-Yates and Mississippi Valley Generating Company $1.87 million in damages. Then, on January 9, 1961, the Supreme Court overturned the award of the Court of Claims on the grounds that the contract was unenforceable because of the existence of a conflict of interest in the role of Adolphe Wenzell as a consultant to the government on the Dixon-Yates contract and as a major officer of First Boston Corporation. The award was overturned despite the fact that the Justice Department did not even attempt to prosecute Wenzell for violating any law or regulation.[49]

The Dixon-Yates scandal was not the only official misconduct controversy to implicate Eisenhower administration officials. On August 1, 1955,

Secretary of the Air Force Harold Talbot resigned after disclosures that after entering the government, he continued to help Mulligan & Company, an engineering firm in which he was a partner, solicit private business.[50] Throughout the controversy Talbot maintained he had done nothing improper, and a subsequent Justice Department investigation determined that he had not violated any federal law or regulation.

Edmund Mansure, the administrator of the General Services Administration (GSA), resigned early in February 1956 after allegations that pressure from the National Republican Party forced him to award GSA contracts to contractors who supported the president and the Republican Party.[51] However, the Mansure controversy received little press coverage, and Congress did not go out of its way to investigate the matter.

On February 15, 1957, Robert Tripp Ross, assistant secretary of defense for legislative and public affairs, resigned after reports that Wynn Enterprises, a company owned by his wife, had received a number of military clothing contracts while Ross served in the government. A subsequent investigation by Congressman Holifield's Government Operations Investigating Subcommittee raised serious questions about the quality of work performed by the Wynn companies.[52]

The last major scandal, and probably the most famous, involved President Eisenhower's Chief of Staff Sherman Adams and erupted in June of 1958. The former governor of New Hampshire admitted to having accepted a number of expensive gifts from private individuals.[53] Throughout the controversy, Chief of Staff Adams denied that these gifts had helped to gain preferential treatment for the donors. Adams admitted, however, that he did contact a number of regulatory agencies on the behalf of Bernard Goldfine, the source of the most valuable gifts. Adams resigned his position on September 23, 1958.[54] President Eisenhower maintained that Adams was not forced to resign, but that he left to save the president the trouble of defending Adams at every public appearance.

The Eisenhower scandals never grew to the proportions of those of the Truman Presidency, but they proved a constant source of irritation to the Eisenhower White House.

PRESIDENTIAL RECRUITMENT AND PUBLIC SERVICE ETHICS

Although the Eisenhower years saw continued preoccupation with conflict of interest matters, they also saw much more concern with problems associated with the recruitment of individuals to fill high-level career and political positions.

The Eisenhower transition team had considerable difficulty convincing private-sector executives to join the administration. Many of those who turned down positions cited conflict of interest regulations, the prohibition on private supplementation of government salaries, and their unwillingness to subject themselves and their families to scrutiny over their personal financial dealings and relationships. It is a reasonable assumption, noted a September 1957 article appearing in *Fortune,* that a number of business executives refused nominations for federal service because of the "conflict of interest bogey."[55]

Even before the election of President Eisenhower, in 1952, John Carson published a study entitled *Executives for the Federal Service: A Program for Action in Time of Crisis.*[56] Carson argued that the Korean War and the worldwide threat of communism required the country to mobilize its best executive talent. However, since four out of five executives refused appointment, he felt that the country was being deprived of the leadership it needed. Besides the problems of inadequate compensation, commitments to private business, insecurity of public employment, and a perceived abuse of public officials by Congress and the media, the Carson study also pointed to the fear of legal reprisals stemming from the inadvertent violation of conflict of interest prohibitions as an increasingly serious problem.[57]

A number of members of Congress interviewed by Carson rejected complaints about over-scrutiny of the backgrounds of presidential appointees. Congress, they maintained, had a Constitutional obligation to identify nominees who might use their public positions to further their own personal interests.[58] These strict supporters of conflict of interest regulation argued that "those businessmen who are not willing to stand up before Congressional committees and the public press to defend their policies and actions just aren't patriotic enough or are unfitted temperamentally to serve in government jobs."[59]

The debate did not end here. The Hoover Commission's 1955 *Report of the Commission on Organization of the Executive Branch on Personnel and Civil Service* pointed to conflict of interest laws as a major hindrance to the recruitment efforts of federal agencies and departments.[60] In particular, the commission criticized the interpretation of the law prohibiting the supplementation of the salaries of government employees as applying to an employee's continued participation in a company pension or stock option plan. Consequently, the Hoover Commission recommended that "the President review the conflict of interest laws to determine whether the intent of such laws can be better achieved by other more positive means that would encourage rather than discourage entry of competent men into public life."[61]

The issue of the impact of conflict of interest law on executive recruitment surfaced again in the 1957 Brookings Institution study, *Executives for Government: Central Issues of Federal Personnel Administration.* Authors Paul T. David and Ross Pollack concluded that the "conflict of interest statutes have restricted far more severely [the recruitment of federal executives] than the requirement for political clearance."[62] The prohibition against continued participation in pension and stock option plans once more received the most criticism.

As in the earlier studies, however, the authors could not supply hard evidence concerning the number of executives who declined appointments because of the conflict of interest laws. Moreover, inadequate compensation and career disruption were still cited most often as the reasons for declining nominations or appointments. Furthermore, in 1958, the Harvard Business School Club of Washington, D.C., published a report on businessmen in government, which listed (1) conflict of interest regulation, (2) inadequate compensation, (3) duration of stay, (4) the difference between the executive process in business and in government, and (5) lack of interest in government as reasons given for declining high-level federal positions.[63] More important, the Harvard report noted that many businessmen refused positions because of the popular notion that individuals took public positions to serve so-called "special interest" groups.[64] Business executives saw no reason to subject themselves to this form of guilt by association.

Interestingly, the Harvard study surveyed businessmen who were serving or had served in federal government and found that 31 percent of the "presently serving" group continued to receive additional compensation or benefits from their pregovernment employer, regardless of the prohibition on supplementation of salaries.[65]

Finally, the report suggested five steps toward restoring public trust in the integrity of businessmen who enter the federal government. The first step was to increase public awareness that most businessmen who enter government have a high sense of integrity. The second was to increase recognition that conflicts of interest are not limited to pecuniary ones. Third was to require businessmen entering government to disclose relevant investment information and require that they disqualify themselves from matters where there is, "or might be, or there is reasonable likelihood that the public believe there might be a conflict of interest." Fourth was to establish stiff criminal penalties for violating conflict of interest laws. The fifth step was to limit mandatory divestiture of financial interests only to situations "where the relationship between the company and the government job are such as to indicate a clear and present danger of a personal conflict."[66]

The Harvard Business Club conflict of interest reform program attempted to steer a middle course. Only in extreme circumstances would divestiture be the remedy for an actual or apparent conflict of interest. Disqualification from matters which would arguably affect the official's financial holdings would be the preferred solution for conflict of interest problems.

Concern over the impact of conflict of interest regulations on executive recruitment thus grew at the same time that pressure increased to do something about the seemingly endless string of officials subject to conflict of interest allegations. The problem was how to strengthen regulations without increasing recruitment and retention problems.

BACK TO SQUARE ONE

Despite the position of the Eisenhower White House that the vast majority of allegations against its officials were politically motivated, the frequency of allegations of poor judgment on behalf of top officials overshadowed White House claims that the president did not tolerate unethical conduct in his administration. However, the moral outrage apparent at the beginning of the decade was gone by its end. Cynicism about the willingness of government to punish officials for misconduct increased. With the White House refusing to take the lead on conflict of interest reform, few in Congress looked forward to a review that might force changes in the way Congress policed its own members.

At the same time, as the Cold War continued and as the country tried to deal with a perceived gap in the scientific and technological competence of its work force, concern grew about the continued ability of the federal government to recruit the best and the brightest individuals as full-time government employees or as consultants.

In sum, the most serious failure of the Eisenhower White House was not its tendency to regard most allegations of official impropriety as politically motivated, but its failure to take a leadership role in developing a consensus on what standards of conduct should apply to federal employees in the second half of the 20th century. Eisenhower entered the presidency promising to restore honesty and integrity to government. He left the state of public service ethics no worse off than when he entered the presidency, but no better off either.

NOTES

1. G. Calvin Mackenzie, *The Politics of Presidential Appointments* (New York: Free Press, 1981), p. 15.

2. Ibid.

3. Elmo Richardson, *The Presidency of Dwight D. Eisenhower* (Lawrence, Kans.: Regents Press, 1976), p. 35.

4. Van Riper, p. 490.

5. Richardson, p. 36.

6. See Philip H. Burch, Jr., *Elites in American History: The New Deal to the Carter Administration* (New York: Holmes and Meier, 1980), pp. 123–46; for biographical data on individual appointments, *see* pp. 434–50. *Also see* Stanley Mann Doig, *Men Who Govern* (Washington, D.C.: Brookings Institution, 1964), p. 31.

7. Richardson, p. 19.

8. Mackenzie, p. 19.

9. Joseph P. Harris, *The Advice and Consent of the Senate* (Berkeley: University of California Press, 1953), p. 119.

10. The prohibition against supplementation of salary was found at Section 1914 of the United States Code. It is presently found at Section 209 of title 18 of the United States Code.

11. Association of the Bar of the City of New York, *Conflict of Interest and Federal Service* (Cambridge, Mass.: Harvard University Press, 1960), p. 97.

12. Cleveland A. Williams, "Senate Confirmation: The Eisenhower Years," (Ph.D. dissertation, Southern Illinois University, 1961), p. 122.

13. Ibid.

14. Section 434, Title 18 of the United States Code read:

Whoever being an officer, agent or member, directly or indirectly interested in the pecuniary profits or contracts of any corporation, joint stock or association, or of any firm or partnership, or business entity, is employed or acts as an officer or agent of the United States for the transaction of business with such business entity, shall be fined not more than $2000 or imprisoned not more than two years or both.

15. Association of the Bar, p. 97.

16. Cleveland A. Williams, p. 124. He also notified the committee of his holdings in other companies that had dealings with the government and of his decision not to sell these stocks because of the tax consequences of such sales.

17. U.S. Congress, Senate, Hearings before the Senate Committee on Armed Services on the Nomination of Charles E. Wilson to be Secretary of Defense, 83d Cong., 1st Sess., 1953, p. 15.

18. *Congressional Record,* 83d Cong., 1st Sess., 1953, p. 545.

19. Williams, p. 110.

20. Association of the Bar.

21. *New York Times,* February 7, 1953, p. 18.

22. *United States Law Week,* 22 (Sept. 8, 1953): 2103. *See also New York Times,* September, 15, 1953, p. 44.

23. The two applicable postemployment statutes were 18 U.S.C. 99 and 18 U.S.C. 284. The amended versions of these prohibitions are currently found at 18 U.S.C. 207.

24. *New York Times,* November 17, 1953 p. 20. The Justice Department charged him with violating the prohibition on former government employees representing private parties before the government found at 18 U.S.C. 284.

25. Association of the Bar, p. 51.

26. *New York Times,* January 30, 1954, p. 1; January 31, 1954, p. 5. Also see *United States* v. *Bergson,* 119 F. Supp. 459 (D.D.C. 1954); Bayless Manning, *Federal Conflict of Interest Law* (Cambridge, Mass.: Harvard University Press, 1964), pp. 189–90.

27. Association of the Bar, p. 51, note 7c. The bill was introduced as H.R. 10.000, 83d Cong., 2d Sess. (1954).

28. Association of the Bar, p. 72, note 1.

29. Robert Donovan, *Eisenhower: The Inside Story,* pp. 332–33. (New York: Harper) 79–80.

30. *Congressional Record,* March 13, 1953, A 785–787.

31. Rule 4: Action in Case of Personal Interest: The *Congressional Record,* March 13, 1953, A 788.

32. Ibid.

33. *See* David A. Frier, *Conflict of Interest In The Eisenhower Administration* (Ames, Ia.: Iowa State University Press, 1969).

34. *See* Aaron Wildavsky, *Dixon-Yates: A Study in Power Politics* (Westport, Conn.: Greenwood Press, 1976. Originally published in 1962 by Yale University Press).

35. Ibid., pp. 17–22.

36. Ibid., pp. 18–19.

37. Ibid., p. 24.

38. Ibid., p. 25.

39. Ibid., p. 27.

40. Frier, p. 55.

41. Ibid., p. 45.

42. Frier, p. 58.

43. Wildavsky, p. 228.

44. Ibid., p. 231.

45. Ibid., p. 252.

46. Ibid., p. 261.

47. Ibid., pp. 262–63.

48. Section 18 U.S.C. 434. The self-dealing criminal prohibition is currently found at 18 U.S.C. 208 of the United States Code.

49. *U.S. Petitioner* v. *Mississippi Valley Generating Company,* 364 U.S. 520 (1961).

50. Frier, p. 83.

51. Ibid., p. 129.

52. Ibid., p. 140.

53. Ibid., p. 192.

54. Ibid., p. 200.

55. "Conflict of Whose Interest?" *Fortune,* September 1957, p. 120.

56. John J. Carson, *Executives for the Federal Service: A Program for Action in Time of Crisis* (New York: Columbia University Press, 1952).

57. Ibid., p. 27.

58. Ibid., pp. 33–34. The comments made were taken from conversations with Congressman Emanuel Celler of New York and Senators Paul Douglas of Illinois and Ralph Flanders of Vermont.

59. Ibid., p. 34.

60. Commission on Organization of the Executive Branch of the Government (Second Hoover Commission), *Task Force Report on Personnel and Civil Service* (Washington, D.C.: Government Printing Office, 1955).

61. Ibid., pp. 40–42. These findings were not based on the results of a questionnaire or survey. The commission reported its general impression gathered from conversations with experts in public administration and government.

62. Paul T. David and Ross Pollack, *Executives for Government: Central Issues of Federal Personnel Administration* (Washington, D.C.: The Brookings Institution, 1957), p. 26.

63. Harvard Business School Club of Washington, D.C., *Businessmen in Government: An Appraisal of Experience* (Washington, D.C.: 1953), p. 26.

64. Ibid., p. 8.

65. Ibid., p. 27.

66. Ibid.

IV

Ethics and the New Frontier

In the autumn of 1958, Congress passed a joint resolution establishing a code of ethics for all federal government employees.[1] The code was identical to the one proposed in 1951. Its directions to public employees and officials were detailed:

1. put loyalty to the highest moral principles and country above loyalty to persons, party, or government department;
2. uphold the Constitution, laws, and legal regulations of the United States and of all governments therein and never be a party to their evasion;
3. give a full day's labor for a full day's pay, giving to the performance of duties earnest effort and best thought;
4. seek to find and employ more efficient and economical ways of getting tasks accomplished;
5. never discriminate unfairly by dispensing of special favors or privileges to anyone, whether for remuneration or not, and never accept, for self or family favors or benefits under circumstances which might be construed by reasonable persons as influencing the performance of governmental duties;
6. make no private promises of any kind binding on the duties of office, since a government employee has no private word which can be binding on public duty;
7. engage in no business with the government, either directly or indirectly, which is inconsistent with the conscientious performance of governmental duties;
8. never use any information received confidentially in the performance of governmental duties as a means for making private profit;
9. expose corruption wherever discovered;
10. uphold these principles, ever conscious that public office is a public trust.[2]

The resolution, as noted by the Senate Committee on Post Office and Civil Service, "impose[ed] no penalties, identif[ied] no new type of crime, and establish[ed] no legal restrictions on anyone." Congress felt it had to do something about government ethics even if the action would have no substantive impact.

FINDING A BLUEPRINT FOR REFORM

Despite the deadlock between Congress and the White House over conflict of interest reform, efforts outside the government to find a solution increased. Funded by the Ford Foundation, a report produced by the Association of the Bar of the City of New York proved to be the most comprehensive and influential. Roswell Perkins, a prominent New York City attorney, chaired the board that studied the conflict of interest problem during the summer of 1960.[3]

The main theme of the report was that any new conflict of interest reforms must be designed to protect public confidence in the integrity of the federal service and at the same time allow the federal government "to obtain the personnel and information it needs to meet the demands of the twentieth century."[4]

Equally important, the panel found that conflicts of interest damaged the public interest by:

1. leading to the award of government contracts on the basis of favoritism rather than merit;
2. destroying the principle of "equal treatment of equal claims"; and
3. further increasing the public perception that public decisions are made to aid special interests instead of the public interest.[5]

While conflict of interest problems were real, however, the current system for regulating conflicts had been made obsolete by the complexities of modern government. Most problems no longer centered on the prosecution of claims but instead dealt with a much broader spectrum of activities that involved the conduct of consultants, part-time experts, advisers with or without compensation, advisory committees, and independent contractors, as well as full-time career and political appointees.[6]

To deal with this new environment, the panel recommended that:

1. Congress replace the scattered conflict of interest statutes with a single integrated statute to cover a broader range of governmental activities;
2. the president demonstrate support for high ethical standards by establishing a small coordinating office in the White House with responsibility for making sure

that federal agencies and departments administered conflict of interest statutes and regulations;[7] and finally,

3. because of the extreme difficulty in obtaining criminal convictions, administrative sanctions would become the preferred method of deterring and punishing conflicts of interest.

At the heart of the proposed program was its emphasis on administrative sanctions instead of reliance on rarely enforced criminal prohibitions, and its position that few federal agencies and departments would pay attention to a conflict of interest prevention program without strong presidential leadership. Although a White House coordinating office would not operate agency programs, it would have responsibility for the preparation of "general regulations on conflict of interest problems applicable throughout the executive branch."[8] It would, in addition, act as a clearing house for information on conflict of interest questions to assure consistency in the operation of ethics programs from agency to agency.

The panel, on the other hand, rejected calls for automatic divestiture and public financial disclosure because of the economic hardship caused by forced divestiture, and because of invasion of privacy concerns associated with public financial disclosure.[9] As an alternative to forced divestiture, the panel urged the greater use of the blind trust managed under strict rules whereby an independent trustee would have full responsibility for making all investment decisions. Further criticizing the idea of public financial disclosure, the panel argued it was a "certain invitation to demagogic political attack[s] of one kind or another upon the rich man as one who is privileged and [who] has lost contact with the mass of citizenry."[10] The panel also maintained that public disclosure would do little to deter individuals intent upon using their positions for personal gain because those individuals would certainly not list financial interests that might raise suspicions. To guarantee compliance, provisions would have to be made to conduct complete financial audits of anyone filing a statement.

In brief, the Association of the Bar of the City of New York took a middle-of-the-road position on conflict of interest reform. Stricter criminal laws, unreasonable divestiture requirements, and intrusive public financial disclosure would do little to restore public trust in the integrity of federal personnel, and would only make it more difficult to recruit essential scientific, technical, and professional employees. Presidential leadership and effective administrative sanctions were the key to preventing conflicts of interest.

In sharp contrast to the middle-of-the-road approach of the report of the Bar Association of the City of New York, a contingent of liberal members of Congress, headed by Congressman Emmanual Celler, demanded much harsher reforms to control special interests which attempted to manipulate public policy through behind-the-scenes contacts. A strong supporter of the New Deal and the Fair Deal, Celler believed that those entering government since the end of the Second World War, particularly presidential appointees, did not have the same degree of loyalty to public service as those who had entered the federal service during 1930s and the war years of the 1940s. For example, Celler believed that without-compensation executives more often than not put the interests of their companies ahead of the national interest.[11]

Under Celler's leadership, the Antitrust Subcommittee of the House Judiciary Committee, in a 1958 study of the effectiveness of existing conflict of interest laws, found existing laws weak and full of loopholes.[12] These findings led Celler in May of 1958 to propose legislation to broaden the scope of the criminal conflict of interest laws to include all matters, and not only the narrow areas of claims and contracts.[13] Although Celler's legislation received little congressional support during the 85th and 86th Congresses, Celler's strong views ultimately had to be dealt with.

By 1960, the split over the direction of conflict of interest reform had become fairly well defined. On the one hand, Congressman Celler and fellow supporters wanted a reform program to attack the perceived problem of the undue influence of special interests on government decision making. Celler expressed little concern over the impact of regulations on the ability of the federal service to attract executive talent, consultants, or intermittent employees. He clearly believed that the revolving door gave private interests the opportunity to steal the government blind through "honest graft." The Celler view paralleled the position taken by liberal Democrats during the early 1950s. The position taken by the Association of the Bar of the City of New York, on the other hand, recognized the seriousness of conflicts of interest, but urged that administrative standards of conduct and sanctions should gradually replace criminal ones as the main tools of conflict of interest enforcement.

The Kennedy White House would face the problem of demonstrating its commitment to high standards of official conduct without crippling the ability of the national government to operate. The Truman and Eisenhower administrations had failed at this task. It remained to be seen whether the Kennedy Administration would have any more success.

NEW INITIATIVES AND THE KENNEDY WHITE HOUSE

Even before his election, John F. Kennedy embraced the need for conflict of interest reform. In a speech on October 17, 1960, at Wittenberg University in Springfield, Ohio, Senator Kennedy declared that "no officer or employee of the Executive Branch shall use his official position for financial profit or personal gain, or reveal to others for their advantage confidential information acquired through his position."[14] Kennedy urged Congress to enact "a simple, comprehensive code on conflict of interest," a code that would eliminate "duplications, inadvertencies and gaps' in existing laws and regulations.[15]

After his narrow victory in November 1960, Kennedy followed up on his Wittenberg pledge by asking a Harvard Law School Professor, Abram Chayes, to recommend specific conflict of interest reforms.[16] According to Professor Chayes, Kennedy wished to avoid the kind of scandals that had plagued the Truman and Eisenhower administrations. Moreover, the president-elect feared that existing laws might hamper his ability to attract good people to serve in his administration. As Chayes explained in an interview with the staff of the Kennedy Library, "the old conflict of interest laws were very hard, particularly on lawyers, scientists, and other people who have this kind of professional relation and then try to be in Government."[17]

Chayes believed that many of the scandals had occurred because the statutes were outdated and because "nobody had put out any Government-wide executive regulations governing the problem in any systematic way."[18] Besides assembling a panel of outside experts to conduct a general review of all the conflict of interest rules and regulations, Professor Chayes recruited Roswell Perkins, who had chaired the Bar Association study, to draft a memorandum outlining the most important problems facing a new presidential appointee.

In a December 23, 1960, letter to Senator Kennedy, Chayes strongly endorsed the reform proposals put forward by Perkins,[19] which generally followed those earlier published in the report by the Association of the Bar of the City of New York. Chayes, however, expressed some reservations about Perkins's recommendation that the president appoint a special assistant with responsibility for reviewing the financial affairs of presidential appointees for conflicts of interest.[20] Instead, Chayes urged the president-elect to appoint a "panel of well-known legal figures outside the Government" to review the financial affairs of appointees for potential conflicts of interest. Chayes believed that an outside panel would provide more credibility than the proposed White House clearance procedures.[21] The Kennedy transition team ultimately rejected this recommendation.

On December 28, 1960, Roswell Perkins forwarded Professor Chayes a nine-page draft of a pamphlet on conflicts of interest, prepared for distribution to incoming presidential appointees. Written by Alex Hoagland and edited by Perkins, the pamphlet reviewed statutory restrictions on:

1. private salary for government work;

2. acceptance of gifts, favors, and hospitality;

3. private services in government-connected matters;

4. private investments and business activities; and

5. disclosure of government information.[22]

Besides outlining current restrictions, the pamphlet warned appointees that "day-to-day changes in . . . private business and financial affairs [could] bring about wholly unexpected and unintended violations of the law."[23] Therefore, it explained, when a potential conflict of interest problem developed, the appointee should immediately consult the agency official responsible for conflict of interest enforcement. In conclusion, the pamphlet admonished appointees to remain above suspicion because:

Our Government is the property of all the people; it exists and it operates only by virtue of their consent and their confidence. As an employee of the Government, you are an employee of all of the people, not your own, and you exercise the power of the people, not your own, and you exercise it for the benefit of the people, not your own. You are their trustees, and you must give them not only your time and your energy; you must not only be impartial, objective, selfless and wholly honest on their behalf; you must, most of all and at all times, so conduct yourself that you will be above suspicion.[24]

In spite of general agreement regarding the merits of Perkins's proposals, doubts arose about the feasibility of implementing them quickly. On January 9, 1961, David Bell, who was assigned to the Bureau of the Budget, wrote Theodore Sorenson to say that the transition team was still considering the merits of Perkins's reform proposals.[25] In a five-page memorandum on "Controlling Conflicts of Interest," the staff of the Bureau of the Budget agreed that the new administration should make conflict of interest reform a high priority. The almost total lack of government-wide leadership, the bureau concluded, made an effective conflict of interest prevention program virtually impossible. Without any central direction, "agencies [had been] largely left free to initiate their own administrative policies."[26] More often than not, reforms came only after "public disclosure of malfeasance or questionable conduct."[27]

However, the Bureau of the Budget memorandum suggested that "a limited approach to the conflict of interest problem would be quicker and easier to prepare, more likely to win early adoption, and could be presented as a first step in dealing with a highly complex subject."[28] Nevertheless, the bureau memorandum admitted that in the long run the Bar Association approach would probably be more effective. The memorandum concluded by recommending the establishment of an interagency working group to review the City of New York Bar proposals and to make suggestions about how they might be made more workable. The White House subsequently decided to go ahead with a series of administrative reforms and delay efforts to get Congress to enact sweeping legislative reforms.

On January 22, 1961, President Kennedy appointed Dean Jefferson B. Fordham of the University of Pennsylvania Law School, Bayless Manning, and Judge Calvert Magruder to an advisory panel on conflict of interest matters. The president gave the panel two months to make its recommendations.[29] On March 22, 1961, the president's panel submitted a report which generally supported a series of White House ethics directives followed by legislative fine-tuning of existing criminal prohibitions. The panel "found no indication of widespread lack of probity or serious departure from basic moral standards in the federal establishment."[30] However, the panel admitted a "very real need to reshape existing controls and to provide more effective tools for their administration" in a way that maintained high ethical standards but did not prevent the government from recruiting important technical and professional talent.[31]

To restore public confidence in the integrity of the federal service, the advisory panel identified five steps. First, the public must demonstrate its intolerance for unethical conduct by reporting any knowledge of it. Second, updated statutes with strong criminal penalties must be imposed to deter the most blatant types of conflicts of interest. Third, a series of executive orders should be issued to deal with conflict of interest violations not meriting criminal penalties. Fourth, the heads of agencies and departments must make it clear that they intend to take action against employees ignoring conflict of interest regulations. Finally, sufficient resources must be committed to provide for an effective administrative program.

Accepting one of the major themes of the Bar Association Report, the advisory panel strongly recommended that the president select a White House official to take responsibility for coordinating the executive-branch ethics program.[32] The White House special assistant on ethics would prepare presidential promulgations and general regulations on government ethics, approve agency ethics regulations, and collect and analyze data on the operation of the executive-branch conflict of interest system.

To help resolve troublesome ethical problems experienced by federal employees and officials, the panel also recommended the creation of ad hoc ethics advisory panels that would issue periodic advisory rulings on day-to-day ethics problems.[33] Equally important, the panel pointed out that without clear standards for problems that fall outside of existing criminal prohibitions, little long-term progress could be made. For instance, to deal with appearance problems created by government employees accepting gifts, it recommended prohibiting both regular and intermittent employees from accepting them if they had "reason to believe that [a] gift would not have been made but for their official position."[34] A broader prohibition would apply only to full-time personnel, and would also prohibit the acceptance of gifts, entertainment, or favors from a donor who conducted business or was believed to be seeking business "relationships with the employee's agency."[35]

Other conduct regulations would prohibit or regulate:

1. use of official information not available to the public for private gain;[36]
2. abuse of office;

3. conflicting outside activities; and

4. private ex parte contacts with government employees.

In brief, it recommended that the president should use a series of Executive Orders to standardize conduct regulations throughout the executive branch and to make sure that agencies and departments enforced them.

The panel reserved much of its criticism for the confusing and antiquated conflict of interest statutes, but rejected major substantive changes in the scope of the criminal prohibitions. For example, the panel recommended broadening the self-dealing prohibition to include all types of matters, and not just matters involving the transaction of business, but endorsed continued use of disqualification instead of mandatory divestiture to resolve self-dealing problems.[37]

With respect to the controversy over the private supplementation prohibition, the panel supported the general policy behind the prohibition, but recommended that the bar be amended "to permit government appointees to continue during their government service their status under group security and insurance programs of their former employers."[38] This proposed change would not permit a former employer to continue to pay the salary of his former employee.

Finally, the report addressed the issue of the revolving door. Specifically, it placed new restrictions on the representation and lobbying activities of former government employees. The panel noted that the conduct of former government employees created an ethical problem because "it is feared that the former employee will have undue influence in his former department; . . . may carry away information that he may use to the detriment of the Government; and it is considered to be immoral and disloyal for the former employee to switch sides."[39]

To deal with these legitimate concerns, the panel proposed that Congress expand the class of covered transactions beyond the nineteenth-century emphasis on claims, and in some situations make "the former employee's exclusion be permanent."[40] By not discussing proposals to restrict general lobbying by former officials, the panel implicitly endorsed the position that postemployment restrictions should be tied to matters which the former official had handled while in government service.

The advisory panel's report apparently received little distribution outside the White House. However, following the general theme of the report, the Kennedy White House shortly thereafter began to issue a series of executive orders on government ethics and map out its position on statutory changes. Outside the White House, John Macy, the new chairman of the Civil Service Commission, played a key role in formulating and implementing the reform program.

REFORMATION AND THE CIVIL SERVICE COMMISSION

Through most of the 1950s, the Civil Service Commission showed little interest in mandating specific ethical standards in federal agencies and departments. The commission provided technical assistance to agencies and departments wishing to develop their own standards of conduct, but did not attempt to determine the effectiveness of agency standards-of-conduct programs.

A commission staff paper, drafted in June of 1959, questioned the value of government-wide standards of conduct. "Only when codes are directed to the problems of a homogeneous group—can [they] be specific enough to furnish real guidance in different situations or—become group standards informally enforced by the group," read the report. Furthermore, the fact that government agencies differed so much made it difficult to draft government-wide standards. Although the commission had the authority to sponsor such conduct regulations, the paper continued, "such a project would require the investment of substantial staff time over a long period."[41]

In lieu of drafting specific government-wide standards of conduct, the paper suggested that the commission might issue general minimum standards which each agency would tailor to deal with the conduct problems of its organization.[42] The staff paper left the impression that the commission did not want the opportunity to administer a government-wide ethics program.

With the appointment of John Macy as chairman of the Civil Service Commission, however, this attitude quickly changed. In early March 1961, following an initial attempt by the Kennedy White House to draft its own memorandum which was met with strong criticism from political appointees,[43] Frederick G. Dutton, special assistant to the president, asked Chairman Macy to help draft an ethics directive for presidential appointees. Dutton asked for recommendations on

1. the acceptance of honoraria for lectures, writing, and other activities;
2. a prohibition on appointees engaging in nongovernmental work as a way of supplementing their governmental income;
3. restrictions on the acceptance of gifts; and
4. a prohibition on acceptance of private reimbursement for travel, meals, hotels, and other travel-related personal expenses.[44]

On March 22, 1961, John Macy forwarded Dutton a series of suggestions and a draft of a presidential letter to appointees on standards of conduct. Chairman Macy strongly advised that the directive be kept general and cover only high-level appointees subject to Senate confirmation. As Macy explained, "The main purpose of the Presidential directive is to furnish guidance to Presidential appointees in making personal decisions in these matters and therefore, would not be so legalistic or technical as to require advice from counsel on fine points."[45] However, the directive would provide more specific guidance on the most troublesome issues, such as the acceptance of gifts.

To avoid appearances of impropriety, a presidential appointee was urged to "keep clearly in mind at all times that when he is making decisions about the acceptance of fees, compensation, gifts, expenses, etc. or about the performance of personal services, he must never make a decision which reasonably may (1) adversely affect the confidence of the public in the integrity of the Government, (2) be regarded as the use of his public office for private gain, (3) result in unequal treatment of citizens at the hands of the Government[,] (4) impede Government efficiency or economy, (5) result in Government policy decisions being made outside the established official channels for making such decisions[, or] (6) cause a loss of complete independence and impartiality on the part of the appointee or his agency."[46]

The Macy memorandum did not specify punishment for an appointee who took actions that violated one of the six general rules of conduct. However, the tone of the section indicates that the president would not tolerate even the appearance of impropriety on the part of his top appointees. Since the president had the authority to remove the majority of presidential appointees without cause, enforcing these broad rules was not a problem.

The second part of the memorandum forbade presidential appointees to accept "fees or remuneration for personal services, speeches, or writings" and prohibited almost all types of gifts, entertainment, lodging, and other favors.[47] However, the proposed rules permitted personnel to accept a meal at a banquet at which the appointee is "appropriately present as a guest."[48]

Chairman Macy and the White House realized that an outright prohibition on the acceptance of all gifts would be unworkable. The proposal thus attempted to distinguish between gifts made because of a personal relationship and those made as the result of the employee's public position. Consequently, the ban applied to situations where the nominee had reason to believe that the source of the gift:

1. "has or is seeking to obtain contractual or other business or financial relationships with the appointee's agency";

2. "conducts operations or activities which are regulated by such appointee's performance, or non-performance of his official duty"; or

3. "offers the gift or remuneration because of the appointee's position with the Government."[49]

The draft directive clearly reflected the view that presidential appointees must remain above suspicion regarding their official duties.

President Kennedy's Message on Ethical Conduct in the Government

On April 27, 1961, President Kennedy sent Congress a message titled "Ethical Conduct in the Government," which announced a series of administrative reforms to deal with conflicts of interest and made preliminary recommendations with respect to the updating of the criminal conflict of interest statutes.[50] Specifically, the message announced that the White House would issue a detailed standards-of-conduct directive for presidential appointees and that government-wide rules would be forthcoming to regulate

1. the acceptance of gifts;

2. the use of inside information for personal purposes;

3. outside employment; and

4. self-dealing by federal personnel.

Until the detailed directives were issued, the message directed all employees, whether full-time or intermittent, to turn down gifts if they determined that "the gift would not have been made except for his official position."[51] In addition, it directed regular employees to turn down gifts if the employee had reason to believe "that the donor's private interests [would] likely be affected by actions of the employee or his agency."[52] It prohibited government personnel from using information not available to the public for personal gain,[53] and admonished personnel not to "engage in outside employment which is 'incompatible' with [their] Government employment."[54]

To deal with the problem of lack of uniformity in agency standards of conduct, President Kennedy directed each agency and department "to issue regulations designed to maintain high moral and ethical standards" and to adapt these "general principles to the particular problems and activity of each agency."[55] Finally, Kennedy announced that in order to provide for government-wide coordination of the ethics reform program, he would designate a single White House official to supervise the implementation of the program. Frederick G. Dutton, special assistant to the president, was subsequently given this responsibility.[56]

The message on ethical conduct reflected a White House decision to adopt a middle-of-the-road approach to ethics reform. By issuing a series of executive orders on standards-of-conduct issues, the White House hoped to head off congressional pressure to enact sweeping revisions of the major criminal prohibitions that might cause an exodus of personnel and further complicate recruitment efforts.

Ethical Booster Shots

On May 5, 1961, President Kennedy released Executive Order 10939, *To Provide a Guide on Ethical Standards to Government Officials*. The order applied to all heads and assistant heads of departments and agencies, full-time members of boards and commissions appointed by the president, and members of the White House staff.

It was not a coincidence that the second part of the order used language almost identical to that of the March 22, 1961, draft memorandum sent by John Macy to Special Assistant to the President Frederick Dutton. The language of the order left little question that nominees were to avoid even the appearance of impropriety related to outside activities and the acceptance of gifts:

No such official shall engage in any outside employment or other outside activity not compatible with the full and proper discharge of the responsibilities of his office or position. It shall be deemed incompatible with such discharge of responsibilities for any such official to accept any fee, compensation, gift, payment of expenses, or any other thing of monetary value, or create the appearance of, or resulting in (1) use of public office for private gain, (2) an undertaking to give preferential treatment to any person, (3) any loss of complete independence and impartiality, (4) the making of a Government decision outside official channels and (5) any adverse effect on the confidence of the public in the integrity of the Government.[57]

To add teeth to these general standards, the order specifically directed covered appointees not to accept honoraria for speeches if the subject-matter was devoted substantially to the responsibilities, programs, or operations of the official's department or agency; or drew substantially on official data on ideas which have not become a part of the body of public information.[58] In other words, a secretary of agriculture who happened to be a national expert on butterflies could accept an honorarium if he spoke on butterfly collecting, but not if he discussed the role of the Agriculture Department in protecting rare butterflies. The order, however, permitted top officials to accept awards given by civil organizations for meritorious public service.

With respect to the restriction on outside activities, the order specifically authorized officials to continue to participate in the activities of charitable, religious, and nonprofit educational, public service, and civic organizations. Recognizing the limited travel funds of some agencies, the order permitted bona fide private sources to reimburse officials for actual travel expenses if the agency made a determination that the reimbursement was consistent with the intent of the order.

Executive Order 10939 established the first uniform standards of conduct regulations for presidential appointees. If appointees did get involved in situations which appeared to involve a conflict of interest, the order effectively forced the White House to rule on the propriety of their conduct.

The Presidential Appointee in the Fishbowl

Besides having to deal with the difficulties of developing a conflict of interest reform program, the Kennedy White House had its own problems with Senate Committees reviewing the financial affairs of its nominees. The Senate Armed Services Committee, for example, required nominees to submit detailed financial disclosure statements of their holdings and continued its practice of requiring nominees to divest themselves of any interests in companies holding defense department contracts. These problems led the Kennedy White House to consider additional measures in an effort to head off problems before the confirmation proceedings.

At the request of the White House, in July of 1961 the Bureau of the Budget drafted a presidential directive on financial disclosure and divestiture for high-level nominees and appointees.[59] The directive proposed to require nominees "to submit statements to the White House containing all essential information about their pension and retirement plans, partnership income, security holdings, and such interests in real property as might involve rights subject to regulation or control by the Government (for example, oil and gas leases)."[60] Appointees would have sixty days after the issuance of the directive to provide the White House with the required disclosure statements. Moreover, any changes in holdings were to be reported within thirty days.

Besides mandating the disclosure of the official's holdings, the directive required that the appointee disclose the financial holdings of his "spouse, child, or a business in which he is serving as officer, director, or other position."[61]

Equally significant, the directive provided for mandatory divestiture of financial interests in certain very limited situations. Without going into detail, the directive required appointees to regulatory agencies to divest themselves of all financial interests in companies which they regulated. Moreover, some divestiture would be required if appointees held financial interests in companies that had very large contracts with the appointee's organization.[62]

Bureau of the Budget Director David Bell emphasized to Special Assistant to the President Feldman that the draft had been prepared to promote discussion within the administration regarding financial disclosure and divestiture. Bell believed that a disclosure program was important "regardless of what action may be required as to divestiture."[63]

The Kennedy White House understood that preconfirmation disclosure would help to identify potential conflict of interest controversies before confirmation proceedings, and that divestiture would greatly simplify finding remedies for problems. However, legitimate concern with privacy issues and the possible impact of disclosure and divestiture on recruitment led the White House to decide against formal financial disclosure or even limited mandatory divestiture.[64] Although formal disclosure programs were not adopted, the Kennedy White House did expand the collection of financial data from nominees as part of the informal nominee clearance process.

Restlessness in the Ranks

By early summer 1961, John Macy had received several requests for assistance from agencies and departments regarding the drafting of their new standards of conduct pursuant to the president's message to Congress.[65] At the urging of Chairman Macy, on July 20, 1961 Presidential Assistant Dutton issued a memorandum entitled "Minimum Standards of Conduct for Civilian Employees." Prepared by the staff of the Civil Service Commission and departmental representatives, the Dutton memorandum combined substantive rules regarding noncriminal conflict of interest situations with directions for the establishment of administrative systems to deal with conflict of interest matters on an agency-by-agency basis. The memorandum also authorized the extension of standards of conduct regulations to part-time and intermittent employees and consultants.[66] It also applied to presidential appointees.

Special Assistant Dutton directed cabinet departments to submit their standards of conduct for review by the end of July, and established an August deadline for other agencies. Dutton and Macy made it clear that the White House and Civil Service Commission would closely oversee the implementation of the order.[67] The memorandum directed agencies to discuss in their standards of conduct all relevant laws and rules on employee conduct, to provide information on how an employee could obtain additional clarification of conduct rules and laws, and to explain disciplinary actions for violations of agency standards of conduct.[68] In sum, the White House expected each agency and department to establish a formal conflict of interest prevention program.

To make sure that employees understood what restrictions applied to them, the memorandum directed agencies to explain the key criminal conflict of interest prohibitions. Specifically, these included prohibitions against full-time and part-time government employees

1. "assisting outsiders in the prosecution of claims against the United States";
2. assisting others for pay in any matter before the executive branch in "which the United States is interested";
3. taking action with respect to matters in which they have a conflicting interest;
4. receiving "outside pay for government work";
5. and participating in certain postemployment activities involving the prosecution of claims against the United States.[69]

Following the provisions of Executive Order 10939, the memorandum required all federal agencies and departments to implement minimum rules regarding conflicts of interest and outside activities, acceptance of gifts, the holding of financial interests, and the misuse of inside government information for personal financial gain.

The Dutton memorandum differed in one major respect from Executive Order 10939. It directed employees and officials to avoid both actual and apparent conflicts of interest. For instance, the memorandum stated that employees "may not engage in any outside employment, including teaching, lecturing, or writing, which might reasonably result in a conflict of interest, or an apparent conflict of interest, between the private interest of the employee and his official government duties and responsibilities."

With respect to the acceptance of gifts, gratuities, or favors, the memorandum directed employees to refuse these if

1. the gift or favor might be "reasonably interpreted by others as being of such value that it could affect his impartiality" in dealing with any person, corporation or group;

2. the employee had reason to believe "that the person, corporation, or group has or is seeking to obtain contractual or other business or financial relationships with the employee's agency";

3. the donor of the gift "conducts operations or activities which are regulated by the employee's agency";

4. the source of the gift "may be substantially affected by such employee's performance or non-performance of his official duty";

5. the source of the gift "is in any way attempting to affect the employee's official actions."[70]

The memorandum went into extensive detail concerning the acceptance of gifts and favors in order to prevent the rules from being interpreted as prohibiting family or purely personal gifts. Besides the clear language directing employees and officials to avoid apparent conflicts of interest, the language of the Dutton memorandum appeared to establish new administrative rules for dealing with self-dealing situations. As noted earlier, federal criminal law at the time did not generally require officials to divest themselves of financial interests that created an actual or apparent conflict of interest, but it did require disqualification from those matters. Moreover, the White House had rejected proposals that would have applied an automatic divestiture rule to certain types of financial interests held by high-level presidential appointees.

One might expect the Dutton memorandum to have incorporated the criminal disqualification rule. However, whether intentionally or inadvertently, this section of the memorandum rewrote federal policy on financial interests and divestiture. The order clearly stated that "employees may not have direct or indirect financial interests that conflict substantially, or appear to conflict substantially, with their responsibilities as Federal employees."[71] The section made no mention of disqualification as a remedy for financial conflicts of interest that conflict substantially. On the other hand, the memorandum affirmed the right of employees "to engage in lawful financial transactions to the same extent as private citizens."[72]

What the Dutton memorandum did achieve was to establish a separate administrative standard for reviewing self-dealing cases. Since the standard was administrative, the Justice Department would not have a role in applying it to conflict of interest cases. Other provisions warned employees not to use inside government information to gain an advantage in any financial transaction, and dealt with misuse of government property and indebtedness by government employees. The White House quickly issued the Dutton memorandum to agencies to force them to revise their own agency standards of conduct and to establish and staff formal ethics programs. It achieved this purpose.

Tying Up the Loose Ends

After the issuing of Executive Order 10939 and the Dutton memorandum, Frederick Dutton and John Macy focused their attention on making sure that agencies and departments completed their standards of conduct and submitted them for review.

A September 27, 1961, memorandum from Presidential Assistant Dutton reminded agencies that they had until October 10 to notify the White House that:

1. "their agency orientation programs for new employees, supervisory personnel, and staff training included a presentation on 'ethics in government' ";
2. "an article has already appeared in your agency's house organ on conflicts of interest and standards of conduct of special concern in your particular field";
3. employee handbooks included a statement on the new standards of conduct; and
4. each department's standards of conduct had been brought to the attention of all employees through the distribution of copies to every employee, or that a copy of the agency's regulations on standards of conduct is kept posted on all departmental bulletin boards."[73]

Subsequently, Dutton forwarded the agency standards and associated compliance reports to John Macy of the Civil Service Commission for review and analysis. On October 26, 1961, Mr. Macy reported a gratifying response from the agencies and also noted that most agencies were doing a good job communicating to their employees the new standards of conduct.[74]

Thus, by the end of 1961, it appeared that the White House and John

Macy had succeeded in implementing a government-wide administrative system for dealing with conflicts of interest on an agency-by-agency basis. Chairman Macy had become the Kennedy Administration's expert on conflicts of interest and employee standards of conduct.

Although the early Kennedy ethics directives covered all executive-branch officials and employees, the focus was clearly on the conduct of presidential nominees and appointees. The White House and John Macy wanted these officials to avoid any suspicion of wrongdoing. Individual agencies and departments could generally be left to police rank-in-file employees, but misconduct by top Kennedy officials could do severe damage to a president who had won office by the barest of majorities.

Therefore, John Macy and the Kennedy White House recognized the important differences between career and political appointees for purposes of conflict of interest regulation. Political appointees were much more likely to get involved in problems concerning the appearance of conflict of interest because many were recruited from outside the government and had little prior government experience. Equally significant, the majority of political appointees planned to return to their private careers and thus found it important to keep their private-sector contacts. Appointees would run into trouble when they failed to recognize that conduct that they regarded as innocent might nevertheless raise questions of bias and favoritism. A president could not afford to have political appointees who failed to understand that their conduct must be above suspicion and not merely in compliance with appropriate laws and regulations.

The next step in the Kennedy Administration reform program was to address the issue of antiquated federal conflict of interest statutes.

NOTES

1. H. R. Con. Res. 175, 85th Cong., 2d Sess. (1958).

2. U.S. Congress, Senate, Committee on Post Office and Civil Service, "Code of Ethics for Government Service," Report on House Concurrent Resolution 175, 85th Cong., 2d Sess; Report No. 1812, July 10, 1958.

3. *New York Times*, May 22, 1958, p. 58.

4. Bar Association Report, chapter 10, p. 1.

5. Ibid., p. 7.

6. Ibid., p. 8.

7. Ibid., p. 188.

8. Ibid., p. 192.

9. Ibid., p. 247.

10. Ibid., p. 254.

11. U.S. Congress, House, Committee on the Judiciary, Antitrust Subcommittee, WOCs and Government Advisory Groups, Hearings, July 25–August 5; August 10; October 25–December 9, 1955; July 26, 1956; 4pts (84: 1–2), Washington, D.C. 1955–1956.

12. Federal Conflict of Interest Legislation, Staff Report to Subcommittee No. 5 of the House Judiciary Committee, 85th Cong., 2d Sess, 1958.

13. H. R. 1257 (85th Cong.).

14. *Congressional Quarterly Weekly*, January 13, 1961, p. 41.

15. Ibid.

16. As part to the Oral History Project of the John F. Kennedy Library, the library staff interviewed Professor Chayes on his role in the Kennedy Administration.

17. Transcript, Abram Chayes, Second Oral History Interview, June 22, 1964, p. 77, John F. Kennedy Library.

18. Ibid.

19. Letter from Abram Chayes to Senator John Kennedy, December 23, 1960, Official File, John F. Kennedy Library.

20. Ibid.

21. Ibid.

22. Letter to Professor Abram J. Chayes, December 28, 1960, Official File, John F. Kennedy Library. Copy of pamphlet attached.

23. Ibid., p. 7 (pamphlet).

24. Ibid., pp. 8–9.

25. Memorandum, David E. Bell for Mr. Sorenson, January 9, 1961, Official File, John F. Kennedy Library.

26. Ibid., attachment to letter, p. 2.

27. Ibid.

28. Ibid., p. 4.

29. Ibid.

30. *New York Times*, January 23, 1961, p. 1; text, January 23, 1961, p. 11.

31. Report, President's Advisory Panel on Ethics and Conflict of Interest in Government, March 22, 1961, Official File, John F. Kennedy Library, p. 2.

32. Ibid., p. 7.

33. Ibid., p. 13.

34. Ibid., p. 16.

35. Ibid.

36. Ibid., p. 38 (Recommendation Twelve).

37. Ibid., p. 22.

38. Ibid., p. 31 (Recommendation Nine).

39. Ibid., p. 33.

40. Ibid., p. 35 (Recommendation Ten).

41. U.S. Civil Service Commission, *Conduct and Conflict of Interest*, June 1959, No. 3055, Office of Personnel Management Archives, Request for Policy Guidance on Bills Relating to Conduct of Federal Employees.

42. Ibid.

43. Memorandum, Frederick G. Dutton for John Macy, March 16, 1961. *Employee Conduct and Ethics*, Civil Service Commission, Program Planning Division, 1961, 3058, Office of Personnel Management Archives.

44. Ibid.

45. Ibid.

46. Ibid.

47. Ibid., p. 3, *Suggested Guide for Governing Activities of Schedule C and other Full-Time Non-Career Appointees within Federal Agencies*.

48. Ibid.

49. Ibid.

50. U.S. President Kennedy, House Document, No. 145, 87th Cong., 1st Sess., Message from the President to the United States Congress relative to Ethical Conduct in the Government, April 27, 1961.

51. Ibid.

52. Ibid., p. 7.

53. Ibid.

54. Ibid., p. 8.

55. Ibid., p. 9.

56. Ibid., p. 10.

57. Executive Order 10939, May 5, 1961.

58. Ibid.

59. Memorandum, David Bell, Director of Bureau of the Budget, for Mr. Feldman, Special Assistant to the President, July 5, 1961, Papers of Myer Feldman, Official Files, John F. Kennedy Library. p. 1.

60. Ibid.

61. Ibid.

62. Ibid., p. 3.

63. Ibid.

64. Chairman Macy of the Civil Service Commission, Nicholas Katzenbach of the Department of Justice, and Presidential Advisor Cyrus Vance also reviewed the directive.

65. Letter, John Macy to Frederick G. Dutton, June 8, 1961, *Employee Conduct and Ethics*, 1961, Office of Personnel Management Library Archives, Document No. 3058.

66. The White House, Washington, Memorandum for Heads of Departments and Agencies, Subject: *Standards of Conduct for Civilian Employees*, July 20, 1961.

67. *Employee Conduct and Ethics*, 1961, Note for the Files, July 20, 1961, Office of Personnel Management Archives.

68. Dutton Memorandum, p. 1.

69. Ibid., pp. 1, 2.

70. Ibid., p. 2.

71. Ibid.

72. Ibid.

73. The White House, Washington, D.C., Memorandum to all Executive Department and Agency Heads, September 27, 1961, Frederick G. Dutton. p. 1.

74. Letter, John W. Macy to Honorable Frederick G. Dutton, October 26, 1961, Official File, John F. Kennedy Library.

V

The Kennedy Administration and Momentum for Reform

CONFLICTS OF INTEREST AND THE JAIL HOUSE

After completing its revision of standards of conduct for presidential appointees and rank-in-file employees, the Kennedy Administration turned its full attention to updating the criminal conflict of interest statutes.

Even prior to the 1960 presidential election, it became clear that sharp differences of opinion existed over how the statutes should be amended. In the early summer of 1960, Congressman John Lindsay introduced legislation to enact the reforms proposed by the Association of the Bar of the City of New York. These reforms placed a higher priority on administrative rather than criminal sanctions by requiring agencies to impose tough administrative sanctions for violations of new statutory prohibitions against acceptance of gifts and other things of value, misuse of information, abuse of office, and outside employment. Agencies would have the authority to impose heavy fines and disbarment penalties on former government employees violating postemployment prohibitions or on private parties found to have given items of value to government personnel. Criminal penalties would remain, but would be used sparingly.[1]

In contrast, Congressmen Celler and McCulloch wanted Congress to strengthen existing criminal prohibitions and enact new ones. For instance, Celler proposed a new lifetime bar prohibiting former officials from representing other parties before the government with respect to matters over which they had exercised some responsibility while in government.[2] A two-year bar against switching sides would also apply to any matter in which the former agency of the employee had a significant interest.[3] More important, the Celler bill included a two-year prohibition on general lobbying by former government officials.[4]

During the spring of 1960, hearings chaired by Congressman Celler considered various reform proposals. Throughout these proceedings, Celler argued that administrative sanctions would not deter wrongdoing because agencies would not impose harsh administrative sanctions on their own personnel, particularly high-level officials. Celler compared the administrative approach to putting the fox in charge of the chicken coop.[5] Only long jail sentences would stop conflicts of interest. In a brief exchange with Congressman John Lindsay of New York, Celler told his young colleague that "the longer you remain here the more you will realize that you cannot expect the agency to enforce conflict of interest statutes through administrative sanctions, you just will not get anywhere."[6] Celler also rejected the argument that the current conflict of interest statutes made it difficult to recruit "able and talented men and women for Government service."[7]

Celler held to this position despite efforts by Roswell Perkins, speaking in support of the reforms proposed by the New York Bar Association report, to persuade Chairman Celler that the current statutes deterred few bent on violating the law because of the extreme difficulty of obtaining indictments and convictions. Aggressive internal inspection programs, Perkins maintained, would catch and punish many more violators.[8]

Besides the disagreement on the matter of criminal versus administrative sanctions, Celler did not agree with the Bar Association's proposal to apply less stringent conflict of interest requirements on intermittent employees than on regular personnel. Perkins strongly supported a two-tier regulatory structure in order to make it easier to persuade experts to take temporary assignments as government consultants or advisers. In contrast, Celler believed that federal agencies and departments used far too many outside consultants. From Celler's perspective, the numerous advisory committees ought to stop hiring private lawyers for part-time work because many of them used their public positions to further their own financial and personal interests. By the end of 1960, positions had hardened over the direction of conflict of interest reform. The new Kennedy Administration tried to break the logjam.

In April 1961, as part of his message on ethical conduct in the government, President Kennedy forwarded Congress the administration's Executive Employees Standards Act, H.R. 7139, which generally followed the recommendations of the president's advisory panel on conflicts of interest. The bill, however, differed considerably from the proposals of the City of New York Bar Association and Congressman Celler.

In spite of the fact that Congressman Celler amended his bill to make it less restrictive on the representation activities of former government employees,[9] the Kennedy Administration recognized that Celler thought the administration bill was too weak. On May 22, 1961, Assistant Attorney

General Nicholas Katzenbach informed Arthur B. Focke, general counsel of the Bureau of the Budget, that four key differences existed between the White House and Celler bills.[10] First, the Celler bill did not distinguish between full-time and intermittent employees. This meant that it would not permit intermittent or regular employees to accept "salary payments from prior employers; i.e., and would make [intermittent employees] subject to the same broad conflict of interest prohibitions as regular employees."[11] Katzenbach and the administration believed that such provisions would make it much more difficult to recruit essential intermittent employees.

Second, the administration strongly opposed Celler's effort to place a two-year representation bar "with regard to matters for which a former Government officer or employee merely had official responsibility as distinguished from those matters in which he participated personally and substantially."[12] Besides further restricting the representation activities of former officials, the administration believed that officials would face a nightmare in determining which matters had been under their official responsibility.

Finally, the Celler bill placed a blanket ban on government employees' rendering assistance with or without compensation to other parties in their dealings with the government. In contrast, the Kennedy Administration supported permitting uncompensated assistance, as long as it did not take the "form of acting as attorney or agency for another."[13] Again, the administration believed the blanket ban on uncompensated assistance could lead to numerous inadvertent violations of the prohibitions by government personnel.

The Kennedy Administration believed its administrative reform program would make stricter criminal rules unnecessary, but that Congress did need to update the existing laws to make sure they applied to a much broader range of governmental activities. Congressman Celler, in sharp contrast, rejected incremental fine tuning. He demanded much stronger measures to stop perceived revolving-door abuses and other steps to make sure that offenders did not slip through loopholes in the criminal conflict of interest laws.

During the early months of 1961, the Defense Department and other federal agencies pressured the White House and the Justice Department to oppose the Celler proposals. Assistant Attorney General Katzenbach assured Defense and other agencies that the administration would oppose the Celler bill, but told them that Celler had made it clear that "no bill except one with Congressman Celler's name on it would be reported to the Committee."[14]

In June 1961 hearings before the House Committee on the Judiciary, Katzenbach continued to lobby hard for the administration's bill. On the matter of criminal versus administrative sanction, the assistant attorney general noted that while the chairman's bill gave "great emphasis to the use of criminal sanctions, the bill introduced by Mr. Lindsay takes the other approach. The Administration's bill lies somewhere in between."[15] On the matter of statutory administrative sanctions, Congress did not need to enact such provisions, since the White House was actively implementing its own administrative standards program.

Katzenbach urged the committee to reconsider its position on the treatment of temporary or intermittent employees. He referred the subcommittee to the position taken by the president's advisory panel that the "range and volume of governmental activities," were dramatically increasing the technological manpower needs of the government and that government must compete with business organizations for qualified personnel. Increasingly, Katzenbach maintained, federal agencies had "to make use of people on a limited basis in the capacity of advisers, consultants, or experts," because they found themselves unable to recruit full-time technical personnel.[16]

The administration bill permitted individuals to serve the government up to 130 days during any consecutive period of 365 days before being classified as a full-time employee and thus becoming subject to the full weight of the criminal prohibitions. The Bar Association of the City of New York defined an intermittent employee as one who performed no more than fifty-two days of service in one year.[17] The Celler bill intentionally made no distinction.

Despite White House pressure, Roswell Perkins continued to press for specific statutory standards-of-conduct regulations and for statutory administrative sanctions. While not doubting the commitment of the administration to the maintenance of high ethical standards, he prophetically warned the committee that a subsequent administration could repeal standards of conduct issued through an executive order or neglect to monitor ethics programs at the agency level. A statutory base, however, would force agency heads to act then and in the future.[18]

Perkins also continued to argue that updating the criminal laws would not result in any more prosecutions or convictions. According to Perkins:

The psychology has been that, unless we can get a criminal indictment under the statute, perhaps we had better not move at all. And our feeling is that the statute should point directly to the responsibility of the agency head to move quickly on a day-to-day enforcement basis.[19]

In other words, when the Justice Department refused to prosecute or could not obtain a conviction, few agencies wanted to impose administrative sanctions for the same conduct.

It soon became apparent that major concessions had to be made on the part of the Kennedy Administration and Congressman Celler if any legislation was to pass Congress. During early June 1961, Assistant Attorney General Katzenbach hammered out a compromise bill with the staff of the Celler Committee, Congressman Lindsay representing the Bar Association of the City of New York, and the Defense Department. On June 6, 1961, Katzenbach notified Myer Feldman, special assistant to the president, of the agreement he hoped would lead to a rapid passage of the conflict of interest reform measure.[20]

The compromise called for the creation of a new class of "special government employees" whose members would be exempt from some of the criminal prohibitions. The bill defined a special government employee as an "officer or employee of the executive branch . . . or of any independent agency or of the District of Columbia who is employed for not more than 130 days in any 365-day period to perform temporary duties."[21] The agreement did not establish separate rules for all of the conflict of interest statutes. It did, however, establish separate rules with respect to the laws prohibiting government employees from representing private parties before the government, with or without compensation, with respect to a matter in which the United States had a direct and substantial interest.[22]

Under the proposed law, a "special Government employee," such as a lawyer serving on the staff of an advisory commission, could continue to pursue legal work on behalf of clients with matters before government agencies. The administration hoped this two-tier approach would make consultants and other experts more willing to take part-time government positions since they could still pursue other business before federal agencies and departments. The compromise left one major problem unresolved, however. That issue involved Celler's insistence on a second postemployment activities bar.

A general agreement had been reached that Congress should enact a lifetime bar on former officials representing outside parties with respect to matters for which the former employee had direct responsibility while serving in government. Using language only a lawyer could understand, the so-called "switching-sides measure" imposed a permanent ban on former employees coming back as a representative of a private party to deal with a specific matter in which the former employee had "participated personally and substantially as a Government employee."[23] Of major significance, the personal and substantial participation could take the form of an approval, disapproval, recommendation, decision, rendering of advice, or investigation.

Congressman Celler, however, refused to scrap a second postemployment activities bar which imposed a two-year disqualification period with respect to matters for which the former employee had official responsibility while in government service. Finally, the compromise left relatively intact the existing prohibitions on supplementing the salaries of government employees[24] and on federal employees taking action with respect to matters in which they have a financial interest.[25] The self-dealing prohibition left intact the preference for disqualification over divestiture. The House passed the compromise bill, H.R. 8140, on August 7, 1961.

The House passage of H.R. 8140 did not satisfy everyone in the executive branch. A number of federal agencies and departments warned the White House that the second postemployment activities provision could cause a mass exodus of top-line technical personnel and make recruitment much more difficult. The strongest criticism came from the Defense Department and other federal employers employing large numbers of scientific and technical personnel.

At a meeting of the Federal Council for Science and Technology, a number of agencies pressed Justice to reverse its position on the postemployment activities provisions in H.R. 8140. At the least, government scientists wanted Congress to incorporate a provision exempting scientific personnel from both parts (a) and (b) of Section 207. Justice made it clear that an amendment of that type might seriously jeopardize final passage of the bill in the current session.[26]

This strong opposition on the part of federal agencies to the postemployment measures in the House bill helped to slow Senate action during the remainder of 1961. Further complicating Senate passage were renewed efforts, during the spring and summer of 1962, to get the Senate to pass a reform program based on the reform proposals of the Association of the Bar of the City of New York with its emphasis on statutory standards of conduct and administrative sanctions.[27] It appeared that the compromise was beginning to fall apart.

A strong advocate of the New York Bar Association proposal, Senator Kenneth Keating, was foremost in doubting whether the White House ethics program would work over an extended period of time. Keating wanted Congress to authorize agency heads to require their employees to file periodic reports on "their non-Government employment or self-employment,"[28] and to punish violators of conflict of interest laws by dismissal, suspension or "such other action as may be appropriate in the circumstances."[29] The administration maintained that agency heads already had the authority to punish violators under existing civil service rules and procedures.

The Keating amendments also gave agency heads the authority to impose administrative sanctions on former government employees who violated the statutory prohibitions, including placing other reasonable conditions on the appearances of former employees before agencies and departments.[30] Interestingly, the City of New York Bar Association proposal for prohibiting intermittent and regular government employees from accepting gifts and gratuities did not include a warning against officials becoming involved with appearances of impropriety.[31] In brief, the administration faced an increasingly serious struggle to convince Congress to enact a moderate reform program.

The 1961 failure of the Justice Department and the White House to push through statutory changes in the conflict of interest laws increased concern among government consultants and experts that they might violate the law if they also acted on behalf of private employers in dealing with federal agencies and departments. To calm these fears, in January 1962 President Kennedy obtained from the attorney general an advisory opinion interpreting the applicability of current conflict of interest laws to intermittent employees such as advisers and consultants.[32]

Armed with this opinion, on February 9, 1962 President Kennedy issued a memorandum detailing the coverage of intermittent employees under current conflict of interest statutes.[33] The memorandum also included provisions for confidential financial reporting for intermittent employees. Then, on February 26, 1962, President Kennedy issued Executive Order 1007, establishing detailed rules and regulations governing the formation and behavior of government advisory committees. The order emphasized the requirement that members must comply with all applicable conflict of interest laws, rules, and regulations.

These issuances had the additional purpose of demonstrating to Congress that the administration intended to hold advisers and consultants to the same high standards it had already applied to presidential appointees and regular government employees. In other words, Congress had nothing to fear from exempting "special Government employees" from certain criminal conflict of interest restrictions.

Continuing the offensive for passage of the statutory reform, in a June 1962 congressional testimony, Deputy Attorney General Katzenbach urged Congress to pass the "special Government employee" exemptions and revisions of the postemployment provisions of H.R. 8140. Although recognizing the legitimate concern of Congress over the loosening restrictions on consultants and advisers, Katzenbach reiterated that the White House, Justice Department, and agencies would closely monitor the conduct of experts and consultants under the provisions of the president's recent memorandum on preventing conflicts of interests involving advisers and consultants. Katzenbach pointed to the fact that the president's directive required intermittent advisers and consultants to submit financial disclosure statements of their financial interests. This requirement did not apply to regular government employees.

Pressure by the Kennedy Administration succeeded. The Senate passed H.R. 8140 on October 3, 1962, without incorporating any of the amendments put forward by Senator Keating.[34] A short time thereafter, the House accepted the Senate version without change. President Kennedy signed the bill into law on October 23, 1962, and the law took effect on January 21, 1963.[35]

REVOLUTION OR REDUNDANCY?

The most striking aspect of Public Law 87–849 is that it made relatively few substantive changes in existing prohibitions. Congress did not enact statutory standard-of-conduct regulations or a provision restricting general lobbying activities by former government officials. Congress did amend certain of the criminal prohibitions to distinguish between intermittent employees, such as advisers and consultants, and regular government employees in terms of criminal liability. The law also codified in Sections 201 and 209 of Title 18 of the United States Code all the major criminal conflict of interest prohibitions. These prohibitions included:

1. restrictions on government employees and officials rendering assistance to private parties in their dealings with the government;
2. regulation of the postemployment activities of former government employees before government agencies;
3. restrictions on self-dealing; and
4. the general prohibition on supplementing the salaries of government employees.

Serving Two Masters and Public Service

The revised language incorporated into Sections 203 and 205 of title 18 of the United States Code replaced the long-standing bar against federal personnel assisting in the prosecution of private claims against the government[36] and a similar restriction prohibiting the receipt of compensation for rendering assistance to private parties in their dealings with the government.[37] In other words, the revised measures left intact general prohibitions against compensated and uncompensated assistance by government employees acting as agents or attorneys for private parties.

By prohibiting government employees and members of Congress "from asking, demanding, soliciting, or seeking compensation for any service rendered in relation to any proceedings, application, request for a ruling or other determination,"[38] involving a matter in which the United States was a party and had a substantial interest, Congress sought to make sure that no loopholes remained in the prohibition. Section 203 made it clear that regular government employees could not go into business for themselves representing others before government agencies in any capacity.

Section 205 prohibited uncompensated assistance by government employees, but not by members of Congress. Again Congress sought to close every loophole. The prohibition would apply to "any proceeding, application, request for a ruling or other determination, contract, claim, etc." This little-noticed change in the law vastly expanded the scope of the prohibition. To reduce the burden of this measure, Congress specifically authorized government employees to render compensated and uncompensated assistance with respect to members of their families as long as the officer or employee did not have substantial responsibility for the matter.

Under the "special government employee" provision passed by Congress, employees who worked more than 60 days "during the immediately preceding 365 consecutive days" were not subject to most of the compensated and uncompensated assistance provisions of Sections 203 and 205.[39] Congress came to accept the administration's position that across-the-board application of the representation prohibition threatened national security by making it much more difficult to recruit and retain part-time expert technical and professional talent.

Switching Sides

The administration was less successful in getting its way on the revision of the postemployment activities laws. On a positive note, the Congress passed Section 207(a), the lifetime disqualification bar. Strongly backed by the administration, the bar applied to "any judicial or other proceeding, application, request or other determination, contract, claim, controversy, charge, accusation, arrest, or other particular matter" where the former employee had participated personally and substantially and where the United States was a party or had a substantial interest.

Congress also passed a second official responsibility postemployment activities prohibition. Section 207(b) restricted representational activities before federal agencies for a period of one year after leaving government with respect to matters under the former government employee's official responsibility "within a period of one year prior to termination of such responsibility." Congressman Celler had argued for a two-year bar applicable to any matter under official responsibility while the individual was in government service.

It is important to note that both postemployment activities bans tied postservice representation restrictions to the former official's previous responsibilities in the government.[40] The Kennedy Administration successfully withstood efforts to impose general lobbying restrictions on former government personnel. In addition, none of the postemployment provisions prevented a government employee from taking a position with any private employer.

Critics of the revolving door found little in the 1962 revision to make them happy. The changes made it clear that the two bars applied to a wide spectrum of government proceedings and not only to the prosecution of claims against the government.

Self-Dealing and Disqualification

Little debate took place over the financial self-dealing prohibition. The revised statute, Section 208, prohibited all full-time and intermittent employees from participating in a governmental matter where the official, or the official's spouse, minor child, partner, or organization in which the official was serving had a financial interest. The statute reflected the policy that "a public official should not be in the position of acting for the Government where his private economic interests are involved."[41] The disqualification requirement is triggered by personal and substantial participation by the employee in government proceedings in which the official has an indirect or direct financial interest. Section 208 does not specifically require divestiture of any financial interest or relationship. Equally significant, the amount of the economic interest is, in theory, irrelevant. Of like importance, Section 208(a) included within the definition of financial interest "any person or organization with whom [the official] is negotiating or has any arrangement concerning prospective employment."[42]

With little fanfare, the Justice Department persuaded Congress to incorporate two escape clauses from the self-dealing prohibition.[43] Under Section 208(b) Congress gave the employee's appointing authority permission to grant a disqualification waiver if the appointing authority made an advance written determination "that interest is not so substantial as to be deemed likely to affect the integrity of the services which the Government may expect from such officer or employee."[44] Moreover, the law authorized the exemption of certain types of financial interests from Section 208 coverage by publishing in the *Federal Register* a rule of general applicability that "the financial interest is too remote or too inconsequential to affect the integrity of the agency's employees generally."[45]

Private Supplementation of Government Salaries

On the issue of prohibiting the supplementation of government salaries, Congress kept intact the general prohibition, but in Section 209(b) it authorized continued participation "in a *bona fide* pension, retirement, group life, health or accident insurance, profit-sharing, stock bonus, or other employee welfare or benefit plan maintained by a former employer." The Kennedy White House fought hard for this major exemption on the grounds that the supplementation ban created an undue hardship for high-level appointees who moved from organizations that had lucrative benefit packages.

In light of the uproar that developed over the conflict of interest crisis during the late 1950s and the initial public position of the Kennedy Administration, it is surprising that Congress made so few substantive changes to strengthen the basic conflict of interest statutes besides making clear that they covered all types of government proceedings. The aggressive implementation of the White House ethics-reform program reduced public and congressional pressure for sweeping statutory reforms. Fear of a mass exodus of technical, scientific, and professional talent also played a role in blocking major changes. Finally, Congress feared that if it enacted stiff new ethics reforms applicable to the executive branch, the public might wonder why it had not policed the conduct of its own members. Because of these factors, Public Law 87–849 constituted a fine tuning of the criminal conflict of interest prohibitions rather than a major overhaul.

The 1962 revision of the criminal conflict of interest laws left unresolved the fundamental problem of imposing criminal penalties for conduct that does not fall within the traditional areas of public corruption and graft. The narrow language of the statutes would continue to act as a major deterrent preventing the Justice Department from prosecuting individuals for violating the prohibitions. Terms such as "particular matter," "substantial participation," and "personal participation" are subject to interpretation. The Kennedy White House hoped that its administrative regulations would rapidly become preferred over the cumbersome criminal statutes for dealing with conflict of interest problems.

THE ADMINISTRATIVE REFORMATION CONTINUES

As the Kennedy Administration moved to get Congress to pass its statutory conflict of interest reforms during the spring and summer of 1962, Civil Service Commission Chairman Macy pushed ahead with efforts to get federal agencies and departments to fully implement their agency ethics programs. By this time, Frederick Dutton had left the White House, and Lee C. White, assistant special council to the president, had unofficially assumed the responsibilities of White House ethics counselor.

In a May 1962 memorandum, Chairman Macy assured Special Council White that the commission was actively monitoring agency compliance with Executive Order 10939, the Dutton memorandum, and the president's recent directive regarding the conduct of intermittent and special government employees.[46] Macy informed White that he had directed the commission's Bureau of Inspections "to determine during the course of regular inspections of personnel management practices"[47] whether agencies were:

1. informing their employees of the standards of conduct;
2. advising new employees of the standards of conduct at the time of employment; and
3. distributing the now required semiannual standards of conduct reminders.

Macy reported that as of April 6, 1962, eighty-nine inspection reports involving units within nine departments and agencies had been received. Analysis of the reports found that "better than 90 percent of the establishments were in compliance with the Executive Orders."[48] Macy concluded that the findings were encouraging, but that it was still too soon to draw any definitive conclusions regarding agency compliance with the president's ethics directives.

Chairman Macy's optimism was premature. Both Macy and the White House had underestimated the difficulty of getting agencies to commit the necessary resources to their ethics programs. Late in the summer of 1962, the House Government Operations Committee asked the Congressional Legislative Reference Service (LRS) to determine the level of agency compliance with President Kennedy's conflict of interest prevention program. Completed in the late fall of 1962, the LRS report found "a lack of uniformity among agencies and unduly lax policies in some agencies." Only eleven of fifty-four agencies surveyed had, in fact, established ethics committees as mandated by the president's message of April 27, 1961.[49] With some concern, James Lanigan, general counsel of the House Government Operations Committee, forwarded these findings to the Justice Department and the Bureau of the Budget.

Harold Seidman, director of the Bureau of the Budget, asked his staff to find a way to assure the "uniform implementation of conflict of interest legislation and standards of conduct." In early December 1962, Seidman's staff reported that the failure of the president to appoint a successor to Frederick Dutton, the former White House ethics coordinator, meant that "no central direction is being provided to agency efforts and no uniformity in agency regulations is being enforced."[50] One can assume that Chairman Macy vigorously disagreed with this finding.

The Bureau of the Budget staff noted, secondly, the failure of the administration to seek legislation to stop ex parte contacts between private citizens and organizations and government officials involved in ongoing administrative proceedings. The president's April 1961 message to Congress urged a statutory prohibition on ex parte communications to protect the fairness and impartiality of the administrative process and to assure the public that secret communications were not shaping government decision making.[51]

Finally, the report to Harold Seidman raised serious questions about the long-term viability of the president's conflict of interest reform program. How extensively would agencies have to revise their standards of conduct in order to make them consistent with Public Law 87–849? Would agencies or the administration "publicize the less stringent post-employment standards applicable under the new law"? How would the changes be brought to the attention of advisers and consultants who "supposedly have been deterred from accepting Government employment"? Would use be made of the provision permitting the president or agency heads to designate certain financial interests of employees "too insubstantial to disqualify an employee from dealing with that entity"? Would special machinery be put into place "to determine the status (in terms of time worked during the year) of advisers and consultants employed by more than one agency"?[52]

The Bureau of the Budget memorandum clearly took the position that many agencies regarded their ethics programs as low-priority items. To get the program back on track, the White House needed to take immediate steps to resolve the administrative problems created by the new ethics law and by the lack of a person in the Executive Office of the president who was responsible for overseeing the implementation of the program.

By early January 1963, congressional displeasure with the White House ethics program had become even more apparent. A January 18, 1963, memorandum from the deputy director of the Bureau of the Budget to Presidential Assistant Lee White reported that the House Committee on Government Operations had asked the bureau to amend the Dutton memorandum by obligating agencies to:

1. "cite, quote, and explain statutes on conflicts of interest in their regulations";
2. require employees to sign a statement that they had read and understood agency standards of conduct;
3. specifically require the establishment of ad hoc ethics committees;
4. "require all, or some categories of employees to report their outside pecuniary interests";
5. "require all employees to report their outside employment"; and
6. require more specific regulations on administrative disciplinary action.[53]

Much of the criticism came from liberal House Democrats who believed the White House had gone back on its word to vigorously enforce the new standards of conduct. To deal with this situation, they wanted limited financial disclosure for government personnel and mandatory divestiture of financial interests creating an actual or apparent conflict of interest.

The deputy director of the Bureau of the Budget advised the White House of the costs and benefits of tightening the requirements of the Dutton memorandum in this way:

The improved protection of the Government's interest in ethical conduct by its employees resulting from more stringent Government-wide minimum standards must be weighed against the time and money required to implement such standards and against the invasion of the employee's privacy which potential changes would entail. Intelligent consideration of particular amendments to strengthen the Dutton Memorandum depends upon an analysis of present agency practice and the administrative burdens and possible loss of personnel from Government service which might result from changes.[54]

Early in January 1963, the White House announced that Presidential Assistant Lee White would take over responsibilities for coordinating the executive-branch ethics program. Then, on January 21, 1963, President Kennedy directed all agencies and departments to review their regulations covering conflicts of interest and ethical conduct to make sure they were consistent with Public Law 87–849 and the Dutton memorandum.[55] The directive gave agencies until March 11, 1963, to submit to Lee White their revised standards of conduct. Finally, the directive informed agency heads that the White House would be issuing a revised memorandum on preventing conflicts of interest on the part of advisers and consultants which would reflect the important changes brought about by the passage of Public Law 87–849. Although the presidential directive addressed most of the concerns of the Bureau of the Budget, the White House rejected imposing financial disclosure for regular government employees.

Finally, on May 2, 1963, President Kennedy reissued the memorandum titled "Preventing Conflicts of Interest on the Part of Special Government Employees."[56] It discussed the applicability of statutory prohibitions to the new class of special government employees, and, equally important, the memorandum reminded agency heads of the financial reporting requirement for special government employees.

Despite the apparent displeasure of the Bureau of the Budget with the role of the commission up to that point, Lee White subsequently asked John Macy to take responsibility for reviewing agency compliance with the president's updated ethics directives.[57] On July 26, 1963, Macy forwarded the White House a preliminary report on agency standards of conduct, indicating that the commission had reviewed about 50 percent of agency regulations on conflicts of interests and employee conduct without finding substantial problems.[58]

Macy also reported to White that a number of other steps had been taken to address complaints about the president's ethics program. First, the commission had prepared and published an easy-to-read pamphlet for distribution to government advisers and consultants on the applicable conflict of interest laws and standards of conduct. Second, an interagency advisory group had been established to explore how information could be exchanged among agencies on the number of days being worked by special government employees in order to determine which employees had exceeded the 130-day limit. Third, the interagency advisory group, with the approval of the Bureau of the Budget, had completed a revision of the financial disclosure form for special government employees.[59]

On September 16, 1963, Macy reported to White that the completed review determined that "the standards as a whole are comprehensive and uniform in subject coverage" and that agencies had "adhered closely to the guidelines of the Dutton Memorandum." Most agencies had also updated their standards to reflect the changes brought about by the passage of Public Law 87–849.[60] Macy painted a positive picture of the condition of the reform program:

Although these standards are basically the same as those submitted in 1961, and range, as they did then, from "adequate, limited coverage" to "excellent comprehensive coverage," it is gratifying to find that most agencies have followed closely the criteria outlined in the Dutton memorandum of July 20, 1961, supplementing them wherever necessary to meet individual agency needs. Agencies appear to be making a strong effort to bring their regulations on conflicts of interest and ethical conduct to the attention of their employees, and, from the reports we have received on agencies throughout the United States, I believe their efforts in this direction have been effective.[61]

In spite of the positive tone of the report, however, Chairman Macy identified a number of weaknesses in agency standards. First, too many regulations used vague and overly technical terms which made "much of the content too high-powered for the average employee to interpret."[62] Second, the absence of specific examples of unethical conduct made it difficult for employees to apply the abstract restrictions. Third, the inclusion of a number of conflict of interest problems under the same heading led to unnecessary confusion. Chairman Macy concluded his report by suggesting that any strengthening in the existing regulations be delayed for at least six months to permit employees to assimilate the changes brought about by the amended conflict of interest laws and to give agencies an opportunity to work out the problems in their programs. After that period, a comprehensive review of the minimum standards of conduct could be conducted to determine how they might be strengthened.[63] Shortly thereafter, Lee White accepted John Macy's recommendation and agreed that consideration of revisions to the Dutton memorandum would be delayed for six months.[64]

On November 22, 1963, with the assassination of President Kennedy, the future of the ethics reform program was placed in the hands of the next president.

ON THE RIGHT COURSE BUT AT HALF STEAM

There seems little doubt that President Kennedy and his administration were committed to effective conflict of interest prevention and enforcement. This commitment, however, was tempered by concern over the impact of regulations on the recruitment of essential personnel. The White House steered a middle course, but not without risk. With little likelihood of increased prosecutions under the criminal statutes, the success of the reform program hinged upon the administrative reforms. An effective program depended upon the willingness of agencies not to leave it up to the Justice Department to deal with conflict of interest allegations.

John Macy believed that this turnabout could be accomplished as long as the White House made clear that it expected agencies to act. Others in the Congress and the administration were not so sure. The 1960 report of the Association of the Bar of the City of New York recognized that no one wanted to go on record to scrap criminal penalties. However, the study also implied that few in the Justice Department believed violations of the main statutes warranted criminal prosecution.

In sum, the Kennedy Administration laid the foundation for a conflict of interest regulation program that combined criminal penalties and administrative enforcement. The Kennedy White House believed that if Congress extended the criminal prohibitions to include a much broader range of conduct, the best and the brightest individuals would stay away from government service. However, the Kennedy White House also realized that conflict of interest allegations could destroy the credibility of the president.

NOTES

1. H.R. 10575.

2. H.R. 3411, 87th Cong. See also U.S. Congress, House, Committee on the Judiciary, Federal Conflict of Interest Legislation, Hearing on H.R. 2157, H.R. 1900, H.R. 2157, H.R. 7556, and H.R. 10575, 86th Cong., 2d Sess., February 17, 18, 19, 24, 25, 26, and March 1, 2, and 3, 1960.

3. The current prohibitions on postemployment representation were found at Section 284 of Title 18 of the U.S.C.

4. U.S. Congress, House, Committee on the Judiciary, Federal Conflict of Interest Legislation, p. 2.

5. Ibid., p. 390.

6. Ibid., p. 392.

7. Ibid., p. 394.

8. Ibid., p. 390.

9. Reintroduced as H.R. 3411 and H.R. 3412.

10. Letter, Nicholas DeB. Katzenbach for Mr. Arthur Focke, May 22, 1961, Papers of James Landis, White House Staff Files, John F. Kennedy Library.

11. Ibid., p. 2.

12. Ibid.

13. Ibid.

14. Memorandum, Carlisle Bolton-Smith for Mr. Landis, May 29, Papers of John Landis, White House Staff Files, John F. Kennedy Library.

15. U.S. Congress, House, Committee on the Judiciary, Federal Conflict of Interest Legislation, on H.R. 3050, H.R. 3411, H.R. 3412, and H.R. 7139, 87th Cong., 1st Sess., June 1 and 2, 1961, p. 31.

16. Ibid., p. 31.

17. Ibid., p. 71.

18. Ibid., p. 117.

19. Ibid.

20. Memorandum, Nicholas Katzenbach for Myer Feldman, June 6, 1961, Papers of Myer Feldman, White House Staff Files, John F. Kennedy Library.

21. U.S. Congress, House, Judiciary Committee, Bribery, graft, and conflicts of interest report, July 20, 1961 (to accompany H.R. 8140) 61 (87th Cong., 1st Sess. H. Rept. No. 748) p. 14.

22. See Sections 203 and 205 of Title 18 of the United States Code.

23. See Section 207(a) of Title 18.

24. *See* Section 209 of Title 18.

25. Section 208 of Title 18 of the United States Code.

26. Letter noted in Memorandum, Harold F. Reis, Office of Legal Counsel, Department of Justice, for Myer Feldman, Special Assistant to the President, August 16, 1961, Papers of Myer Feldman, White House Staff Files, John F. Kennedy Library.

27. U.S. Congress, Senate, Committee on the Judiciary, *Conflicts of Interest*, Hearings on H.R. 8140, 87th Cong., 2d Sess., June 21, 1962.

28. Ibid., p. 10.

29. Ibid., Section 402(a), Administrative Enforcement as to Current Employees.

30. Ibid., Section 402(b).

31. Ibid.

32. Opinion of the Attorney General of the United States, *Conflict of Interest Statutes: Intermittent Consultants or Advisers*, January 31, 1962.

33. U.S. President (John F. Kennedy), 1961–1963, Memorandum to Heads of Executive Departments and Agencies, *Preventing Conflicts of Interest on the Part of Advisers and Consultants to the Government*, The White House, February 9, 1962.

34. Cong. Rec. 20905–21 (Daily Edition, October 3, 1962).

35. *See* Roswell Perkins, "The New Federal Conflict of Interest Law," *Harvard Law Review* 76 (April 1963): 117.

36. Section 205 replaced Section 283 of Title 18 of the U.S.C.

37. Section 203 replaced Section 281 of Title 18.

38. Section 203(c) of Title 18 of the United States Code.

39. Sections 203(c) and 205(2) of Title 18.

40. Roswell Perkins, "The New Federal Conflict of Interest Law," p. 1155.

41. Ibid., p. 1129.

42. Ibid., p. 1132.

43. *See* Sections 208(b)(1) and (b)(2) of Title 18 of the United States Code.

44. Section 208(b) of Title 18 of the United States Code.

45. Ibid.

46. Memorandum, John W. Macy for Lee C. White, May 2, 1962, White House Staff Files, Papers of Lee White, John F. Kennedy Library.

47. Ibid.

48. These were Agriculture, Air Force, Federal Aviation Administration, Health, Education and Welfare, Navy, and the Treasury Department.

49. Memorandum for Harold Seidman, Director of the Bureau of the Budget, December 12, 1962, White House Staff Files, Lee White, John F. Kennedy Library.

50. Ibid., p. 2.

51. Seidman Memorandum, December 12, 1962, p. 2.

52. Ibid.

53. Memorandum, Deputy Director, Bureau of the Budget, for Mr. White, January 18, 1963, White House Staff Files, Papers of Lee White, John F. Kennedy Library.

54. Ibid., p. 3.

55. The White House, Memorandum for the Heads of Executive Departments and Agencies, Subject: *Conflicts of Interest and Ethical Standards of Conduct*, January 21, 1963.

56. U.S. President (John F. Kennedy), 1961–1963, Memorandum, *Preventing Con-*

flicts of Interest on the Part of Special Government Employees, the White House, May 2, 1963.

57. Memorandum, Lee C. White for Mr. John W. Macy, Jr., May 15, 1963, White House Staff Files, Papers of Lee White, John F. Kennedy Library.

58. Memorandum, Mr. John W. Macy for Lee C. White, July 26, 1963, White House Staff Files, Papers of Lee White, John F. Kennedy Library.

59. Ibid.

60. Letter, John W. Macy to Honorable Lee C. White, September 16, 1963, White House Staff Files, Papers of Lee White, John F. Kennedy Library, pp. 1–2.

61. Ibid., pp. 2–3.

62. Ibid., p. 3.

63. Ibid., pp. 3–4.

64. Memorandum, Lee White for Honorable John W. Macy, September 27, 1963, White House Staff Files, Papers of Lee White, John F. Kennedy Library.

VI

After Kennedy: The Ethics Program in Limbo

The absence of serious scandals during the Kennedy Administration may have been the result of good luck, an exceptionally loyal work force, or an increased sensitivity for conflict of interest problems brought about by the administration's conflict of interest prevention program.[1] At any rate, the death of President Kennedy placed in limbo the future of the White House-directed ethics program. Consequently, toward the close of November 1964, Chairman of the Civil Service Commission John Macy began to push the White House to decide the future of the program.

Further complicating the situation, on November 27, 1963, the Holifield Subcommittee of the House Armed Services Committee issued a report entitled *Avoiding Conflicts of Interest in Defense Contracting and Employment.*[2] The report noted the flow of personnel between the Defense Department and the three branches of the armed services and major defense contractors, and urged "that the Bureau of the Budget and the Civil Service Commission develop a uniform requirement for the filing of such financial statements by all senior Government personnel whose work affects procurement and contracting."[3] The disclosure requirements would apply equally to regular and intermittent personnel.

On November 30, 1964, Chairman Macy wrote to Bill Moyers of the White House staff, urging that "immediate action be taken under the leadership of the White House staff to review existing policy guidance on ethical standards for officials and employees of the Executive Branch."[4] This review, Macy suggested, should lead to the early issuance by President Johnson of an Executive Order on standards of conduct.

Macy argued that without a strong show of support from the president it would be difficult to keep the program alive. He noted that more than a

year had elapsed since he and Lee White had agreed to conduct a comprehensive six-month review of the program.

Macy recommended that the review should, at a minimum, cover

1. conflict of interest;

2. dual employment;

3. acceptance of compensation for speaking and writing based on knowledge gained
   through official duties;

4. acceptance of gifts or services from those with whom business is conducted; and

5. disclosure of private holdings and securities by government employees.

Because of the controversial nature of a number of the ethics-related issues,
Macy suggested that the review be limited to a relatively small number of
administration officials.[5]

With the approval of the White House, the Programs and Standards Unit
of the Civil Service Commission conducted an exhaustive review of the
executive-branch ethics program and uncovered no substantive problems.[6]
The staff review did recommend the issuance of a new executive order on
standards of conduct to eliminate confusion created by the overlapping
provisions of Executive Order 10939, the Dutton memorandum and President Kennedy's special government employee conflict-of-interest directive.[7]

The commission staff also gave limited support for financial disclosure
for individuals occupying sensitive positions. For instance, the proposed
standards of conduct Executive Order required procurement officers to file
because they had the opportunity to use their positions to help defense
contractors. To protect the privacy rights of public servants, the statements
would not be subject to public inspection.[8]

The subsequent draft order, prepared during December 1964, gave the
Civil Service Commission overall responsibility for "all regulations, inter-
pretations, and program appraisals for the entire scope of the Executive
Order."[9] These rules would cover the activities of full-time presidential
appointees, regular employees, and part-time experts and consultants. Simply, the Civil Service Commission would take over formal responsibility
for the ethics program.

To assure uniformity from agency to agency, Macy asked the staff to
incorporate minimum standards for agency financial disclosure statements,
provisions to protect the privacy of such information, requirements that
presidential appointees file statements detailing their holdings by corporate
entity, and clearer rules regarding the acceptance of meals and entertainment
by employees engaged in contracting.

During the time Chairman Macy and the commission worked on a plan
for updating the executive-branch ethics program, rumors of widespread

gift giving by defense contractors involving high-level government personnel increased. The General Accounting Office (GAO) developed the most damaging evidence as the result of investigations conducted during 1963 and 1964 and directed at uncovering excessive profits, cost overruns, delays, and other suspected irregularities by major defense contractors.[10]

Prior to this point the General Accounting Office had generally restricted its defense-related reviews to federal organizations. During this period, however, the GAO began an aggressive program to review the conduct of private contractors. This included controversial requests to review the records of contractors as well as on-site inspections. Many of the contractors subject to investigations complained that the GAO did not have the expertise to evaluate their performance and was conducting a witch-hunt.

These and other investigations again raised serious questions regarding the impact of the "alleged buddy relationships of military and civilian officials in the military establishment and related agencies . . . with private industries," on the efficiency and the integrity of defense procurement.[11] Repeating the concerns voiced during the First and Second World Wars, critics of the buddy relationship maintained that the opportunity for lucrative, private defense-related jobs made government personnel reluctant to criticize the procurement practices of defense contractors.

As the commission staff worked on a draft of the executive order on standards on conduct during late 1964, Chairman Macy directed it to include an additional presidential directive requiring government contractors to file quarterly reports of any gifts or entertainment furnished to government employees.[12]

A proposed presidential statement to accompany the contractor gift reporting requirement clearly demonstrated the growing frustration with the gift giving practices of government contractors.

It is a matter of great concern to me that there continues to be reports that organizations which do business with the government extend gifts, entertainment, and favors to government under questionable circumstances. No practice that I know of can do more to harm the confidence of American citizens in the integrity and impartiality of our Government.

This practice must be stopped.[13]

As subsequently drafted, the section required all departments and agencies to collect quarterly reports from contractors and their subcontractors with respect to providing government personnel with gifts, gratuities, labor, entertainment, loans or anything of value. The corporate-gift-reporting requirement was similar to one proposed by the Bar Association of the City of New York in its 1960 report.[14]

Expecting little opposition to the revised standards of conduct, Chairman Macy, in late January, 1965, forwarded the latest draft of the order to Kermit

Gordon, Director of the Bureau of the Budget. Besides being designed to codify "existing executive branch standards relating to ethical conduct and conflicts of interest," the draft, Macy explained, provided for

1. confidential financial reporting limited to high-level Presidential appointees and certain regular employees concerned with procurement and contracting activities;
2. the filing of quarterly reports as to "gifts, gratuities, or favors, entertainment, or loans provided to or for any officer or employee of the Government by government contractors";
3. and turning oversight responsibility for the ethics program to the Civil Service Commission.[15]

During this period, John Macy continued his push for more forceful action against defense contractors who provided government employees with gifts, entertainment, and other favors. He asked the general counsel of the Bureau of the Budget, Arthur Focke, to determine whether the Internal Revenue Service could issue regulations denying business expense deductions for gifts and entertainment of government personnel. Focke reported that Sheldon Cohen, commissioner of the Internal Revenue Service, agreed that such action could be taken if the president requested it.[16]

By early March it had become clear that the Bureau of the Budget had a serious problem with the approach put forward by the Civil Service Commission. First, the bureau found little reason to distinguish between high-level presidential appointees and regular employees with respect to the standards of conduct regulations. The commission draft incorporated separate standards of conduct sections for presidential employees, regular employees and special government employees. Second, the bureau proposed to keep the previous presidential directives in force and to use the new order only to modify or supplement them. Third, and to the dismay of the commission staff, the bureau proposed establishing across-the-board gift acceptance exemptions, instead of giving agency heads limited authority to grant case-by-case exemptions. Fourth, and even more disturbing from the commission's perspective, the bureau deleted the section requiring gift reporting by government contractors.[17] Finally, the bureau made a number of major changes in the financial reporting provisions of the draft executive order.

During much of April 1965, Chairman Macy, Arthur Focke, and Justice Department representatives Norb Schlei and Sol Lindenbaum hammered out a compromise draft. On April 9, 1965, Arthur Focke forwarded the compromise draft to Lee White at the White House.[18]

Even though Macy believed that full-time presidential appointees should adhere to higher standards of conduct than regular federal employees, he agreed to the establishment of general standards applicable to all regular employees. Recognizing the statutory changes made by Congress, the compromise order contained a separate section dealing with conflicts of interest and "special government employees." The Budget Bureau then agreed to the revocation of all prior presidential directives on conflicts of interest and standards of conduct. The compromise eliminated Macy's proposal for the reporting of gifts to government employees by government contractors. That proposal proved too touchy to handle, and there were serious questions about how such a provision could be enforced. In spite of Macy's failure to gain acceptance of the corporate-gift-reporting requirement, he received little opposition to the proposal giving the commission general oversight responsibility for the executive-branch ethics program.

Along with a draft of the order, General Counsel Focke sent a message warning the White House that a major public scandal might erupt shortly over the gift-giving practices of major defense contractors. The GAO was circulating a draft report alleging that a number of defense contractors had spent millions of dollars on gifts and entertainment for government officials. Moreover, the report revealed that many businesses had deducted these expenditures on their taxes as legitimate business expenses, a practice not prohibited under current Internal Revenue regulations. General Counsel Focke summarized the contents of the report:

The GAO has received the records of the plants or divisions on 20 prime contractors doing business almost exclusively with the Government and has found that more than $3 million was spent during 1963 in providing gratuities and entertainment. The report implies that most of the expenditures were, in the nature of things, for entertainment of Government employees. It suggests that, even though some of the expenditures might not be reimbursable by the Government or included in the contractors' costs, the Government nevertheless bore approximately 50 percent of the burden of such expenditures by reason of tax deductions claimed by the contractors.[19]

Equally troublesome, the GAO report cited numerous instances of government employees accepting items such as "hunting trips, golf outings, meals, cocktails, tickets to sporting events, etc."[20]

According to the Focke memorandum, the General Accounting Office would recommend some drastic measures to stop this type of irresponsible corporate behavior. These measures included automatic penalties for contractors who entertained government employees, regardless of intent; stronger penalties for government employees taking items of value from defense contractors; and an extensive investigation by the Internal Revenue Service of defense contractors' business-related tax deductions.[21]

The release of the report, Focke feared, would create a storm of controversy over the ability of the new Johnson Administration to keep government contractors honest. Calls for tougher conflict of interest measures would certainly follow. Finally, Focke informed Lee White that the Justice Department continued to oppose the confidential reporting provisions of the order and that, therefore, a final decision on financial reporting would have to be made at the White House.

The Focke memorandum to Lee White left the impression that there had been general agreement on the content of the executive order. In reality, the Civil Service Commission harbored some hard feelings over the language of the order. In a mid–April memorandum to Chairman Macy, L. V. Meloy, general counsel for the Civil Service Commission, granted that the commission could live with the latest draft, but that problems remained which might seriously reduce the effectiveness of the disclosure program.

The most serious problem involved procedures for collecting financial disclosure statements. The commission wanted to require presidential nominees to file disclosure statements shortly after the announcement of their nomination in order to identify potential conflict of interest problems before confirmation proceedings. However, the Bureau of the Budget successfully blocked this filing requirement on the grounds that Senate committees might demand these statements, and that because committees collected their own financial data, conflicting statements might be submitted creating additional problems.[22] The draft, consequently, gave covered employees up to ninety days to file. This extended time would make it next to impossible for the commission to use these statements to detect possible conflict of interest problems prior to confirmation. However, the order did not prevent the White House from requiring financial data from prospective nominees or appointees.

On April 15, 1965, Lee White notified President Johnson that John Macy, Norb Schlei of Justice, and the Bureau of the Budget had reached agreement on a new standards–of–conduct executive order.[23] Concerned about the impact of the forthcoming GAO report of defense contractor practices, White thought it wise to get the order signed and released as quickly as possible. To speed up release, he recommended that the president ask only "one or two Cabinet officers to take a good look at it."[24] Finally, White advised President Johnson that Sheldon Cohen, the Internal Revenue Service commissioner, was thinking of issuing regulations limiting corporations from deducting as a business expense the cost of entertaining government employees. Subsequent correspondence indicates that Lee White sought the immediate review of the order by the attorney general as a further method of expediting its release.

As if the prospect of a damaging GAO report were not enough, early April 1965 saw a high–level appointee to the Commerce Department accused of using inside information to speculate on the stock market. A complaint by the Securities and Exchange Commission alleged that Herbert Klotz, a Commerce Department assistant secretary, had made profits by speculating in Texas Gulf Sulphur stock by using inside information. Although Klotz denied using confidential inside information for stock speculation and claimed that he bought the stock on the basis of secondhand information received from a Commerce Department secretary, he resigned his position three days after the SEC formally charged him with insider trading.[25]

On April 27, 1965, Deputy Attorney General Ramsey Clark informed Lee White that Justice believed the order dealt adequately with the issues raised by the Klotz controversy. Clark argued that a specific presidential directive on stock speculation would raise serious questions regarding the adequacy of earlier ethics-related directives. On the other hand, Clark doubted that financial reporting would help to detect conflicts of interest, because those intent on wrongdoing would not report certain information. More important, Clark argued that these financial reports might be "the source of embarrassment to the Administration if wrongdoing was discovered at a later date in connection with a reported investment."[26] In other words, the reporting requirements, it was argued, would raise public expectations that somehow financial reporting would prevent all conflicts of interest. This expectation was impossible to realize since the order made no provision for the auditing of the financial affairs of employees and officials.

On April 28, 1965, Lee White asked the president to make a series of final decisions regarding substantive parts of the order. These included:

1. the regulation of appearances of conflicts of interest as well as actual conflicts;
2. disclosure of government information for personal gain;
3. a specific prohibition against stock speculation to deal with the problem raised by the Klotz controversy; and
4. a financial disclosure statement.[27]

THE APPEARANCE OF SELF-DEALING

The 1961 Dutton memorandum, as noted, included a provision stating that employees "may not have direct or indirect financial interests that conflict substantially, or appear to conflict substantially, with their responsibilities and duties as Federal employees."[28] The broad Dutton language on appearances had not been applied in the early presidential directive to high-level political appointees. Lee White and other administration officials understood the implications of this change. Because many officials of the White House Office, the Budget Bureau, and the Council of Economic Advisers have very broad, government-wide responsibilities, noted White, the Dutton language might preclude these employees and officials from holding financial interests in anything. On the other hand, the deletion of the appearance language, White also noted, would create a large gap in the standards of conduct by "not precluding individuals from financial interests which conflict or appear to conflict with their governmental responsibilities."[29] Dutton recommended, and the president accepted, the inclusion of the Dutton appearance language.

FREEDOM OF SPEECH AND INSIDE INFORMATION

Lee White then asked President Johnson to decide on language to regulate the use of government information by government personnel. The draft sent to the White House prohibited employees from unauthorized disclosure of official information not available to the general public. On the other hand, it specifically stated that nothing in the order "shall be construed as directing any employee to withhold unclassified information from the press or public."[30] In contrast to the newly proposed language, the Dutton memorandum contained a much broader rule against the release of unauthorized information. It read, "Employees may not discuss official information without either appropriate general or specific authority under agency regulations."[31]

White reported to President Johnson that Abe Fortas, at the time with the law firm of Arnold, Fortas, and Porter, strongly preferred the broader language of the Dutton memorandum. Fortas maintained that the new language would create undue confusion in the government, since government employees would be led to believe that "they should make information freely available to the press so long as there is no conflict of a personal financial interest."[32] The broader language, therefore, would provide the administration with additional leverage in controlling the unauthorized release of information. President Johnson accepted the recommendation that the language of the Dutton memorandum be retained.

STOCK SPECULATION AND THE GOVERNMENT EMPLOYEE

Before the issuance of the Dutton memorandum, John Macy had received White House permission to repeal President Roosevelt's 1937 letter on stock speculation. The Klotz case renewed concern that government standards of conduct dealt inadequately with the problem. However, Lee White advised the president that Section 201(c) of the order, which was taken directly from President Kennedy's Executive Order 10939, adequately dealt with the speculation issue. Specifically, it stated the prohibition against taking actions that "might result in, or create the appearance of (1) using public office for private gain, (2) giving preferential treatment to any organization or person, (3) impeding government efficiency or economy, (4) losing complete independence or impartiality of action, (5) making a government decision outside official channels, and (6) affecting adversely the confidence of the public in the integrity of the Government."[33]

Instead of referring specifically to stock speculation in the executive order, White recommended that during background briefing the administration could stress that the financial reporting requirements along with provisions for reviewing financial problems with employees would "bring forcefully to the attention of employees their special obligation to consider financial transactions in the view of their government capacity."[34] Even more important, under the order's appearance standard, agencies would have the authority to take action against questionable stock speculation by government personnel. The president agreed with the decision to omit any reference to stock speculation in the order.

PRIVACY RIGHTS AND FINANCIAL DISCLOSURE

Finally, Lee White recommended that President Johnson approve the confidential reporting program despite substantial opposition to the program. The Justice Department, for example, continued to doubt the effectiveness of confidential reporting and believed that sooner or later a conflict of interest scandal would occur to shake public confidence in the disclosure program.[35] White argued, however, that the benefits outweighed possible costs because the White House needed more financial information on nominees since Senate committees increasingly required nominees to submit detailed financial disclosure statements. In addition, if the president required disclosure for high-level executive-branch personnel, then Congress might be prodded to adopt a similar measure. Since the system would be confidential, little opposition was expected from government personnel. In the end, President Johnson approved the financial reporting provision.

Even after making the key substantive decisions regarding the Order, however, Johnson had reservations about the tone of the directive. Consequently, he asked Lee White to send copies of the final order to Abe Fortas and Justice E. Barrett Prettyman, senior circuit judge of the United States Court of Appeals.

What transpired probably led Lee White to consider whether he should be in another line of employment. Judge Prettyman issued a scathing response attacking key provisions of the order as fundamentally unfair to the average civil servant, who would find it next to impossible to determine what was permitted and what was prohibited, because of the vagueness of the code. The letter read in part:

I assume that when you asked me to comment on the draft you meant to get my frank opinion; my understanding was tacitly upon that condition. So I am sorry I agreed, because my opinion is quite critical, and adverse criticism of somebody else's work is always unpleasant to me.[36]

Judge Prettyman argued that the draft was too complicated, too obscure and confused in places, and too severe in certain respects. He reserved his harshest criticism for the use of phrases such as "substantially affecting," "motivated by," "create the appearance of," and "might reasonably result in." The justice maintained that it was beyond reason to expect the average citizen or government employee to understand these terms. "The Order," he wrote, "contains many expressions which are usually frightening to the normal well-meaning person, traps for the unwary, and escape hatches for the intentional malefactor."[37]

Judge Prettyman then turned his wrath on the financial disclosure requirements of the Order. Again quoting from the justice's letter to Lee White:

Sections 306, 401, and 403 seem to be (1) unnecessarily severe and (2) probably drastically obstructive to service in the Executive Branch whether as specialists or as regular employees. These sections represent a total negation of personal or family privacy for these people. The order covers all career employees . . . from the highest to the lowest . . . and their households.[38]

The sheer "bulk of the reports, renewable quarterly, is appalling," Prettyman added.[39]

Instead of adopting an overly complex and intrusive standard of conduct, Prettyman proposed as an alternative an advisory opinion system to help build up a body of precedents regarding permissible and impermissible official conduct. Made up of distinguished individuals from inside and outside the government, the ethics advisory panel would "render opinions on specific problems of agency ethics from time to time." Published anonymously, their opinions were to become an "impartial, permanent, invulnerable vehicle ready at hand for handling of these difficulties."[40]

After receipt of Prettyman's harsh criticism of the executive order, Lee White informed President Johnson that he was forming an emergency ad hoc task force recruited from Justice and the Civil Service Commission to deal with the objections.[41] By May 7, 1965, White reported that the task force had eliminated "some of the unessential and confusing sections."[42] Although the task force simplified some of the language in the order, it did not substantially change the tone or content of the directive. Lee White continued to press the president to release the order as quickly as possible in order to offset the expected public criticism resulting from the forthcoming release of the General Accounting Office's report on questionable business practices by major defense contractors.

Consequently, on May 9, 1965, President Johnson announced the issuance of Executive Order 11222, "Prescribing Standards of Ethical Conduct for Government Officers and Employees."[43] The announcement stated that the country could not tolerate "conflict of interest or favoritism—or even conduct which gives the appearance that such actions are occurring—and it is our intention to see that this does not take place in the Federal Government." President Johnson also announced that Chairman John Macy and the Civil Service Commission would have primary responsibility for implementing the provisions of the order.[44]

The message gave no hint of serious problems with defense procurement or of other problems with the ethics management system. For reasons not divulged, the General Accounting Office did not make public its report of questionable practices by defense contractors. The Internal Revenue Service did not publicly announce a program to stop defense contractors from deducting expenses related to the entertainment of government employees as business expenses, and the suggestion that government contractors make quarterly reports on their gifts to government personnel never surfaced again.

THE BUREAUCRATIZATION OF ETHICS MANAGEMENT

The order removed the White House from the day-to-day management of the program. It merged standards of conduct for high-level appointees with those for regular employees, and thus eliminated the special emphasis the Kennedy Administration had placed on the conduct of top political appointees. In theory, the establishment of a confidential reporting program gave agency ethics officers the ability to head off conflict of interest problems disclosed on annual financial reports. By requiring agencies to formally appoint designated agency ethics officials, the administration hoped that ethics management would achieve a higher priority.

Although the order gave these designated agency ethics officers responsibility for reviewing most disclosure statements, the chairman of the Civil Service Commission would have the job of reviewing the statements of agency heads, certain appointees in the Executive Office of the president, and "each full-time member of a committee, board, or commission appointed by the President." However, since new appointees had ninety days after confirmation to file their disclosure statements, these statements would be of little help to the White House in checking the financial affairs of nominees for conflicts of interest prior to confirmation.

The second part of the order set forth standards governing the conduct of executive-branch personnel. The section specifically addressed the issues of:

1. acceptance of gifts, entertainment and favors;
2. outside employment, teaching, and writing;
3. financial self-dealing; and
4. "use of Government information for private personal gain."[45]

On the issue of acceptance of gifts, entertainment, and favors, Section 201 of the order directed employees to apply the three-part test first used in Executive Order 10939. Specifically, according to the order, an employee should reject anything of value if the source of the item

1. has, or is seeking to obtain, contractual or other business or financial relationships with his agency;

2. conducts operations or activities which are regulated by his agency; or

3. has interests which may be substantially affected by the performance of his official duty.

In order to provide for some flexibility in the application of the three-part test, the order specifically authorized agencies to exempt from the gift-acceptance prohibition:

1. things of value given because of an obvious personal or familiar relationship;

2. food and refreshments provided "in the ordinary course of a luncheon or dinner or other meeting or inspection tours where an employee may properly be in attendance";[46]

3. loans from banks and other financial institutions provided on customary terms.

Section 202 prohibited outside employment "which might result in a conflict, or an apparent conflict, between the private interests of his employee and his official government duties."[47] Section 203 prohibited employees from having financial interests that "conflict substantially, or appear to conflict substantially with their responsibilities and duties as Federal employees."[48]

Without question the most sweeping and confusing section was Section 201(c). It directed employees to avoid any action, "whether or not specifically prohibited by" Section 201's restrictions on the acceptance of gifts, which might result in or create the appearance of:

1. using public office for private gain;

2. giving preferential treatment to any organization or person;

3. impeding government efficiency or economy;

4. losing complete independence or impartiality of action;

5. making a government decision outside official channels; or

6. adversely affecting the confidence of the public in the integrity of the government.[49]

The broad appearance standard of the order gave federal agencies the authority to punish employees for almost any conduct that violated any of the six principles listed above. There is little question that the White House and the Civil Service Commission believed that action could be taken against both career and appointed officials under the broad appearance-of-impropriety standard.

Implementing the Mandate

Predictably, the media initially focused their attention on the new financial disclosure requirements of the order. On May 10, 1965, the *Washington Post* reported that about 200 high-level administration officials would be required to file confidential disclosure statements. These would include "cabinet officers, agency heads, Presidential appointees, certain members of the White House staff, and each full-time member of a committee, board, or commission appointed by the President."[50] The *Post* also reported that the president had delegated to the Civil Service Commission the responsibility for determining which other government employees and officials would be required to submit financial statements to their agencies for review.

On the same day, the *Washington Evening Star* reported that "work on the new order [had] been under way since the first of the year and was not triggered by any special concern over a decline in Government ethics, officials said."[51] Neither paper mentioned or even hinted at the existence of the GAO draft report on defense contractor gift-giving practices.

Implementing the order proved a slow process. Not until the beginning of 1966 would most agencies complete their standards-of-conduct revisions.[52] Even then, most submitted regulations identical to the model regulations issued earlier by the Civil Service Commission.

Besides the drafting and submission of agency standards of conduct, commission regulations directed each agency to:

1. furnish all regular and special government employees copies of its revised code within ninety days of its approval by the commission;

2. furnish all new regular and special government employees with a copy of revised regulations on their entrance to duty; and

3. inform employees about where they might receive help regarding application of the code to their particular situations.[53]

The most controversial part of implementation involved the decision by the commission to require confidential financial reporting by:

1. employees paid at a level of the Federal Executive Schedule;

2. employees in grade GS–16 or above of the general Schedule Personnel System or in higher comparable positions;

3. employees in hearing examiner positions; and

4. "employees in positions specifically identified in the agency regulations as positions the basic duties and responsibilities of which require the incumbent to exercise judgment in making or recommending a Government decision or in taking or recommending a Government action in regard to, contracting or procurement, administering or monitoring grants or subsidies, regulating or auditing

private or other non–Federal enterprise, and other activities where the decision or action has an economic impact on the interests of any non–Federal enterprise."[54]

The guidelines provided by the commission required automatic disclosure only by high–level appointees, career executives, and hearing officers. However, tens of thousands of other employees could fall within the category of employees making decisions with an impact on the economic interests of any non–Federal enterprise. As this fact became apparent to the agencies, opposition grew to the scope of the reporting requirement.

For instance, the Internal Revenue Service (IRS) did not want to require its lower-grade revenue agents to file. The IRS argued that its extensive safeguards were much more effective than the very limited disclosure required by the commission. These requirements, adopted after the 1952 Internal Revenue Bureau scandal, included background investigations, net worth statements at the time of entrance on duty, annual review of income tax reports, and a very effective Internal Security Division.[55] The minimal disclosure required by the executive order would only constitute extra paperwork. Other agencies expressed similar complaints, yet, the Civil Service Commission refused to alter its guidelines. Not until the end of 1966 did the agencies finish implementing disclosure requirements.

Although the new disclosure program was the only means most agencies had to review the financial affairs of regular employees for financial conflicts of interest, the expanded White House clearance process instituted by John Macy for screening individuals for appointments to presidential positions provided much more comprehensive information.

After Johnson's 1964 election victory, Macy installed a computerized system for evaluating the qualifications of prospective appointees. As soon as President Johnson had selected individuals for nomination and before the president announced the nomination, Macy and the White House personnel office supervised extensive background checks on them. These checks included a full-field FBI investigation and additional checks to ensure that candidates had paid their taxes and were not "encumbered by potential conflicts of interest." These background checks sometimes resulted in the president changing his mind about a nominee.[56] Since nominees had ninety days after entering government service to file their confidential statements under the executive order, the order could not be used to screen new nominees for actual or apparent conflicts of interest. The White House thus continued to rely on financial information collected by its Personnel Office.

THE PRIVACY RIGHTS BACKLASH

During 1966, the collection of information dealing with the private lives of federal employees and officials raised serious concerns over the privacy rights of public employees. These included criticisms of the new confidential financial reporting program, and of polygraphs, personality tests, and questionnaires asking for information on the personal lives of employees or applicants for federal positions.[57] Senator Sam Erwin of North Carolina took the lead in attacking these methods of government information gathering.[58]

The initial reports regarding Executive Order 11222 left the impression that disclosure would be required of only a few hundred top-level presidential appointees, but by the middle of 1966, criticism increased dramatically as it became apparent that agencies were requiring tens of thousands of employees to file.[59] Some members of Congress even criticized the ethics counseling system for invading the privacy rights of employees.[60]

On June 23, 1966, Senator Erwin wrote to Chairman Macy asking for detailed information on the financial reporting program. The letter also took the position that the reporting program invaded the privacy rights of federal employees and officials.[61] Chairman Macy, in response, informed Senator Erwin that 9,000 employees occupying Federal Executive Salary Schedule GS–16 or above, or holding hearing examiner positions, were automatically required to file. Because the disclosure program was not fully implemented, however, Macy was not able to provide the total number of statements collected. A subsequent survey of some forty federal agencies conducted by the Erwin subcommittee revealed that these agencies alone required 68,000 employees to submit forms.[62]

Senator Erwin also complained about the practice of larger agencies of delegating to supervisory personnel the responsibility for reviewing the disclosure statements. Employees complained to Erwin that supervisors might develop an increased antipathy towards employees because of their financial holdings.[63] Agencies defended the delegation of review responsibility on the grounds that supervisors were in the best position to know whether there might be a conflict between the duties of the employees and their financial interests.

With thirty-three Senators cosponsoring the legislation and with major support from federal employee organizations and the American Civil Liberties Union, on August 9, 1966, Senator Erwin introduced a bill "To Protect the Constitutional Rights of Employees of the Executive Branch of the Government and to Prevent Unwarranted Governmental Invasions of Privacy." It proposed, among other restrictions on information gathering, to limit mandatory financial disclosure "to top officials and employees directly connected with such matters as contracts and tax settlements." It failed to obtain passage, and Erwin reintroduced the bill during the 1967 legislative session.[64]

Faced with this strong negative publicity, the commission moved quickly to reduce the number of employees required to file disclosure statements. New regulations issued early in 1967 permitted employees to appeal a designation of their position for disclosure. There would be no disclosure for positions of GS–13 or below unless the agency notified the commission in writing that disclosure was necessary "to protect the integrity of the Government and avoid employee involvement in a possible conflict of interest situation." For those employees occupying positions of GS–13 or above, automatic disclosure would apply only to positions with responsibility for:

1. contracting or procurement;
2. administering or monitoring grants or subsidies;
3. regulating or monitoring grants or subsidies; or
4. having an economic impact on nonfederal enterprises.[65]

Between the summer of 1966 and early 1968, agencies sharply reduced the number of statements required to be filed. For instance, the Agriculture Department reduced its required statements from 18,000 to 5,000, and the Department of Treasury reduced them from 7,971 to 1,700.[66] Similar reductions took place in almost all the large federal agencies and departments.

Throughout this period, Chairman Macy strongly resisted legislative efforts to limit financial disclosure. He criticized the "current exclusive emphasis on the protection of individual rights with no concurrent recognition that individuals also have obligations."[67] Macy also emphasized that only a handful of employees and officials had complained about financial disclosure. The value of the statements, according to Macy, far outweighed their intrusion on the privacy rights of employees.

The reduction in the number of disclosure statements and increased sensitivity by federal agencies to employee privacy concerns helped to reduce pressure for legislative action. The most lasting effect of the controversy over financial reporting and the invasion of privacy was the diversion of attention from the full implementation of Executive Order 11222 at the agency level.

MORALITY AND ADMINISTRATION: THE END OF AN ERA

In a December 18, 1968, memorandum, John Macy informed President Johnson that "the combination of making the standards [of conduct] known to all concerned with the Government's business and of providing counsel within the Government about the application of the standards to individual cases [had proven to be] a most effective means of preventing conflict of interest situations."[68] Chairman Macy also reported to President Johnson that a recent Civil Service Commission survey of agency ethics programs determined that agencies believed their programs were effective and promoted "unusually high standards of honesty, integrity, impartiality, and conduct . . . essential to the proper performance of the Government business."[69] Macy also informed the president that the commission planned further improvements, however.

First, the commission planned to collect information on how agencies applied their standards-of-conduct regulations. A summary of these cases would be used in annotated instructional material to help facilitate government-wide consistency in the operation of ethics programs. Second, the commission planned to establish training courses for "agency counselors, deputy counselors, and other administrators involved in the ethics program." Third, orientation programs for government personnel would place a greater emphasis on conflict of interest education. Finally, agencies would be required to file reports of all conflict of interest violations with the commission. According to Macy, these steps would "assure coordinated action at the highest levels of Government so that any necessary corrective action may be promptly directed."[70] Shortly after forwarding this memorandum, Macy accepted an appointment by President Johnson to head the Corporation for Public Broadcasting.

Over a period of eight years, Chairman Macy worked with two Democratic presidents and transformed the regulation of conflicts of interest in the federal service. The various presidential directives gave individual agencies and the Civil Service Commission extensive powers to control actual and apparent conflicts of interest. It is significant that neither the Kennedy nor the Johnson Administration became embroiled in a major conflict of interest controversy. Chairman Macy clearly believed that this record was, in large measure, the result of the ethics program.

Nevertheless, the optimistic assessment of Chairman Macy was not entirely justified. The problem of government employees receiving unauthorized gifts, entertainment, and other items of value remained serious. Furthermore, even after almost eight years, the Civil Service Commission still had trouble getting federal agencies and departments to devote adequate resources to their ethics programs.

Finally, the most serious problem remained—the lack of any assurance that future administrations would place the same priority on adherence to both the criminal and administrative conflict of interest prohibitions. Past experience had demonstrated that most federal agencies would operate an aggressive conflict of interest prevention program only under strong White House and Civil Service Commission pressure.

Critics of the administrative approach to conflict of interest regulation continued to believe that self-regulation would not work. Only vigorous outside supervision could control abuses still prevalent at the federal level. The long-term success of the program implemented during the Kennedy and Johnson years would depend heavily on the attitude of succeeding presidents toward public service ethics.

NOTES

1. Comer Van Woodward, *Responses of the Presidents to Charges of Misconduct* (New York: Delacorte, 1974), pp. 375–86.

2. U.S. Congress, House, *Avoiding Conflicts of Interest in Defense Contracting and Employment*. H. Rept. no. 917, 88th Cong., 2d Sess., 1963.

3. Ibid., p. 14.

4. Memorandum, John W. Macy for Honorable Bill D. Moyers, November 29, 1964, Lyndon B. Johnson Library.

5. Ibid.

6. U.S. Civil Service Commission, Internal Memorandum, Subject: "Review of Executive Branch Standards on Ethical Conduct," to Chairman Macy, December 9, 1964, pp. 2–3.

7. Ibid. *Also see* U.S. President (John F. Kennedy), 1961–1963, *Memorandum, Preventing Conflicts of Interest on the Part of Special Government Employees*, The White House, May 2, 1963.

8. U.S. Civil Service Commission, Internal Memorandum to Chairman Macy, "Review of Executive Branch Standards of Ethical Conduct," December 9, 1964, p. 3.

9. Memorandum, John Macy for Messrs. W. B. Irons, W. V. Gill, and O. G. Stahl, Subject: "New Executive Order on Standards of Ethical Conduct," December 14, 1964, p. 1.

10. See Frederick G. Mosher, *The GAO: The Quest for Accountability in American Government* (Boulder, Colo.: Westview Press, 1979) pp. 153–58.

11. Ibid., p. 155.

12. Memorandum for John Macy, Subject: "Proposed Executive Order and Presidential Memorandum on Ethical Conduct," January, 1965.

13. Draft, *Memorandum, The White House*: To the Heads of All Executive Departments and Agencies Reporting of Gifts and Entertainment, Given to Federal Officers and Employers, January, 1965 (no date given).

14. *See* Statute 9 of the 1960 Report of the Association of the Bar of the City of New York, p. 295.

15. Letter, John W. Macy to Honorable Kermit Gordon, Director of the Bureau of the Budget, January 27, 1965 (Unpublished Civil Service Commission Document).

16. Memorandum, Arthur B. Focke for John Macy, February 25, 1965, White House Staff Files, Lyndon Baines Johnson Library.

17. Memorandum, Evelyn Harrison for Chairman Macy, March 5, 1965, Subject: "Budget Bureau Redraft of Executive Order on Ethical Conduct" (Unpublished Civil Service Commission Document), p. 1.

18. Memorandum, Arthur Focke for Special Counsel to the President, April 9, 1965, White House Staff Files, Lyndon Baines Johnson Library, p. 3.

19. Ibid., p. 5.

20. Ibid.

21. Ibid.

22. Memorandum, L. C. Melroy for Chairman Macy, April 13, 1965, Subject: "Proposed Executive Order on Ethical Conduct" (Unpublished Document, Civil Service Commission).

23. Memorandum, for the President from Lee White, Executive Order on Ethical Conduct for Federal Employees, April 15, 1965, Lyndon Baines Johnson Library.

24. Ibid.

25. *New York Times*, April 23, 1965, p. 1.

26. Memorandum, Deputy Attorney General Ramsey Clark for Jack Valenti, April 27, 1965, Lyndon Baines Johnson Library.

27. Memorandum, Lee White for President, April 28, 1965, White House Subject Files, Lyndon Baines Johnson Library.

28. The Dutton Memorandum, p. 2.

29. Memorandum, Lee White for President, April 28, 1965, White House Subject Files.

30. Ibid.

31. Dutton Memorandum, p. 2.

32. Memorandum, Lee White for President, April 28, 1965, White House Subject Files, p. 3. Quotation is Lee White's interpretation of the Fortas position.

33. Ibid., p. 3.

34. Ibid., p. 3. Lee White also informed the president that the Justice Department believed Section 201(c) dealt adequately with the Klotz problem.

35. Ibid., p. 4.

36. Letter, Judge E. Barrett Prettyman for Lee White, May 3, 1965, White House Subject Files, Lyndon Baines Johnson Library.

37. Ibid.

38. Ibid., p. 3.

39. Ibid., p. 3.

40. Ibid., p. 5.

41. Memorandum, Lee C. White for the President, May 3, 1965, White House Subject Files, Lyndon Baines Johnson Library.

42. Memorandum, Lee White for the President, May 7, 1965, Subject: "Executive Order on Conflicts of Interest," White House Subject Files, Lyndon Baines Johnson Library.

43. The White House, Statement of the President, May 10, 1965, Executive Order 11222.

44. Ibid., p. 1.

45. Executive Order 11222, Prescribing Standards of Ethical Conduct for Governmental Officers and Employees, pp. 1–2.

46. Ibid., p. 1.

47. Ibid., pp. 1–2.

48. Ibid., p. 2.

49. Ibid., p. 1.

50. *New York Times*, May 10, 1965, p. 1.

51. *Wall Street Journal*, May 10, 1965, p. 5.

52. Chester Newland, "Federal Employee Conduct and Financial Disclosure," *The Record*, 1965, p. 171. *See* 5 C.F.R. 735 (1966).

53. Ibid.

54. Ibid., p. 172.

55. Newland, p. 171.

56. Calvin McKenzie, *The Presidential Appointments Process*.

57. David Rosenbloom, *Federal Service and the Constitution* (Ithaca, N.Y., Cornell University Press, 1971), p. 211–17.

58. U.S. Congress, Senate, Committee on the Judiciary, "Protecting Privacy and Rights of Federal Employees," Report 519, 90th Cong., 1st Sess., p. 3 (August 21, 1967). Referenced subsequently as Erwin Report.

59. Ibid., p. 26.

60. *Congressional Record*, CXII, no. 114, July 18, 1966.

61. Unpublished Civil Service Commission Document.

62. Erwin Report.

63. Newland, p. 174.

64. Sen. Bill 3803, 89th Cong., 2d Sess., Aug. 9, 1966, reintroduced as S. 1035.

65. 5 C.F.R. 403(a).

66. U.S. Congress, House, Post Office and Civil Service Committee, Hearing before the Subcommittee on Manpower and Civil Service, Privacy and the Rights of Federal Employees, 90th Cong., 2d Sess., on S. 1035, June–July, 1968, pp. 27–36.

67. Civil Service Commission Annual Report, 85, p. 38.

68. Memorandum, John Macy for the President, December 18, 1968, White House General Subject Files, Lyndon Baines Johnson Library.

69. Ibid., p. 3.

70. Ibid.

VII

The Nixon Years and the Loss of Public Confidence

Between 1969 and August of 1973 the ethics program assembled during the Kennedy and Johnson administrations fell apart because of White House, Civil Service Commission, and agency neglect. However, impetus for the Ethics in Government Act of 1978 would come from Watergate and not from problems with conflict of interest regulation.

RECRUITMENT, CONFLICTS OF INTEREST AND CONFIRMATION

President-elect Nixon approached his transition into office in the same way as President Eisenhower sixteen years earlier. Nixon and his staff believed that an entrenched, liberal federal bureaucracy would block the new president's efforts to reduce the size of the federal government and make it more efficient. Nixon made clear on several occasions that through his key appointments he planned "to take firm command of [the] federal bureaucracy."[1] However, the Nixon transition team underestimated the trouble it would have in recruiting top-flight, private executive talent to take control.

As Eisenhower had found, disruption to private careers, low federal executive salaries, family opposition to moving to Washington, and the glass-house atmosphere of Washington deterred many sought-after candidates from accepting high-level positions in the Nixon Administration. Many of these potential candidates feared that a democratically controlled Senate, hostile to Nixon, would examine their personal and financial backgrounds with a microscope for any evidence of impropriety or conflicts of interest as an excuse to block their nominations.

Frederick Malek, who took over the operation of the White House Personnel Office in early 1971, complained in an interview that recruitment was extremely difficult because "typically, the kind of person we want is not looking for a government job. He's happy where he is, doing something constructive, making more money than we can offer him and has great advancement potential. Many are in their mid–30s earning six-figure incomes."[2]

A Heightened Sensitivity and Senate Confirmation

The Kennedy and Johnson years saw few conflict of interest controversies associated with Senate confirmation proceedings. When problems did arise, nominees frequently agreed to divest themselves of certain holdings or place them in blind trusts. The Kennedy White House, for example, worked out a deal with the Senate Armed Service Committee that allowed Robert S. McNamara, nominee for the position of secretary of defense, to use a blind trust to shield himself from direct control over investments that might be affected by his decisions in that post.[3]

Since no formal rules existed regarding the use of blind trusts, blind-trust terms were often worked out through negotiations involving the White House, the Office of Legal Counsel of the United States Department of Justice, and the appropriate Senate committee. This practice continued into the Nixon years.

Senate committees quickly confirmed the majority of Nixon nominees. However, a few well-publicized confirmation battles demonstrated that a vocal minority in the Senate believed nominees with close ties to organizations having substantial business with the federal government would place their private interests and the interests of their former business associates before the interest of the public.

Most of the controversies centered on the steps a nominee would take to eliminate an actual conflict of interest or an appearance thereof. Previous administrations had argued that nominees should not be forced to divest themselves of large financial holdings because of the severe tax implications. Flexible use of disqualification agreements or blind trusts usually was adequate to take care of any conflict of interest problem. However, critics of these remedies argued that there was no way to guarantee that officials would disqualify themselves from matters in which they had a financial interest and that no laws or regulations governed the establishment of blind trusts.

The typical blind-trust agreement required the nominee to place the offending financial interests in a trust and appoint a trustee to make investment decisions regarding the trust corpus. The agreement gave the trustee the authority to make any reasonable investment decision without influence from the nominee. Finally, the trustee agreed not to inform the nominee about the details of investment decisions.

When President Nixon nominated David M. Kennedy, chairman of the Board of Continental Illinois Bank, as secretary of the treasury, a number of Senators wanted Kennedy to sever all connections with the bank and sell all his stock in it. Because of the capital gains implications of such a move, however, Kennedy refused to sell his bank stock. Besides, federal criminal law did not require Kennedy to divest himself of bank stock to become secretary of the treasury. It required only that he avoid making any decision that could directly or indirectly affect the value of the stock. But a disqualification agreement was of little value, since the secretary of the treasury had to make daily decisions affecting the banking industry. The fact that Section 203 of Executive Order 11222 stated that employees may not have "direct or indirect financial interests that conflict substantially, or appear to conflict substantially with their responsibilities and duties as Federal employees," was apparently of little interest to the White House or the Senate Finance Committee.

When the Committee rejected Kennedy's offer to place his stock in a trust managed by Continental, Kennedy offered to designate an independent trustee other than the bank, to require the trustee to diversify the trust so that the bank stock would constitute no more than half the value of the corpus of the trust, and to give up his "option to purchase additional Continental stock prior to taking the oath of office."[4] This arrangement satisfied the majority of the Finance Committee and of the Senate.

Senator Albert Gore, however, found these measures inadequate because the Senate had no way to force Kennedy to live up to the terms of the agreement. Gore argued that Congress should enact legislation to strictly regulate the use of blind trusts if nominees were going to be allowed to use them as an alternative to full divestiture.[5]

The nomination of David Packard as deputy secretary of defense raised similar conflict of interest questions. A founder of Hewlett-Packard Corporation, one of the nation's largest defense contractors, Packard and his family held or controlled Hewlett-Packard stock valued at some $300 million.[6]

Packard balked at complying with the rule of the Senate Armed Services Committee that nominees dispose of holdings in any company with over $10,000 or more in contracts with the Department of Defense. To do so would have resulted in millions of dollars in capital gains taxes for the Packard family, and dumping such a large number of shares on the market would have seriously depressed the value of stock held by other stockholders.

Departing from the established policy, the Armed Services Committee permitted Packard and his family to keep the stock in Hewlett-Packard. In return, Packard agreed to put the stock in a trust for the duration of his term in office and, more important, to allow any increase in the value of the trust corpus (the stock) and any income from the stock to automatically go to charitable beneficiaries.

Once again, Senator Gore criticized the Armed Service Committee for making an exception to its $10,000 divestiture rule. Gore argued that the presence of conflict of interest was "as plain as the nose of your face" because Hewlett-Packard had millions of dollars worth of contracts with the Department of Defense.[7] In spite of Gore's objection, the Senate confirmed the nomination of David Packard by a vote of 82 to 17, reflecting the nominee's outstanding reputation rather than approval of the arrangement.

Predispositional Conflicts of Interest and the Government Regulator

Besides growing restlessness in the Senate over ad hoc remedies for nominees' conflict of interest problems, the early 1970s saw the publication of a number of private and congressional studies criticizing federal regulatory agencies for being biased in favor of those subject to regulation. These reports attributed much of the regulatory bias to the fact that many regulatory agencies employed individuals who had previously worked for regulated industries, and to the belief that many government regulators wished to increase their chances for lucrative postgovernment service employment.[8]

Richard Wagman, chief counsel of the Senate Government Operations Committee, was a strong supporter of the theory of regulatory capture and maintained that "the biggest question is how can agencies be better insulated from the industries they regulate."[9] To deal with this problem, the committee wanted tighter controls on ex parte contacts between regulator and regulated industries, and additional restrictions "that would curb the practice of [employees] moving directly from government agency jobs to regulated industries, and *vice versa*."[10] Other reforms put forward to remedy regulatory bias included greater public access to nonclassified government information, open-meeting laws, public financial disclosures by top officials in all three branches of government, strict campaign finance laws, and public financing of elections.

Besides the reform agenda put forward by the Senate Government Operations Committee, in 1975 the House Oversight and Investigations Subcommittee of the Interstate and Foreign Commerce Committee began an aggressive investigation of the operations of federal regulatory agencies. Even before completion of the subcommittee's study, Congressman John E. Moss, who chaired the subcommittee, introduced the Independent Regulatory Reform Act of 1975, which among other reforms required regulatory agencies to "adopt conflict of interest rules that would prevent members from transferring directly from Government to jobs in regulated industries."[11]

A five-part study, *Federal Regulation and Regulatory Reform*, was released by the House Interstate and Foreign Commerce Subcommittee on Oversight and Investigations on October 3, 1976,[12] and found that most regulatory agencies were doing a good job. However, its review of nine major federal regulatory agencies also found that "all suffered from the common defect of unresponsiveness to the public."[13] The study attributed this unresponsiveness in large measure to the "primary attention to the special interests of regulated industry and lack of sufficient concern for under represented interests."[14]

Acceptance of the theory of regulatory capture was also reflected in the February 9, 1977, release by the Senate Governmental Affairs Committee of its *Study on Federal Regulation*.[15] Many of the most serious regulatory failures could be attributed to the administrators, the report concluded.[16] The reason for poor leadership was explained by the fact that "there has not been a broad representation of individuals of various backgrounds, talent, and outlook on the commissions" and that the "comparatively large number of regulators have come directly from regulated industries."[17]

Again, it was proposed that postemployment restrictions be strengthened to "assure that former regulators who leave to enter the regulated industry maintain an arms-length relationship with their former agency after government service."[18] Congress could accomplish this by prohibiting former regulators from contacting their former agencies with respect to any matter for a period of one year following termination of services with an agency or department on any matter of business then pending before the agency.[19] A requirement that former federal officials report subsequent employment with companies or firms that have been or may have been subject to regulation by the employee's former agency would provide hard data on the extent of the revolving door. Furthermore, comprehensive public disclosure would let the public judge whether an actual or only an apparent conflict of interest existed. It is interesting to note that the reforms put forward during the 1970s were almost identical to those proposed by the Douglas Committee in 1952.

In sharp contrast to the theory of regulatory capture, another view of regulatory reform emerged during the mid–1970s. Conservatives argued that Congress should let the marketplace regulate most industries unless there was a clear threat to public health and safety. They saw no justification for heavy regulation of banks, transportation companies, and the communications industry. The market-oriented reformers argued that American business should be forced to compete rather than allow government to carve up the nation's "economic pie." Less government regulation would reduce the market for those selling their services as influence peddlers.

As the *Congressional Quarterly* noted in 1976, regulatory reform meant different things to different people:

There was continuing debate over what regulatory reform should mean. Conservatives generally focused on eliminating what they considered to be a growing number of unnecessary and burdensome federal controls on business, such as pollution emission limits, product safety regulations, and work place safety rules. Liberals tended to defend health and safety regulations, while calling for greater independence and public responsiveness on the part of federal agencies.[20]

In the aftermath of the Watergate scandal, liberal regulatory reformers found themselves in a strong position to get congressional action on their reform agenda. Conservatives found themselves fighting a delaying action.

PUBLIC SERVICE ETHICS AND ADMINISTRATIVE NEGLECT

On October 10, 1973, Congressman John E. Moss of California, chairman of the House Interstate and Foreign Commerce Committee, asked the General Accounting Office to conduct a comprehensive review of the regulatory practices of the Federal Power Commission (FPC) because of his belief that the FPC favored the interests of the natural gas industry rather than those of the public when it approved large natural-gas rate increases.[21]

On September 13, 1974, Congressman Moss released a General Accounting Office report which was highly critical of the management and regulatory practices of the Federal Power Commission. Chapter Six of the report, entitled "Breakdown in Safeguards to Prevent Conflicts of Interest,"[22] painted a picture of a major regulatory commission that apparently did little to enforce its own standards of conduct and had failed to collect confidential financial disclosure statements for a number of years. Equally damaging, the GAO found that a number of high-level commission officers who had failed to file disclosure statements held financial interests in companies that the GAO believed could be affected by actions of the FPC.[23]

Even before the public release of the report, the FPC moved to diffuse the expected public criticism by directing some nineteen officials to sell certain securities. In addition, the FPC asked the Department of Justice to determine whether any of these officials might have violated any of the criminal conflict of interest prohibitions.[24] Unfortunately, the damage had already been done. Members of Congress used these initial findings to launch a widespread investigation of the status of agency ethics programs. These investigations disclosed that many agencies and departments had effectively put their ethics programs on the shelf and that the Civil Service Commission had not objected to this willful negligence.

Congressman Moss used the GAO's findings as the basis for requesting a much broader inquiry into agency ethics programs. In an August 30, 1974, letter to Elmer Staats, comptroller general of the United States, Moss wrote:

On August 22, G.A.O. briefed me on the results of a ten month study, done at my request, at the Federal Power Commission. One finding was that the overwhelming majority of top F.P.C. officials required under F.P.C. rules to file financial disclosure statements to prevent possible conflicts of interest had failed to do so, and that this situation was endemic at the agency. . . . This shocking state of affairs has come into being over the past five and a half years at the F.P.C., as your report reveals. It is not an unreasonable surmise to believe that similar circumstances prevail at other Federal agencies. A wide-ranging examination of similar requirements and compliance in the area of financial disclosure seems very much in order.[25]

The Congressman from California then asked the comptroller general to examine the financial disclosure systems of almost every major federal regulatory agency.

The scope of the inquiry spread when, on October 16, 1974, the Senate Government Operations Committee asked the GAO to evaluate the effectiveness of ethics programs in a number of independent federal regulatory agencies and commissions.[26] Then, on November 11, 1974, Congressman Benjamin S. Rosenthal of New York's 8th District requested GAO audits of ethics programs in eleven federal agencies and departments.[27] Congressman Rosenthal also asked the GAO to examine "the nature and extent of recent enforcement, if any, of the conflict of interest laws by the Civil Service Commission and the Department of Justice."[28]

The Salvage Operation at the Civil Service Commission

Realizing that the forthcoming GAO report on the Federal Power Commission and other reports on agency ethics programs would be highly critical of the Civil Service Commission, the commission moved during the summer of 1974 to attempt to reestablish some control over agency ethics programs. For instance, in early July 1974, Anthony L. Mondello, the commission's general counsel, sent a memorandum to agency ethics counselors reminding them of the importance of their programs and requesting a report on the status of their ethics programs. Then, in January 1975, the commission appointed David Reich to coordinate the management of agency ethics programs. During 1975, Reich conducted a number of day-long ethics seminars to discuss how agencies should deal with a variety of conflict of interest problems.[29] In spite of the position taken by Commission Chairman Macy during the 1960s, the commission maintained it did not have the authority under Executive Order 11222 to force agencies to improve their ethics programs.

Information gathered by commission officials found that most of the designated ethics officers had a poor working knowledge of the criminal conflict of interest statutes, agency standards of conduct, and the financial disclosure program. Even more alarming, the commission found that these positions had an extremely high turnover rate and that only a few agencies had full-time ethics counselors. By early 1975, the commission understood that most agency ethics programs were in very poor condition.

Although the commission did try to rebuild confidence in its ability to oversee the ethics program, these efforts met with skepticism in Congress. More important, a consensus began to develop to the effect that administrative standards of conduct just could not control conflicts of interest. Only a more effective system of enforcing criminal prohibitions would deter wrongdoing. Simply stated, the standards of conduct experiment had failed.

ETHICS MANAGEMENT AT THE FORD WHITE HOUSE

In the aftermath of the Watergate break-in, Gerald Ford faced the difficult task of restoring public confidence in the presidency and the federal government in general. The Ford White House realized that its nominees would have to pass the closest examination of their personal and financial backgrounds of any candidates yet subjected to Senate confirmation. Consequently, the administration devoted a tremendous amount of time checking the backgrounds of prospective nominees.

Equally important, the White House realized that even minor conflict of interest problems would be likely to receive an inordinate amount of attention from the media. For instance, on September 26, 1974, the *New York Times* reported that Phillips Petroleum Company executive Robert C. Bowen, who was on loan to the Treasury Department as part of the Federal Executive Interchange program, might have been actively involved in influencing oil and propane regulation.[30] The disclosure surfaced as part of an investigation of the Executive Interchange Program by the Regulatory Activities Subcommittee of the House Committee on Small Business.[31]

The subcommittee wanted to know whether Bowen might have violated the self-dealing prohibition of Section 208 of Title 18 of the United States Code, or Treasury Department standards of conduct. On October 3, 1974, Secretary of the Treasury William Simon told the subcommittee that Mr. Bowen had done nothing improper since he had not participated in any policy decisions while working for the Treasury Department and Federal Energy Administration.[32]

Although the Treasury and Justice Department found nothing improper in Bowen's conduct, the subcommittee investigation determined that agencies participating in the Executive Interchange Program spent little time checking the backgrounds of participants for conflicts of interest or informing these temporary executives of the conflict of interest rules and regulations by which they were required to abide. Finally, the report raised serious questions about agency recruiting of executives who work for companies heavily regulated by the agency in question.

On the heels of the Bowen controversy, there arose a much more serious dispute over the nomination of Andrew Gibson to be administrator of the Federal Energy Administration. After the resignation of Richard Nixon, President Ford gave William N. Walker responsibility for all White House

personnel matters.[33] Concern about heading off any embarrassing nominations led Walker and the White House Personnel Office to expand standard background checks. As expected, these clearance procedures created
considerable delay in sending nominations to the Senate.

In a hurry to appoint his own head of the Federal Energy Administration,
Ford apparently ordered Gibson's nomination sent to the Senate before all
the background checks had been completed. On November 7, 1974, a few
days after the president announced the nomination, the *New York Times*
reported that Gibson had a ten-year separation agreement with his former
employer, Interstate Oil Transport Company of Philadelphia. Reportedly,
Gibson would receive one million dollars over a ten-year period.[34] The
report immediately raised questions about whether the separation agreement
constituted an illegal supplementation of the salary of a government employee or official. It is an understatement to say that the disclosure caught
the Ford White House off guard. A day after the *Times* report, White House
Press Secretary Ron Nessen told the press that President Ford had not known
about the separation agreement and that Ford would reconsider the nomination in light of the new information.[35] The Gibson nomination controversy became even more confused when the White House admitted, on
November 10, that some White House aides had known about the separation
terms before the president announced the nomination, but that the president
had had no knowledge of the separation agreement.[36] On November 13,
1974, at the request of Mr. Gibson, President Ford withdrew the nomination.

These two controversies did not end the conflict of interest problems of
the Ford Administration. A steady stream of press reports focused public
attention on the revolving-door issue and on the practice of government
employees accepting gifts and entertainment from individuals, companies,
and organizations having financial dealings with the federal government or
subject to government regulation. It began to appear that almost no one
paid attention to agency standards of conduct.

The *New York Times* reported on September 7, 1975, that 350 out of
several thousand employees of federal regulatory agencies once worked for
industries they now regulated. The article also noted that a number of former
government regulators had taken important positions with regulated industries over recent years.[37]

Early in 1976, a probe by the Joint Committee on Defense Production
revealed that several civilian Pentagon officials had accepted free entertainment at a Maryland hunting lodge maintained by the Northrop Corporation, a major defense contractor.[38] At public hearings called by the Joint
Committee in February 1976, members of the committee questioned the
presidents of Northrop and Rockwell International Corporation regarding
their gift-giving and entertainment practices.[39] Although Defense Department standards of conduct generally prohibited department personnel from

accepting such favors, the two presidents maintained that their companies had done nothing wrong. In fact, they claimed that these company-sponsored meetings improved the working relationship among the Defense Department, defense contractors, and other government agencies.[40] They suggested that Congress should encourage retreats, not attack them.

It soon became known that other government officials had accepted favors from major defense contractors. It was particularly embarrassing when Robert E. Hampton, chairman of the Civil Service Commission, confirmed a published report that he had accepted free hospitality at a hunting lodge leased by Rockwell International.[41] Because the Civil Service Commission had no direct dealings with Rockwell International, Chairman Hampton maintained that his conduct did not violate the commission's standards-of-conduct regulations.

Shortly after the Hampton disclosure, the press reported that the controversial secretary of agriculture, Earl Butz, had recently been the guest of Southern Railway Company at a company-owned hunting lodge. Although the secretary denied any wrongdoing, he agreed to pay Southern Railway one-half the cost of the trip after the Department's deputy counsel held that the secretary had violated the department's standards of conduct regulations.[42]

During the same period, Senator William Proxmire released the results of his own investigation which identified fifty-five high-ranking Defense Department officials who had visited hunting lodges operated by Rockwell International and Ratheon.[43] After completion of its investigation, the Defense Department later reprimanded a number of these officials for clearly violating Defense Department standards-of-conduct regulations.

Finally, in March 1976, President Ford's National Campaign chairman, Howard H. Calloway, acknowledged that while he was secretary of the army he had discussed with Agriculture Department officials a plan to expand his Colorado ski resort by leasing federal land controlled by the Agriculture Department.[44] The controversy forced Calloway to take a leave of absence from the Ford campaign. A subsequent investigation cleared Calloway of any charges of official wrongdoing.

The Ford White House did begin work on plans to restructure the conflict of interest program, but it had little time to finalize and implement an ethics reform program of its own as the result of the 1976 election victory of Jimmy Carter.

OVERHAULING CONFLICT OF INTEREST MANAGEMENT

The General Accounting Office reports on ethics programs released between 1974 and 1977 played a major role in convincing Congress of the need to overhaul the executive-branch conflict of interest prevention program.[45] Although most agencies under attack argued that they had already reformed their programs, the damage had been done.

For instance, the GAO found that the Civil Aeronautics Board (CAB) had failed to collect required disclosure statements for 1970, 1971, and 1973. In addition, the report noted that the CAB had no system in place to resolve conflicts revealed in the course of reviews.[46] By the end of 1976, the General Accounting Office had released nine additional reports of careless management of agency ethics programs during the Nixon years.[47]

Common Cause and Protecting the Public Interest

Along with the General Accounting Office, Common Cause, the Washington, D.C.-based, nonprofit public interest lobbying organization also pushed for a major overhaul of ethics management through most of the 1970s. In October 1976, it issued a report entitled *Serving Two Masters: A Common Cause Study of Conflicts of Interest in the Executive Branch*. Common Cause accused federal agencies of letting private interests shape federal policy making by refusing to enforce restrictions on conflicts of interest. The American public, Common Cause argued, could no longer trust federal agencies to act on the public's behalf because of their general unwillingness to control conflicts of interests.

This theme is clearly reflected in the summary of the report's findings:

Our findings point to potential conflicts of interest, and the possibility of serious agency bias, throughout the executive bureaucracy. High level employees were found to have stock holdings that conflicted with their duties; a disproportionate number of officials came to government from the industry regulated by their agency; and numerous public employees leave government to go to work for private interests with which they had direct dealing.[48]

From the position of Common Cause, the conflict of interest problem involved not only financial conflicts of interest but also those caused by associational bias. If agencies "draw high percentages of their top-policy makers" from such regulated enterprises, these policy makers are almost certain "to inherit industry biases or accept industry's point of view on key policy issues."[49] Any reform program must deal with both financial and associational conflicts of interest.

At the top of Common Cause's reform agenda was public financial disclosure for top officials in all three branches of government. The failure of the confidential disclosure program provided Common Cause and other supporters of public financial disclosure with strong ammunition for their argument before Congress. Since agencies could not be trusted to collect and review confidential disclosure statements or to punish officials for conflicts of interest, public access could force action.

Under the Common Cause proposal, federal law would require public financial disclosure by federal employees and officials in positions classified at GS–15 or higher. Covered officials would have to report:

1. all sources and amounts of income;

2. companies or organizations in which they have a financial interest;

3. all assets, liabilities, gifts, honoraria, patent rights, and agreements on future employment; and

4. previous nongovernment employment.[50]

In response to arguments that public disclosure would drive badly needed talent out of government and make it even more difficult to recruit qualified individuals, Common Cause countered that public disclosure at the state level had not caused an exodus of government personnel. More important, the group argued, government did not need individuals who were unwilling to sacrifice a small amount of privacy in order to help restore and maintain public trust in the integrity of public officials.

Also high on the list of proposed Common Cause reforms was making divestiture rather than disqualification "the presumed remedy in all cases where an employee has a financial interest that conflicts with his duties."[51] Disqualification agreements, it insisted, did not work, because no feasible method existed to guarantee that officials would disqualify themselves. Furthermore, because of the absence of statutory requirements, blind trusts were not an adequate substitute for divestiture.

To deal with the serious problem of associational conflicts of interest, Common Cause sought much stronger curbs on the lobbying of former government officials before government agencies and departments. Specifically, it advocated a general prohibition on former government employees representing private parties before their former agencies on any matter for a period of two years after leaving government service. The two-year cooling-off period, Common Cause believed, would reduce "influence peddling" activities because former personnel would have much less to sell on the influence-peddling market.

In addition, Congress could help to reduce associational conflicts of interest by prohibiting certain classes of federal employees from taking jobs with government contractors or organizations regulated by the individual's former government agency for a period after leaving government service.[52]

The primary themes of the Common Cause report were not new. They reflected a sincere belief that unregulated special interests threatened the ability of government institutions to protect the public interest. In the aftermath of the Watergate scandal, such views found many more adherents inside and outside government.

Conflict of Interest Reform: Costs and Benefits

By coincidence, in late 1976 the Commission on Executive, Legislative, and Judicial Salaries also issued a report that indirectly dealt with conflict of interest reform.[53] On November 29, 1976, the commission's Task Force on Public Conduct, which was chaired by Mortimer Caplin, former commissioner of the Internal Revenue Service, reported to Peter G. Peterson, Secretery of the Treasury, that the Public Conduct Task Force advocated:

1. more comprehensive financial disclosure;
2. higher executive salaries to reduce pressure on officials to earn outside income;
3. rejection of automatic divestiture;
4. the continued use of blind trusts and disqualification agreements; and
5. the possible subjection of former federal employees "to a blanket one-year bar prohibiting them from appearances before their former government agencies on new matters as well as old."[54]

The panel's position on public financial disclosure was to keep statements confidential if the filing body determined "that (i) no conflict exist[ed] and (ii) the demands of individual privacy outweigh[ed] the public's right to know."[55] In other words, the task force opposed automatic public financial disclosure.

The final commission report incorporated many of the recommendations of the Public Conduct Task Force as well as some additional ones. As a precondition to future salary increases, the commission proposed the establishment of a new and stringent code of public conduct, "so that the painful process of restoring public confidence of the governed can begin with tangible evidence that the era of Watergate is finally over."[56] The commission proposed to apply a new code of public conduct to all three branches of government. This would include:

1. substantial public disclosure of the financial affairs of senior public officials in all branches;
2. rigorous restrictions on outside earned income, assuming that Congress significantly raised executive salaries;
3. appropriate and accountable expense allowances "to reassure the public that once appropriate allowances have been granted, the expenditures reported are indeed being made for the permitted and specified purposes and not as a mask for substitute income";[57]
4. uniform postservice employment for all three branches to deal with the revolving door problem; and
5. vigorous and consistent auditing "so as to ensure that these requirements are fully enforced and that all information disclosed under the Code of Public Conduct is regularly and adequately audited and publicly reported."[58]

Without question, the most interesting aspect of the treatment of the public integrity issue by the Executive Compensation Commission is the relationship it made between conflicts of interest and executive compensation. It was felt that compensation comparable to that of the private sector would greatly reduce the need for presidential appointees to leave the federal service after only a short period of time. Equally significant, a large increase in executive compensation would permit strict limitations on any outside earned income received by top government policy makers.

As a means of building public support for its reform program, the commission recommended that President Ford appoint an advisory board or panel to draft a new public service code of conduct for swift legislative consideration. The Ford Administration, however, did not act on this recommendation.

In summary, the commission took a middle-of-the-road position on conflict of interest reform. Better administration and limited statutory changes, it contended, could prevent most conflicts of interest. Radical changes would make it even more difficult to recruit and retain top-flight executive and scientific personnel.

THE ETHICS BATTLEFIELD

Between 1969 and 1976, few substantive changes were made in conflict of interest regulation, but Watergate and accompanying disclosures of official misconduct left the impression that the White House and most federal agencies and departments had ignored the issue of government ethics. It appeared that the gains made during the Kennedy and Johnson Administrations had been lost. The problem was how to restore public confidence.

NOTES

1. G. Calvin Mackenzie, *The Politics of Presidential Appointments*, (New York: Free Press, 1980), p. 47.

2. Don Bonafede, "Nixon Personnel Staff Works To Restructure Federal Policies," *National Journal*, 3 (November 12, 1971): 2446.

3. U.S. Congress, Senate, Committee on Armed Services, Hearing on Armed Services, Hearing on the Nomination of Robert S. McNamara as Secretary of Defense Designate, January 17, 1961, 87th Congress, 1st Sess., pp. 10–11.

4. *Congressional Record* 115, p. 1293, January 20, 1969.

5. Ibid., p. 1294.

6. Mackenzie, p. 100.

7. *Congressional Record* 115, p. 1675, January 23, 1969.

8. Mark Green, ed., *The Monopoly Makers: Ralph Nader's Study Group Report on Regulation and Competition* (New York: Grossman, 1973); Louis M. Kohlmeier, Jr., *The Regulators: Watchdog Agencies and the Public Interest* (New York: Harper and Row, 1969).

9. *Congressional Quarterly Almanac*, 1975, p. 587.

10. Ibid., p. 587.

11. *Congressional Quarterly Weekly*, February 17, 1975, p. 688.

12. *New York Times*, October 3, 1976, p. 21.

13. These were the Securities and Exchange Commission (SEC), Federal Trade Commission (FTC), Environmental Protection Agency (EPA), Federal Power Commission (FPC), Interstate Commerce Commission (ICC), Food and Drug Administration (FDA), Federal Communications Commission (FCC), Consumer Products Safety Commission (CPSC), National Highway and Transportation Safety Administration (NHTSA).

14. Cited in *Congressional Quarterly Almanac*, 1976, p. 513.

15. *Congressional Quarterly Almanac*, 1977, p. 551. *See also* U.S. Senate, Committee on Governmental Operations, *Study on Federal Regulation*, 95th Cong., 1st Sess., January 1977.

16. *Congressional Quarterly Almanac*, 1977, p. 551.

17. U.S. Senate, Committee on Governmental Operations, *Study on Federal Regulators, Volume I. The Regulatory Appointments Process*, 95th Cong., 1st Sess., January 1977, p. vii.

18. Ibid.

19. Ibid., p. 52.

20. *Congressional Quarterly Almanac*, 1976, p. 512.

21. U.S. General Accounting Office, *Federal Power Commission: Need for Improving the Regulations of the Natural Gas Industry and Management of Internal Operations*, B–180228 (U.S. Government Printing Office, 1977), ·September 13, 1974.

22. Ibid., p. 31.

23. Ibid., p. 39.

24. *New York Times*, September 19, 1974, p. 65.

25. Unpublished letter from Congressman John E. Moss to Elmer Staats, Comptroller General of the United States, August 30, 1974.

26. Letter, United States Senate, Government Operations Committee, Subcommittee on Budgeting, Management and Expenditures, to Elmer Staats, Comptroller General of the United States, October 16, 1974 (unpublished document).

27. Letter, Congressman Benjamin S. Rosenthal to Elmer Staats, Comptroller General of the United States, November 11, 1974. The eleven agencies were the FDA, ERDA (Energy Research and Development Agency), FDA, CAB (Civil Aeronatics Board), Interior, Agriculture, Defense, Transportation, Housing and Urban Development, Commerce, and Treasury.

28. Ibid.

29. *See* Comptroller General of the United States, "Action Needed to Make Executive Branch Financial Disclosure System Effective," February 28, 1977, FPCD–77–23 for discussion of reforms implemented by the Civil Service Commission and Executive Branch agencies.

30. *New York Times*, September 26, 1974, p. 55.

31. U.S. Congress, House, Committee on Small Business, Subcommittee on Energy and Environment, *Conflict of Interest Problems within the Presidential Executive Interchange Program*: Hearing before Subcommittee, 94th Cong., 1st Sess., December 3, 5, 1975.

32. *New York Times*, October 3, 1974, p. 24.

33. Mackenzie, p. 57.

34. *New York Times*, November 7, 1974, p. 1.

35. *New York Times*, November 8, 1974, p. 1.

36. *New York Times*, November 10, 1974, sec. IV, p. 21.

37. *New York Times*, September 7, 1975, p. 36.

38. *New York Times*, January 24, 1976, p. 1.

39. U.S. Congress, Joint Committee on Defense Production and the Department of Defense. *Industry Relations: Conflict of Interest and Standards of Conduct*, Hearing, 94th Cong., 2d Sess., February 2 and 3, 1976 (Washington: U.S. Government Printing Office, 1986).

40. *New York Times*, February 3, 1976, p. 37.

41. *New York Times*, January 16, 1976, p. 31.

42. *New York Times*, February 7, 1976, p. 29.

43. *New York Times*, February 4, 1976, p. 55.

44. *New York Times*, March 14, 1976, p. 1.

45. *New York Times*, September 17, 1974, p. 29.

46. Comptroller General of the United States, *Effectiveness of the Financial Disclosure System for Civil Aeronautics Board Employees Needs Improvement*, U.S. General Accounting Office, FPCD–76–6, September 16, 1975, p. 8.

47. These reports dealt with the FDA, the U.S. Geological Survey, the International American Foundation, the FAA (Federal Aeronautics Administration), the Department of Commerce, SBA (Small Business Administration), the Export-Import Bank, the FCC and TVA.

48. Common Cause, *Serving Two Masters: A Common Cause Study of Conflicts of Interest in the Executive Branch* (Washington, D.C.: October, 1976), p. 1.

49. Ibid., p. 1–2.

50. Ibid., p. 6.

51. Ibid., p. 7.

52. The proposed law read that executive employees in GS–15 and higher levels should be prohibited from accepting employment for a period of two years after leaving their agencies with any company or organization which had been affected by a proceeding (rule-making, adjudication, licensing, contracting) in which they participated personally and substantially.

53. Commission on Executive, Legislative and Judicial Salaries, *Report of the Commission*, December, 1976.

54. Ibid., p. 84.

55. Ibid., p. 82.

56. Ibid., p. 2.

57. Ibid., p. 2.

58. Ibid., p. 2.

VIII

The Carter Presidency and Ethics Reform

During the 1976 presidential campaign, candidate Jimmy Carter promised to restore public trust in the integrity of government. In a speech before the American Bar Association on August 19, 1976, Carter declared, "If I become President, I will never turn my back on official misdeeds. I intend to take a new broom to Washington and do everything possible to sweep the house of government clean."[1] Carter announced his support for public financial disclosure for high-level government officials and for a law to limit the movement of persons employed by federal regulatory agencies into heavily regulated industries.

Even before Carter's August speech, the Carter staff began work on a plan to restructure executive-branch conflict of interest regulation. Jack Watson, a close aide to Carter, asked John L. Moore, an Atlanta attorney and a Carter supporter, to draft a reform program which subsequently became the administration's blueprint for reform.[2]

On November 19, 1976, Hamilton Jordan told reporters that Carter appointees would have to subscribe to a new code of ethics, "be prepared to serve full terms of office,"[3] and possibly file public financial disclosure statements. A week later, Jody Powell, President-elect Carter's press secretary, told reporters that Carter was near a decision on legislative proposals which were designed to check the movement of individuals from regulatory agencies to regulated industries, and vice versa.[4]

The realities of a presidential transition soon made the Carter transition team think long and hard over what reforms it should actually implement or propose. Early in December 1976, Charles Kirbo, attorney and adviser to Jimmy Carter, told reporters that the transition team hoped the Senate Committees would not automatically require Carter nominees to divest themselves of holdings that might create a conflict of interest problem. Instead, he urged committees to occasionally allow disqualification agreements or blind trusts as legitimate alternatives.[5]

Then, on January 4, 1977, President-elect Carter announced new ethical guidelines for all top nominees and for several thousand other political appointees and career bureaucrats in key policy-making positions. The policy statement accompanying the guidelines read, "It [will] be the policy of the Carter-Mondale Administration to appoint and nominate for appointment only persons of high ability who will carry out their official duties without fear or favor and with an equal hand, unfettered by any actual or apparent conflicts of interest."[6]

In keeping with this promise, the guidelines required nominees for Executive Level I and II positions, cabinet members, and a limited number of heads of other federal organizations to divest themselves of any financial interests if the holding of such interests would force these individuals to disqualify themselves from any official duties. The guidelines also mandated divestiture by these top officials "where the nature of the holding or liability is such that it will be broadly affected by governmental, monetary, and budgetary policies."[7] However, the establishment of a blind trust would be the equivalent of divestiture if the trust met certain stiff requirements. These included:

1. a clearly independent trustee;
2. a trust containing only diversified assets;
3. the maintenance of a diversified portfolio by the trustee;
4. limitation of information to the official to what was necessary for the completion of income tax returns; and
5. barring the official from exercising any control over the management of trust assets.

Officials occupying Executive Level III positions were urged, though not required, to divest themselves of financial interests when "disqualification would seriously impair the capability of the officer to perform the duties of the office to which the individual was nominated."[8]

A third set of rules established guidelines for continuing financial relationships with former employers. The supplementation of salary guidelines was designed to head off confirmation disputes over payments from former employers. Although Section 209 of Title 18 of the United States Code permitted continued participation in preexisting retirement, health and stock option plans, Senate committees had become increasingly critical of nominees who happened to be entitled to large severance payments precisely at the time when they decided to accept a nomination to a high-level federal position.

Under the guidelines, a Carter official could receive payments if he were part of a "pre-existing established plan" tied to past performance. Even if it met the above requirements, any payment "in excess of a range of a $50,000 to $75,000 would need careful examination."[9]

The Carter guidelines also required high-level appointees to agree to disclose their net worth, their assets and liabilities, and the assets and liabilities of their spouses and minor children. However, the Carter transition team hedged on whether these statements would be subject to public inspection.

Finally, the Carter guidelines sought to limit the lobbying activities of Carter officials by requiring nominees to sign an agreement stating that for a one-year period following termination of government service, they would not "make any formal or informal appearance before"[10] their former agency and that for a two-year period after leaving government service they would file financial disclosure statements with the government. The Carter White House did not explain how it would enforce this provision.

John Gardner, president of Common Cause, praised the newly announced guidelines as "a major breakthrough in the fight to eliminate conflicts of interest in the executive branch."[11] However, not everyone agreed with this glowing assessment of the reform measures. A *New York Times* editorial, for example, thought that President-elect Carter might have gone overboard in his zeal to restore public confidence in government and to control conflicts of interest. The editorial read:

Much of the new code is commendable. The problems it deals with are real: unsavory connections between Government procurement and former officials; shameless traffic through the 'revolving door' between regulatory agencies and industry. But in his haste to address such abuses, the President-elect has promulgated rules that are needlessly, even harmfully general and rigid. They risk the loss of able potential recruits, nuisance and travail for those who take policy jobs, and perhaps even political embarrassment for himself.[12]

Besides noting the potential impact of the rules on recruitment, the editorial called the requirement that former officials file financial disclosure statements for a period of two years after leaving government service "utopian and ill-considered."[13] Equally significant, the *Times* questioned the need for a one-year prohibition on former top officials contacting anyone in their former agencies with respect to any matter. The editorial asked, "Why should a former Justice Department lawyer specializing in say, antitrust, be forbidden for a year to participate in a Federal tax case?" It continued, "Such readily imaginable difficulties illustrate the shortcomings of a government-wide, blunderbuss approach, and the virtue of pursuing, instead, an agency-by-agency evaluation of rules."[14]

While the *New York Times* was criticizing the Carter guidelines as overzealous, the Carter White House was considering amending Executive Order 11222 to require public financial disclosure by tens of thousands of federal officials and employees.[15] The proposed order required a complete listing of affiliations, a listing of all sources of income, and a net worth statement. It also required similar information from the official's spouse and minor children.

To obtain an outside evaluation, John Moore asked conflict of interest expert Roswell Perkins, to give his opinion on the public disclosure order. In a February 1, 1977, letter Mr. Perkins sharply criticized key elements of the order and argued that the 1960 findings of the Association of the Bar of the City of New York report on conflicts of interest, which had rejected public financial disclosure as a remedy, remained "completely sound."[16] In Perkins's words:

The issue is not disclosure *vs.* non-disclosure, because there is no reason not to require the fullest possible disclosure of financial information to the people *who need to know* within the department or agency where the employee works and the Civil Service Commission and/or the Justice Department.[17]

Since the principal objective of any disclosure program is to eliminate both real and apparent conflicts of interest, argued Perkins, it is hard to see how public disclosure would help to accomplish those objectives. Therefore, "unless public disclosure is essential to achieve these ends an appointed official's income and sources of income should be his personal business, just like that of any other citizen."[18]

Perkins understood that the General Accounting Office reports on agency confidential disclosure systems and the Common Cause report, *Serving Two Masters*, had created support for public financial disclosure to force agencies and the Civil Service Commission to do their job. However, as he told Moore, the idea that public disclosure would help to solve the administrative problem is "so patently absurd as to require no discussion."[19] As a reasonable alternative to public disclosure, Mr. Perkins recommended that the Executive Order require each agency to publish the names of all individuals required to file disclosure statements as well as the names of individuals who failed to file.

On another matter, Perkins agreed with Moore that President Carter should place a new ethics office in the White House. This was identical to the recommendation made in 1960 by Perkins and the Association of the Bar of the City of New York report.

In his letter to Perkins, Moore had also argued that within a year of the issuance of the disclosure executive order, the White House would have a good idea of its impact on recruitment of executive personnel. Perkins disagreed with this conclusion, stating:

The effect on such recruitment will be too subtle, because the reasons for avoiding Government service are always cumulative. A Government official who is already considering leaving Washington might say to himself: 'This is the thing which will tip the scales for me. The climate of public service is bad enough, and now they make me do something no other citizen has to do and for no discernible purpose.' A comparable scenario may well exist in connection with those being recruited for Government.[20]

Mr. Perkins suggested that the new administration reconsider its proposals "in the total perspective of staffing the Executive Branch for the long pull."[21] The White House, he thought, could surely find a less drastic way to get agencies to pay attention to their ethics programs.

In addition to the critical response of Mr. Perkins, the Justice Department informed the White House that the Privacy Act probably barred the president from releasing financial disclosure statements filed by employees and that, in its opinion, Congress needed to pass legislation authorizing public financial disclosure.[22] Shortly thereafter, President Carter shelved plans to issue the public financial disclosure executive order and directed the Justice Department and staff to draft legislation to provide for public financial disclosure. In May 1977, the White House sent the Ethics in Government Act to the Hill.

In May 1977, the White House released the statements of twenty White House aides. Despite pressure from the media, the White House refused to release any other statements on the grounds that there was insufficient staff to prepare the release of hundreds of other statements filed by Carter appointees.

Even more embarrassing for the Carter White House, the filling of top positions proceeded at a very slow pace. The new ethics guidelines unquestionably complicated recruitment and conflict of interest clearance. Before sending the name of a presidential nominee to the Senate, the Carter White House required a prospective nominee to:

1. authorize a full-field FBI background investigation and a Civil Service Commission security investigation;
2. sign a form authorizing the release of tax records kept by the Internal Revenue Service; and
3. complete a questionnaire requiring the disclosure of detailed information "about the applicant's personal and financial background, future employment plans and potential conflicts of interest."[23]

If the collected information uncovered a potential conflict of interest problem, the White House counsel needed time to advise the prospective nominee on the steps necessary to bring the individual into compliance with the Carter guidelines, federal laws and regulations, and to prepare the individual for the rigors of the Senate confirmation process.

Michael H. Cardozo served throughout the Carter Administration as the person in the White House counsel's office responsible for examining the financial background of potential nominees for possible conflicts of interest. According to Cardozo, out of 720 initial cases, 100 proved difficult to resolve.[24] Cardozo reported that many prospective appointees with large financial holdings often had to hire outside counsel to complete the required disclosure statements and to assist in the reorganization of their portfolio to eliminate an actual or apparent conflict of interest problem.

CONGRESS MOVES CAUTIOUSLY TOWARD ETHICS REFORM

Between the resignation of Richard Nixon in August 1974 and the inauguration of Jimmy Carter in January 1977, Congress considered but failed to enact ethics-related reform legislation. However, the period did see the outlines of a reform program take shape. First and foremost, reformers wanted investigations of high government officials to be conducted outside the Justice Department. The Watergate Reform Act of 1975 provided for the establishment of an independent Office of Public Attorney to investigate and prosecute charges of official misconduct against high-level government officials.[25] Second, Congress reluctantly moved toward requiring public financial disclosure for high-level officials in all three branches of government, and third, support increased for additional legislation to deal with the revolving-door problem. On July 21, 1976, the Senate passed the Watergate Reform Act of 1976 by a vote of 91 to 5, which included provisions addressing the concerns discussed above.[26] However, the House failed to act on the Senate measure.

On February 1, 1977, Senators Abraham Ribicoff and Charles Percy reintroduced ethics reform legislation as the Public Officials Integrity Act, Senate S. 555. With a strong advocate of ethics reform in the White House, they hoped for speedy congressional approval of their legislation.

In late February 1977, the General Accounting Office issued a report recommending a major overhaul of the executive-branch ethics program. Although the GAO refrained from taking an official position on the issue of public financial disclosure, it expressed its strong support for the establishment of a new executive branch Office of Ethics to have responsibility for:

1. issuing uniform standards of ethical conduct and financial disclosure regulations;

2. developing a new financial disclosure statement;

3. auditing agency financial disclosure programs to assure their effectiveness;

4. issuing periodic advisory opinions on ethical conduct;

5. investigating allegations of unethical official conduct unresolved at the agency level; and

6. coordinating an ethics information and education program.[27]

Then, on May 3, 1977, President Carter sent Congress the Ethics in Government Act, which proposed public financial disclosure for high-level executive-branch officials, the establishment of an Office of Government Ethics located within the Civil Service Commission, and new restrictions on appearances of former government personnel before government agencies and departments.[28]

The most interesting aspect of the president's legislative proposal involved the role of the proposed ethics office. Headed by a presidential appointee subject to Senate confirmation, the new agency would have responsibility for:

1. issuing general conflict of interest guidelines;

2. making recommendations to the president regarding needed changes in conflict of interest law and regulations;

3. monitoring agency and individual compliance with applicable laws and regulations; and

4. directing the government-wide ethics education program.

However, the proposal fell far short of establishing an independent office with full responsibility for criminal and civil conflict of interest matters. Although the office would have overall administrative responsibility for the ethics program, and although the director of the office would have authority "to order corrective action in agency programs and individual cases,"[29] the Justice Department would have final authority over criminal investigations and prosecutions of conflict of interest violations. The Justice Department obviously did not want to give the Civil Service Commission any jurisdiction over criminal prosecutions of high-level government officials.

Equally important, the Carter proposal left unclear how the director would go about punishing a presidential appointee for violating standards of conduct regulations. Presidential nominees or appointees, for the most part, serve at the pleasure of the president; consequently, they can be removed only by the president. In theory, the director of the proposed Ethics Office could only ask the president to punish or dismiss a guilty official.

The Carter White House and the Justice Department clearly did not want to centralize all responsibility for conflict of interest matters in the proposed Ethics Office. The office was to perform a general coordinating function, and leave day-to-day mangement to individual agencies and departments, and criminal matters to the Department of Justice or with a "special prosecutor" when necessary.

On the issue of new revolving-door prohibitions, the proposals turned out to be weaker than anticipated. Making an already confusing statute even more confusing, President Carter asked Congress to extend from one year to two years the prohibition on a former official's appearing before an agency on a particular matter which was previously under his or her "official responsibility" during the final year of government service.

Instead of supporting a ban on officials taking jobs with certain private concerns having substantial dealings with federal agencies and departments, the administration proposed an across-the-board antilobbying provision prohibiting high-level former officials from contacting their former agency on any matter in a representational capacity for a period of one year after leaving government service.

At the close of the message, President Carter endorsed legislation requiring the Department of Justice to ask the Court of Appeals in Washington to appoint a special prosecutor in cases where there is reason to believe a high-level executive-branch official has violated a criminal law.

Between January and May of 1977, it became apparent that, as had occurred in previous administrations, the Carter White House was becoming increasingly concerned that drastic changes in conflict of interest laws and regulations could create a federal manpower crisis.

The White House Makes Its Case

Early in May 1977, the Senate Governmental Affairs Committee held hearings on S. 555, the Public Integrity Act, and on the recently introduced Ethics in Government Act. Those testifying on behalf of the Carter proposals generally supported some legislative reforms, such as public financial disclosure and stronger postemployment activities restrictions. However, they also stressed the need, as the Kennedy Administration had done in 1961 and 1962, for Congress not to overregulate and not to eliminate all flexibility for working out conflict of interest problems involving high-level officials.

For instance, John Moore, Jr., who had become chairman of the board of the Export-Import Bank, urged the committee not to prohibit blind trusts as a substitute for divestiture, but to give the new Ethics Office the authority to issue strict rules patterned after those already being followed by Carter Administration officials.[30] As Moore explained:

At a minimum, it is expected that these rules would require that the assets initially placed in the trust be relatively diversified and marketable, that the trustee is truly independent, not directed to retain particular assets or otherwise restricted, and the reporting individual and his spouse and minor children are fully insulated from further knowledge of trust assets and transactions.[31]

The emphasis placed by the Carter Administration on administrative flexibility did not receive overwhelming congressional support. Many in Congress doubted whether the proposed Ethics Office could force agencies and departments to pay attention to their ethics programs. Congress, consequently, struggled over how to force the proposed Ethics Office and individual agency ethics programs to enforce applicable laws and regulations.

Senator Lawton Chiles of Florida fought for a provision in the Public Officials Integrity Act requiring the Ethics Office to operate a formal ethics advisory service which would issue opinions on ethical conduct issues. Over time, Chiles believed, these opinions would help to provide valuable guidance for employees and officials to determine whether certain conduct violated any law or regulation.[32] Not unexpectedly, the Carter White House and the Justice Department opposed the service because of the staff needed to operate it and, more important, because Justice did not want a unit of the Civil Service Commission issuing advisory opinions on federal criminal law.

During the same Senate hearings, Fred Wertheimer, vice president for operations at Common Cause, argued that to be effective, the new ethics division must have audit and subpoena powers to permit it to conduct ethics investigations, and must be headed by a presidential appointee subject to Senate confirmation. Moreover, the office must also have clear statutory authority to:

1. review and approve agency ethics regulations;
2. conduct investigations of conflict of interest controversies;
3. evaluate agency enforcement procedures;
4. take appeals from agency decisions or actions; and
5. order corrective steps by employees and agencies when necessary.[33]

Moreover, to guard against an office unwilling to act, Wertheimer wanted Congress to give "non-governmental parties . . . standing to sue to enforce any conflict of interest or financial disclosure statute."[34]

Common Cause also disagreed with the Carter White House on the blind trust and divestiture issues. It wanted divestiture to become the preferred method of conflict of interest avoidance and Congress to enact strict statutory requirements for its establishment and operation.

On June 27, 1977, the Senate passed the Public Officials Integrity Act of 1977, requiring public financial disclosure for high-level officials in all three branches of the federal government and strict statutory rules for the establishment of blind trust guidelines. Although the act established an Ethics Office to be located within the Civil Service Commission, the Senate showed much more interest in provisions providing for appointments of special prosecutors to investigate charges of official misconduct against high-level officials. The Senate also took action to tighten revolving-door restrictions, but not in the way the Carter White House wanted.

In the first place, the Senate amended the lifetime prohibition on switching sides, Section 207(a) of Title 18 of the United States Code, to apply to "informal" as well as "formal" proceedings. The Carter Administration supported the inclusion of informal proceedings, but had serious problems with the language of the law that appeared to apply the lifetime ban to all forms of aiding and assisting, including assistance rendered away from an informal or formal government proceeding. The Senate wanted to stop the practice of former officials taking private positions and then helping private interests behind-the-scenes with specific matters that the former official had worked on while in government.[35] The Carter White House believed that such a law would be impossible to enforce and would create panic among high-level officials.

The Senate also increased the "official responsibility" bar from one to two years, but limited its aiding and assisting prohibition to assistance made at a government proceeding. Finally, the Senate passed a new one-year ban on former high-level officials contacting their former agency on any matter. In addition to providing criminal penalties, the Senate bill gave agencies the authority to administratively disbar a former official for up to five years for violating a postemployment provision. The Carter White House hoped the House would delete or water down the off-scene assistance prohibition.

Legislative Fragmentation and the House

Instead of finding House consideration of its bill easy going, the Carter White House found widespread disagreement on what the Ethics Act should look like. Before any bill could pass the House, the Select Committee on Ethics, the Post Office and Civil Service Committee, the Armed Services Committee, and the House Judiciary Committee each had to report part of the bill because different portions of the bill fell under their separate jurisdictions.

Ultimately, the strongest opposition to the White House approach came from the House Subcommittee on Employee Ethics and Utilization, chaired by Representative Patricia Schroeder of Colorado. The subcommittee wanted Congress to enact strict statutory requirements for all aspects of the ethics program. For example, instead of having confidential disclosure for some employees and public disclosure for others, the subcommittee bill mandated public disclosure as far down as GS–12 which, in theory, would have covered 500,000 federal employees and officials.[36]

Equally significant, Congresswoman Schroeder proposed to give the director of the Office of Ethics authority to appoint and supervise all agency ethics counselors; that is, agency ethics officers would work for the Ethics

Office, not for individual agencies and departments.[37] In order to increase the accountability of the Ethics Office, the subcommittee would require the Office of Government Ethics to review and approve all public disclosure statements, not only those submitted by presidential nominees. If enacted, this single provision would have required a huge increase in the planned size of the Ethics Office.

Besides its major disagreements with the White House over the content of the Ethics Act, the Schroeder subcommittee asked why so few high-level officials and former officials had been prosecuted for conflict of interest violations. Under close questioning from the subcommittee, Russell T. Baker, chief of the Public Integrity Section of the Department of Justice, admitted that it was extremely difficult to prosecute individuals for conflict of interest violations:

It would not be an exaggeration to state that conflicts of interest have caused si-multaneous frustration to the prosecutors, agencies, Government employees, and the public. The frustration faced by the prosecutors seems to stem primarily from the fact that we are dealing with poorly drafted statutes containing loopholes and vaguely defined prohibitions, criminal sanctions which are frequently overly severe for the conduct involved, and inadequate coordination of criminal and administrative sanctions.[38]

Mr. Baker insisted that Justice Department attorneys often "felt prose-cution was inappropriate because the felony sanction was too severe, given the nature of the conduct involved in the particular case." In other words, the charges had little "jury appeal." Furthermore, Baker maintained that Justice Department attorneys "would have pursued a less severe sanction, such as a misdemeanor prosecution, a civil fine, or administrative action, had such alternative been available.[39] This testimony basically supported the findings of the Association of the Bar of the City of New York in its 1960 report.

In September 1977, Robert J. Lipshutz, counsel to President Carter, in-formed Congresswoman Schroeder that the White House opposed a number of provisions in the subcommittee's bill. First, he criticized Schroeder's plan to place agency ethics counselors under the direct control of the director of government ethics because it ran counter to the well-established rule that programs dealing with internal governance are effective only if each agency head receives "both a strong mandate and unequivocal authority to carry it out."[40] He regarded the Schroeder plan as entirely untested.

Second, Lipshutz argued that confidential reporting should continue for designated employees below GS–16 until the administration had time to assess the impact of the public reporting program. Finally, the White House saw no reason to require the Ethics Office to review all public disclosure forms since the proposed law would require review by the appropriate designated agency ethics officer.

The bill subsequently reported by the full Post Office and Civil Service Committee attempted to take into consideration some of the White House complaints. Public disclosure would extend down to GS–16 or equivalent positions, but would also include Schedule C presidential appointees paid below the rate of a GS–16. On the other hand, the Committee established a statutory confidential reporting system for lower-level positions and required that these officials file the same comprehensive statements as those covered by public disclosure.[41]

However, in a major rebuke to the White House, the bill gave the director of the Ethics Office the authority to appoint and direct seventy-five ethics counselors. "It is essential," the committee argued, "that those individuals responsible for monitoring and administering the program, the agency ethics officers, be accountable to one person."[42]

On November 2, 1977, the Committee on the Judiciary reported on H.R. 1, the Ethics in Government Act of 1977, which generally pleased the White House because of its similarity to the administration's Ethics Act. To protect against the misuse of disclosure statements, the president's Ethics Act made it unlawful for any person to inspect, obtain, or use a report for:

1. any unlawful purpose;
2. any commercial purpose;
3. determining or establishing the credit rating of any individual; or
4. directly or indirectly soliciting money for any political, charitable, or other purpose.

The Judiciary Committee added language requiring that each person requesting to inspect or obtain a statement provide the appropriate agency with detailed information on the person or organization requesting the information. In addition, agencies and the Ethics Office would be required to destroy the statements after five years.[43]

As noted, the Carter White House disagreed with the Senate action applying the lifetime postemployment bar to off-scene assistance. To reduce the impact of this provision, the White House convinced the House Judiciary committee to delete this part of the lifetime bar and replace it with a new Section 207(b)(ii), which would apply a two-year aiding and assisting prohibition with respect to matters in which the former high-level officials had been personally and substantially involved. However, the new prohibition appeared to cover both on–scene and off-scene assistance.

The little noticed struggle over the off-scene assistance prohibition suggests that the Carter White House was becoming increasingly apprehensive about the impact of conflict of interest reform. Besides the potential problems of enforcement and the possible exodus of top officials, the administration had a difficult time arguing that off-scene assistance should not be limited.

Further complicating legislative consideration of the postemployment activities proposals was the fact that the Carter Administration proposed a two-tier system for determining which officials would be covered by the new aiding and assisting and the one-year no-contact prohibitions. The statutes would apply automatically to executive-level positions, political appointees in positions classified at GS–16 or above, and military officers in grade 0–6 or above. In addition, the legislation gave the director of the Ethics Office the thankless task of designating other positions for coverage if they had significant decision- or policy-making responsibility.[44]

Chairman Danielson of the Judiciary Committee had problems with giving an administrative agency responsibility for deciding which positions would be subject to the new criminal measures. However, on October 7, 1977, Larry H. Hammond, deputy assistant attorney general, informed Chairman Danielson that the Justice Department found nothing unconstitutional about the delegation amendment.[45] With this assurance, the committee incorporated the administration's new postemployment proposals.

Not all members of the Judiciary Committee found the bill reported by their committee praiseworthy. The most vocal criticism came from Republicans who believed that many of the proposals were intended to make it more difficult for Republican administrations to fill key positions with individuals having strong ties to business community. Congressman Charles Wiggens of California, for example, argued that in order to protect the privacy rights of government officials, Congress should require only "the minimum amount of personal information necessary to reveal actual or potential conflicts."[46]

Congressmen Carlos Moorhead, Robert McClory, and Thomas Kindness attacked the Carter Administration's "naive attempt to deal with what it perceives as the problem of the 'revolving door' in Government service."[47] The three reserved their harshest criticism for the new, one-year cooling-off period, which they found particularly punitive. Taken as a whole, they argued that these reforms would seriously "hamper the ability of Federal Government to attract bright, young people, as well as experienced professionals, for high-level policy positions."[48]

By August, 1977 three years after the resignation of Richard Nixon, confusion still reigned in Congress over ethics reform. This was particularly true in the House, where jurisdictional battles threatened to block any legislation. Furthermore, as happened in 1962, the White House came under increasing pressure from federal agencies to reconsider some of the reforms because of their potential impact on recruitment and retention of key executive, scientific, and professional personnel.

The failure to pass ethics reform legislation proved embarrassing for Congress and the Carter White House. To deflect some of the criticism, in March of 1977 the House passed H.Res. 287, requiring all House members to file annual statements of their financial holdings, and to comply with regulations on the acceptance of gifts, foreign travel, the use of office accounts funded with surplus campaign funds, and the misuse of the franking privilege, having Congress pick up the cost of congressional mailings. Even more controversial, beginning in 1979, the resolution established an outside-earned-income cap of $8,625, or approximately twenty percent of the congressional salaries of $57,500.[49]

Since many Congressmen used income from speaking and other activities to supplement their salaries, the earned-income limitation proved particularly unpopular. Consequently, by the spring of 1978, considerable support had developed in the House to scrap the outside-income limitation. One way to do this was to hold ethics legislation hostage, a threat that led the House leadership to delay full House consideration of a compromise ethics bill.

Late in September 1978, the House finally got around to debating ethics legislation. The bill considered by the House gave the Carter Administration most of what it wanted and was very similar to legislation passed by the Senate more than a year earlier. However, the House did make a number of important changes.

Throughout Senate and House consideration of these measures, the Defense Department expressed concern that they might seriously hamper the free flow of information between former officials working for defense contractors and the government. To deal with this problem, the compromise legislation permitted former officials to obtain exemptions on a case-by-case basis to permit them to transfer scientific and technical information without violating the law.

Congressman Samuel Stratton argued that the remedy of case-by-case exemptions did little to allay fears of top government scientists who he feared might leave the government in droves as, under the administration bill, "the scientist [would] not know whether the exemption is to be granted until after completion of his Government employment."[50] This argument convinced the House to accept a Stratton amendment exempting from the provisions of 18 U.S.C. 207(a), (b), and (c), "the making of communications solely for the purpose of furnishing scientific or technological information."[51]

Besides the issue of the transfer of technical information, the controversial one-year no-contact ban caused a revolt on the floor. As Congressman Wiggins argued, the new bar demonstrated a belief on the part of Congress that government officials will not have "the guts or the objectivity or integrity to make a proper decision."[52] Taking advantage of this sentiment, Congressman Robert Eckhardt convinced the House to give agencies the authority to exempt from the new one-year no-contact bar "any person in good standing in a licensed profession, if certain conditions regarding ethical conduct are met."[53] The main requirement was that the profession provided for the removal of the professional's license for unethical practices. This last-minute change effectively gutted the general lobbying prohibition.

Throughout the debate, Congressman George Danielson, Chairman of the House Judiciary Committee, had defended the new postemployment provisions and urged his colleagues not to destroy their effectiveness by a series of amendments. Congress, he argued, should pass the new one-year no-contact bar to shield employees from being forced to decide between working for the public interest and possibly helping out an old friend. As Danielson explained:

I should say, that we are trying to keep the foxes out of the chicken coop. It does not do any good to say that the particular fox is not going to eat any of the chickens, because the chickens do not believe it. You and I may believe it, but the chickens do not. Let us keep the fox out of [the] hen house. That is exactly what this is for. If we chip away these restrictions one by one, the fox is going to fly. That is certain.[54]

In addition to the provision about the transfer of technical information, Congressman John Ashbrook succeeded in getting the house to impose an earned-income limitation on all executive-branch employees compensated at a rate of GS–16 or above. The limit would equal no more than fifteen percent of the official's salary.[55] If members of Congress, he argued, were required to live under an earned-income limitation, the same rule should apply to high-level executive personnel.

Other amendments would not fare so well. For instance, the House rejected amendments that sought to exempt high-level career officials from public financial disclosure and to give the director of the Office of Government Ethics the authority to appoint and direct agency ethics officers.

Chairman Danielson led the opposition to the Schroeder amendment on the supervision of agency ethics officers. He told the House that the passage of the amendment would create "an absolute bureaucratic monster."[56] The bureaucratic monster, Danielson argued, would be the establishment of "a sort of independent police force, a band of roving commissars, who will be sprinkled throughout the various Government agencies willy-nilly on a rotating basis to look under every leaf and twig."[57] Congressman Leo Ryan, supporting Danielson's position, made it clear that he saw no reason for creating a "priesthood" of ethics counselors. These "mullahs of the U.S. Government," Ryan maintained, would tell the various agencies "what ought to be."[58] After long debate, on September 30, 1978, the House passed the Ethics in Government Act of 1978.

THE ETHICS IN GOVERNMENT ACT OF 1978

It took a month for House and Senate conferees to work out differences between the House and Senate versions of the ethics reforms. On

October 28, 1978, President Carter signed the act into law.[59] Contrary to public impression, the law made few substantive changes in criminal or administrative conflict of interest provisions. These involved the new postemployment activities prohibitions. On the other hand, Congress enacted changes that, in theory, improved methods for checking the financial affairs of officials for conflicts and, when necessary, for conducting unbiased investigations of allegations of wrongdoing in high places. These procedural changes did, however, dramatically alter the way in which government employees, particularly presidential appointees, entered the federal service.

The act required public financial disclosure for high-level officials in all three branches of the federal government, but the conferees deleted a provision requiring random audits of statements. Congress also placed strict statutory restrictions on the use of blind trusts as an alternative to divestiture or disqualification agreements.

The law established a new Office of Government Ethics within the Office of Personnel Management, giving it responsibility for overseeing the management of the executive-branch program for preventing conflicts of interest. This included reviewing the disclosure statements of presidential nominees and approving blind trusts. However, Congress did not give the office day-to-day responsibility for agency ethics programs or the authority to audit disclosure statements.

More by default than by a conscious decision, Congress left it to the new Ethics Office to interpret and enforce the standards of conduct issued under Executive Order 11222. The conferees also accepted the Senate provision requiring the Ethics Office to operate a formal advisory service.

With respect to the new postemployment activities prohibition, the conferees saved the one-year no-contact bar, 18 U.S.C. 207(c), by deleting the exception for licensed professionals. To get this concession, however, a compromise was struck limiting automatic coverage only to officials who served in executive-level positions. Other officials who had occupied positions above a GS–17 or equivalent, or 0–7 or above, as well as certain officials below those classifications, would be subject to the antilobbying provision only if they had occupied a position that the director of the Ethics Office had found to have had significant decision-making or suspervisory responsibility.

From the perspective of Congress, the most important public integrity reform involved the amendments to Title 28 of the United States Code, which provided a mechanism for the appointment of temporary special prosecutors to investigate high-level wrongdoing.

It is difficult to understand how the 1978 Ethics Act came to be regarded as landmark legislation tightening conflict of interest restrictions: It did nothing of the kind. Public financial disclosure and the special prosecutor provisions, however, did open the entire subject of conflict of interest regulation to much greater media and public scrutiny. As a result, those un-familiar with the regulations assumed that most did not exist prior to the Ethics Act.

IMPLEMENTING THE MANDATE

The implementation of the Ethics Act, with the exception of interpreting the new postemployment prohibitions, primarily involved restructuring the process of identifying and resolving conflict of interest problems. A public disclosure form needed to be drafted, distributed, and explained. Thousands of positions needed to be reviewed to determine which had significant decision-making and supervisory responsibility. Blind trusts established prior to the act needed to be reviewed to see whether they complied with the new statutory requirements, and work needed to begin to set up an advisory opinion service and to evaluate the effectiveness of agency ethics programs.

It is important to remember, however, that the act left intact the other ethics power centers. The Public Integrity Section of Justice kept its overall responsibility for criminal conflict of interest matters. The Office of White House counsel kept its responsibility for reviewing the backgrounds of nominees for conflict of interest problems and for working with nominees to resolve problems. Designated agency ethics officers kept day-to-day management responsibility for their ethics programs and had the additional responsibility of reviewing public financial disclosure statements. The new Ethics Office could not implement its part of the program without the cooperation of other important members of the growing ethics bureaucracy. However, a new crisis quickly forced the Carter White House to put im-plementation of the Ethics Act on hold.

Ethics Reform and Bureaucratic Sabotage

By late November 1979, the White House began to receive reports that thousands of high-level officials planned to leave the government to avoid public financial disclosure and the new postemployment restrictions. A number of agencies and departments, particularly the Defense Department, urged the White House and the Office of Personnel Management to move quickly to issue regulations interpreting the financial disclosure and post-employment requirements in order to reduce some of the panic associated with the passage of the Ethics Act. On January 15, 1979, the White House announced it had selected Berhardt Wruble, the principal general counsel of the Army, to set up the new office and act as its temporary director.[60] Still, concern mounted over the threatened exodus.

On January 31, 1979, the *Washington Post* reported that the "Stiffened

Federal Law May Make Officials Quit." The article stated that "hundreds of government officials—scientists, educators, and researchers—may resign this spring to avoid coming under a stringent new code of ethics aimed at curbing conflicts of interest."[61] Officials complained the loudest about the new two-year restriction on "aiding, assisting, counseling, advising in representing." If Section 207(b)(ii) of Title 18 of the United States Code applied to off-scene assistance, many believed their private opportunities would dry up. Even President Carter's Secretary of Health, Education, and Welfare, Joseph A. Califano, publicly asked the president to postpone the effective date of the law and have some hearings on it.[62] Mr. Califano made it clear that he hoped Congress would act to amend the law.

Some members of Congress jumped on the ethics repeal bandwagon. Senator Patrick Moynihan, for example, responded with alarm over the *Washington Post* article:

I simply wish to state that I think we passed a law that had much more in it than we originally realized, and that in the name of ethics in Government, we are making service to Government impossible for ethical people. I believe the administration was the originator of this effort. I think we had better pay attention to it before we look up and suddenly find that we have not only lost so many absolutely indispensable people, but that we cannot replace them.[63]

On February 5, 1979, an editorial in the *Washington Post* argued that the nation and Congress had seriously overreacted when it passed the Ethics Act, and that the postemployment reforms specifically were bound "to cause an exodus of decent and valuable people from office."[64] The editorial urged the administration and Congress to support a "generous" interpretation of the new ethics measures. It even suggested that Congress and President Carter support amendments to the new revolving-door measures.

The strongest bureaucratic criticism of the ethics reforms came from within the Defense Department. The February 1979 issue of *Air Force Magazine*, for example, reported that "USAF officers queried . . . denounced the new statute, branding it 'a slap in the face' to officers generally, 'blatantly unfair,' 'a disaster,' and worse."[65] The officers saw the new revolving-door restrictions as "new doors being slammed on full-time and consultant jobs that experts retiring from the services had expected to land." Finally, the article argued that the new measures could cause "a great loss of expertise for defense contractors, a loss that could translate into development and production problems and eventual higher costs to government."[66]

Some key members of Congress, however, rejected calls for emergency changes in the Ethics Act. On February 16, 1979, Senator Abraham Ribicoff wrote to President Carter and to Director Wruble maintaining that Congress had carefully considered the impact of the reforms and that the reforms had received the "full support of the President and the Department of Justice."[67]

A memorandum accompanying the February 16th letter informed the president that the Congress had no intention to "prevent a Federal employee from taking any position with any firm or organization which he chooses when he leaves the government."[68] The Congress intended to apply the new aiding-and-assisting prohibition only "to those matters in which a former high-ranking official had been personally and substantially involved." In other words, it did not intend "to restrict involvement in general matters which may have fallen under an employee's official responsibility while he was in government service."[69] However, the prohibition was intended to apply to off- as well as on-scene assistance for the two-year period. If the White House and the leadership in the House and Senate believed that this clarification would calm the storm, they were mistaken.

During March 1979, stories of impending doom continued to appear in the national media. For instance, *Newsweek* reported that thousands of officials had already set in motion the process of getting out of the government.[70] *Science Magazine* reported that the Ethics Act had thrown the federal science establishment into a state of panic.[71]

Early in March 1979, Congressman Danielson introduced legislation to delay the effective date of the new restrictions for six months. Congressman Carlos Moorhead introduced legislation to repeal the one-year no-contact bar and to amend the aiding and assisting prohibition so that it would not apply to off-scene assistance.[72] Shortly thereafter, the *Congressional Quarterly Weekly* reported that the administration believed the two Congressmen had introduced the bills to pressure the Office of Government Ethics to issue regulations interpreting the scope of the new prohibitions more narrowly.[73]

To expedite the start-up of the office, Acting Director Wruble brought with him from the Department of Defense a staff of nine lawyers and other support personnel. Working out the draft regulations was not easy. Wruble worked closely with the Department of Justice and the Carter White House, as the Ethics Office attempted to put into simple English the very complex postemployment and financial disclosure requirements of the Ethics Act.

On April 3, 1979, the Office of Government Ethics issued its interim regulations on the revolving-door provisions of the Ethics Act. These regulations contained numerous examples of permissible and impermissible conduct by former employees under the four prohibitions.[74] Along with these regulations, the White House proposed a number of technical amendments to clear up some confusion regarding the intent of the Ethics Act.[75]

The administration sought a number of significant substantive changes. First, the White House asked Congress to narrow the scope of the new "aiding and assisting" prohibition, found at Section 207(b)(ii) of Title 18 of the United States Code, by making it clear that it would not apply to any type of assistance rendered away from an informal or a formal government proceeding. Defending these "technical amendments," in April 1979 testimony before the Senate Judiciary Subcommittee on Administrative

Law and Governmental Relations, Director of the Office of Personnel Management Alan Campbell argued that the present aiding-and-assistance language would be extremely difficult to enforce, that it might subject former high-level officials "to loose allegations that, behind closed doors, they said the wrong things," and that organizations doing business with the government might stop "hiring former senior government employees burdened by such restrictions," because they might be accused of using these former officials in an illegal manner.[76]

Deputy Secretary of Defense Charles Dutton testified that he had two people turn down senior positions because they decided to wait until Congress took action on reform proposals.[77] Secretary of Health, Education and Welfare Joseph Califano predicted "the departure of some 100 officials from his department" because new regulations would make it very difficult for former officials from his department to find outside work that did not require them to keep in close contact with Washington.[78]

An April 6, 1979 *Washington Post* editorial commented on the history of the Ethics Act and argued that the reformers had inadequately considered the consequences of their reforms:

By now one can predict that when reformers set out to purify some part of public affairs, they will prescribe strong remedies and then find out that those remedies are too harsh, and all back awkwardly to a more sensible plan. . . . Predictably, the law's drafters now maintain that the most drastic readings of the law were not what they had in mind at all. And after much travail and considerable craftsmanship, the new Office of Government Ethics has indeed produced regulations that construe the law in much more reasonable and limited—though inevitably complicated ways. If the regulations and amendments are adopted, as they should be, the administration and Congress will wind up in a much better place—indeed, one better in some respects than they deserve. . . . Next time around, we hope the champions of public virtue will think twice before they pass a comparable "reform."[79]

On April 9, 1979, by voice vote, the Senate passed the Carter Administration's technical amendments intact.[80]

To speed House consideration of the amendments, in late May the Carter White House agreed to support an exemption from the new postemployment prohibitions for high-level officials who [go] to work for colleges and universities, medical research and treatment facilities, or state and local governments."[81] Moreover, the Carter White House agreed to a second amendment sharply limiting the number of positions automatically subject to the new "aiding and assisting by personal presence at" prohibition and the one-year no-contact bar to executive-level positions and military positions of 0–9 and above. Congress gave the director of the Ethics Office responsibility for determining which positions at the level of GS–17 or above in the Senior Executive Service, and which positions of active duty commissioned officers assigned to pay grade at 0–7 or 0–8, had significant supervisory or policy-making responsibility.

Congress completed action on the amendments on June 15, 1979, and President Carter quickly signed the changes into law.[82] The White House and Congress had been forced to make major substantive changes in the Ethics Act because of panic over a possible massive exodus of essential talent, but neither Congress or the Carter White House waited to see whether the fear was justified.

Shortly after Congress completed action on the amendments to the Ethics in Government Act, Acting Director Wruble returned to his position with the Army. In November 1979, President Carter nominated J. Jackson Walter to become the first permanent director of the Office. Staffing of the office was not completed until late fall of the same year. Within a short time, Director Walter made it clear that as long as agencies operated effective programs, his office would keep out of day-to-day matters. The small staff and budget meant that the office could provide only expert assistance. Its statutory duties would take all its manpower.

President Carter assumed the presidency promising to clean up the government, but the Ethics in Government Act of 1978 left the executive-branch system for regulating conflicts of interest basically unchanged in terms of the substantive limitations on official conduct. It added a few players to the conflict of interest prevention and enforcement game, and mandated procedural reforms which forced major changes in the way the White House and agencies dealt with conflicts of interest.

However, the Carter Administration fell into the trap of seeing ethics in terms of compliance with the criminal conflict of interest statutes. Provisions for a special prosecutor and public financial disclosure would certainly result in the detection and prosecution of officials and former officials who attempted to use their public positions for personal gain. Unfortunately, Congress and the White House failed to understand that the major problem related to criminal convictions involved the vague and confusing language of the major criminal statutes.

Moreover, Congress and the Carter White House lost sight of the fact that most allegations of wrongdoing by top officials did not reach the level of a criminal violation, but rather involved appearance of impropriety. The Ethics Act did little to deal with an equally vague and confusing set of standards of conduct regulations.

Finally, Congress and the Carter White House failed to realize that the Ethics Act would raise public expectations. Out of all the officials who go in and out of government, some must be guilty of a conflict of interest, the reasoning went. If investigation after investigation continues the pattern of finding impropriety but no illegality, public skepticism is bound to increase and pressure for tighter statutes will certainly follow.

The major shortcoming of the Ethics Act was its failure to revise all the substantive criminal and administrative conflict of interest prohibitions to eliminate confusion and ambiguity. Instead it gave the public the false impression that procedural reforms would end ethical problems in government service.

NOTES

1. *New York Times*, August 10, 1976, p. 15.
2. Bruce Adams and Kathryn Kavannagh-Baran, *Promise and Performance: Carter Builds a New Administration* (Lexington, Mass.: Lexington Books, 1981), p. 87.
3. Robert G. Kaiser, "Carter Appointees May Have to Reveal Some Financial Details," *Washington Post*, November 19, 1976, cited in Adams and Kavannagh-Baran, p. 83.
4. *New York Times*, November 30, 1976, p. 1.
5. *New York Times*, December 2, 1976, p. 50.
6. *New York Times*, January 5, 1977, pp. 1, 17.
7. Ibid.
8. Ibid.
9. Ibid.
10. Ibid.
11. *New York Times*, January 5, 1977, p. 16.
12. *New York Times*, January 8, p. 18.
13. Ibid.
14. Ibid.
15. Draft Executive Order, Public Financial Disclosure, January, 1977 (unpublished document).
16. Letter, Roswell B. Perkins for John L. Moore, February 1, 1977 (unpublished document).
17. Ibid.
18. Ibid.
19. Ibid.
20. Ibid.
21. Ibid.
22. *Congressional Quarterly Almanac*, 1977, p. 529.
23. Mercer Cross, "Delay on Top Jobs: Good or Bad?" *Congressional Quarterly Weekly*, March 5, 1977, p. 397.
24. Adams and Kathryn Kavannagh-Baran, p. 91.
25. U.S. Congress, Senate, Committee on Government Operations, *Watergate, Part I: Reorganization and Reform Act of 1975*, Hearings on S. 496, 94th Cong., 1st Sess., 1975, July 29–31.
26. *Congressional Quarterly Almanac*, 1976, p. 423.
27. Comptroller General of the United States, *Action Needed to Make the Executive Branch Financial Disclosure System Effective*, FPCD–27–23, February 28, 1977.
28. Message to Congress, President Jimmy Carter, May 3, 1977, regarding the Ethics in Government Act.
29. H.R. 6954.
30. U.S. Congress, Senate, Committee on Governmental Affairs, *Public Integrity*

Act of 1977, Blind Trusts and Other Conflict of Interest Matters. Hearing on S. 555, 95th Cong., May 3, 4, and 5, 1977, p. 156.

31. Ibid.

32. Ibid., p. 144.

33. Ibid., p. 113.

34. Ibid., p. 115, Section 308(e) of S. 555.

35. U.S. Congress, Senate, *Public Officials Integrity Act of 1977*, S. Rept. 170 to accompany S. 555, 95th Cong., 1st Sess., 1977, pp. 151–52.

36. See generally, U.S. Congress, House, Committee on Post Office and Civil Service, *Federal Ethics and Financial Disclosure*, Hearing before the Subcommittee on Employee Ethics and Utilization, on H.R. 6954 and H.R. 3928, 95th Cong., June 16 and 23, 1st Sess., 1977.

37. Ibid.

38. Ibid., p. 2.

39. Ibid., p. 5.

40. Letter, Robert J. Lipshutz for Congressman Patricia Schroeder, September 8, 1977 (unpublished document).

41. U.S. Congress, House, *Federal Employee Financial Reporting and Disclosure*, H. Rept. 642, part 1, to accompany H.R. 6954, 95th Cong., 1st Sess., 1977, p. 26.

42. Ibid., p. 33.

43. U.S. Congress, *Ethics in Government Act of 1977*, H. Rept. 800 to accompany H.R. 1, p. 5.

44. Ibid., p. 33.

45. Letter, Larry A. Hammond, Deputy Assistant Attorney General for Chairman E. Danielson, October 7, 1977 (unpublished document).

46. U.S. Congress, *Ethics in Government Act of 1977*, H. Rept. 800 to accompany H.R. 1, p. 99.

47. Ibid., p. 102.

48. Ibid., p. 104.

49. *Congressional Quarterly Weekly*, April 29, 1978, p. 1043.

50. *The Congressional Record*, September 27, 1978, p. 31983.

51. Ibid.

52. Ibid.

53. Ibid., p. 31992.

54. Ibid., p. 31990.

55. Ibid., pp. 32006, 32008.

56. Ibid., p. 31996.

57. Ibid.

58. Ibid., p. 31997.

59. P.L. 95–521, October 26, 1978.

60. *Washington Post*, January 16, 1978, p. C2.

61. *Washington Post*, January 31, 1979, p. A3.

62. *New York Times*, March 8, 1979, p. A1.

63. *Congressional Record*, Senate, January 31, 1979, p. 250.

64. *Washington Post*, February 5, 1979, editorial, p. A20.

65. "The Disastrous Ethics in Government Law," *Air Force Magazine*, February, 1979.

66. Ibid.

67. *Congressional Record*, February 21, 1979, S 1613. Memorandum on the "Aiding and Assisting in Representation Provisions of 18 U.S.C. 207(b)."

68. Ibid.

69. Ibid.

70. "A Federal Brain Drain," *Newsweek*, March 5, 1978, p. 51.

71. "Stringent New Ethics Law Worries Government Scientists," *Science Magazine*, March 9, 1979, p. A8.

72. *Congressional Quarterly Weekly*, March 25, 1979, p. 513.

73. Ibid.

74. *Federal Register*, April 3, 1979, p. 19974, 5 C.F.R. 737.

75. *Congressional Quarterly Weekly*, April 7, 1979, p. 631.

76. *Congressional Record*, Senate, April 4, 1979, p. 3871.

77. "Battle Shaping Up on Job Curbs for Ex-Federal Employees," *New York Times*, April 3, 1979, p. 13.

78. Ibid.

79. *Washington Post*, April 6, 1979, editorial. p. 28.

80. *Congressional Quarterly Weekly*, April 14, 1979, p. 702.

81. *Congressional Quarterly Weekly*, May 26, 1979, p. 1033.

82. *Congressional Quarterly Weekly*, June 23, 1979, p. 1246.

IX

Conflict of Interest and
the Reagan Administration

Shortly after the election victory of Ronald Reagan on November 4, 1980, the president-elect appointed Pendelton James, head of a Los Angeles executive recruiting firm, to head the personnel selection operations for the transition.[1] As James would later admit, the complexities of conflict of interest regulation caught the transition team off guard and contributed to lengthy delays in the filling of top cabinet and sub-cabinet posts.[2]

Within a few days of the Reagan election, J. Jackson Walter, Director of the Office of Government Ethics, sent the Reagan transition headquarters a comprehensive memorandum outlining conflict of interest clearance requirements.[3] The office subsequently worked closely with the transition counsel, Fred Fielding, to review the financial affairs of Reagan nominees for potential conflicts of interest and working out solutions for identified problems.[4]

By early December 1980, the slow progress in making appointments led Edwin Meese, the transition director, to point to conflict of interest regulation as one of the major reasons for the delay. According to Meese:

Because . . . of the conflict-of-interest regulations and the requirements of various committees on the Hill, it's no longer as it used to be where a President calls up a cabinet member, he consults with his wife, and he calls him back in 24 hours, and the deed is done. It's now a situation where any prospective Cabinet member . . . has to sit down, literally, with a lawyer, his banker, his accountant . . . and it often takes as much as a week, in which he himself is figuring out how he can comply with all the regulations.[5]

By late January 1981, frustration over conflict of interest clearance led Fred Fielding, council to the president, and Attorney General William

French Smith to announce that the White House might ask Congress to amend parts of the 1978 Ethics Act, particularly the part on public disclosure requirements.[6] Moreover, the Reagan Justice Department argued that the special prosecutor provisions of the Ethics Act might violate the separation of powers doctrine of the Constitution because only executive-branch officials can constitutionally prosecute criminal violations. In other words, the Reagan White House argued that its administration had to deal with a whole series of substantive changes in conflict of interest rules and regulations which seriously hindered its ability to implement the president's mandate. This impression was a distortion of what the Ethics Act actually had accomplished.

TRANSITION AND THE ETHICS ACT

A 1985 survey conducted by the Presidential Appointee Project of the National Academy of Public Administration found that "the average number of weeks to complete the appointment process [had] grown steadily in each of the five past administrations."[7] While the Johnson Administration in 1964 took an average of seven weeks, the Reagan White House took close to fifteen weeks. Some of the delay was attributable to clearance rules mandated by the Ethics Act of 1978.

When President Reagan began to staff his administration, his transition team continued the practice of requiring prospective nominees to authorize FBI full-field investigations and to complete a detailed personal data statement. The data statement form asked "lengthy questions on such matters as [their] previous involvement . . . in criminal or civil litigation, [their] business associations . . . and any other information which if made public, might prove harmful or embarrassing to the nominee or the President."[8]

In addition to internal White House clearance requirements, however, the Ethics Office informed the Reagan transition team that nominees had five days to file their disclosure statements with the designated agency ethics officer where the nominee would be working. The DAEO (Designated Agency Ethics Officer) then reviewed the statement for possible conflicts of interest, certified that conflicts of interest were not found or had been resolved, and then forwarded the statement to the Ethics Office for further review. Before sending the statement to the appropriate Senate committee responsible for confirmation, the director of the Ethics Office was required to certify "on the basis of information contained in the report that the nominee is in compliance with appropriate laws and regulations," or, if the contrary were true, that the director was unable to certify such a statement.[9] In theory, lack of certification does not prevent the Senate from confirming a nominee, but in practice, Senate committees have not recommended confirmation without a positive Ethics Office certification.

Since negotiations between the Ethics Office and the White House over certification are not public record, it is impossible to tell how much pressure has been exerted in either direction as part of the certification process. It might be noted, however, that the Ethics Office has never sent a Senate Committee a disclosure statement without a positive certification.

Besides the certification process, the Reagan White House learned that the public could inspect disclosure statements fifteen days after their initial filing. The public inspection provision meant it was extremely risky to announce a nominee without first resolving all conflict of interest problems. As expected, this process frequently required informal negotiations between the Office of White House Council, the nominee, the appropriate DAEO, the Office of Government Ethics, and possibly the Justice Department.

The Reagan White House also found that the scope of the disclosure angered a large number of nominees. In 1985, a National Academy of Public Administration report referred to the disclosure form, SF 278, as a "pale green monstrosity" and a "confusing, excessively detailed hurdle... few presidential appointees are able to negotiate successfully on the first attempt."[10]

As if these procedures were not enough, the Reagan White House found that it could no longer negotiate blind trust agreements with the appropriate Senate committee. As noted, the Ethics Act sharply limited the use of blind trusts as an alternative to divestiture or disqualification, and the Ethics Act gave the OGE (Office of Government Ethics) primary responsibility for approving their establishment.[11]

The Ethics Act opened to much more detailed public examination the process of reviewing the financial affairs of presidential nominees for conflict of interest problems. This represented a radical departure from past practices.

MORALITY AND ADMINISTRATION: THE EARLY YEARS

Through most of 1981, the Reagan White House, the Justice Department, and the Ethics Office discussed the possibility of getting Congress to amend the Ethics Act to reduce the burden of public financial disclosure. Any hope of getting Congress to approve changes became unlikely, however, as allegations of misconduct against high-level Reagan officials began to multiply.

In May 1982, the press revealed that shortly before taking office, Attorney General William French Smith had received a $50,000 severance payment from Earle M. Jorgenson, a California steel firm on whose board of directors Smith had served before becoming attorney general.[12] Throughout the short controversy, Smith maintained that the payments were entirely proper because they involved payments for past service. Nevertheless, he subsequently returned them.

The controversy stimulated heated discussion over the unwillingness of top Reagan appointees to separate their public and private lives in order to avoid the appearance of impropriety. For example, in an editorial entitled "A Conservatism of Convenience," David S. Broder accused supporters of the severance arrangement of accepting "the morality of the marketplace as the measure of public rectitude."[13] In another editorial, Richard Cohen criticized the attorney general for not seeing "that what he could do as a private citizen, he can no longer do" as a public servant.[14] On the other hand, columnist Joseph Kraft attributed the criticism to politics. Referring to the recession of 1981–1983, Kraft argued that "if the Reagan policies had worked, the complaints against Smith would find no echo. But so far, at least, the policies have not paid off. And in the absence of achievement beneficial to the many, the ethic of success looks like mere greed on the part of the few."[15]

It was the Richard Allen affair, which came to light in November 1981, that reopened the debate over standards of conduct. The affair involved the acceptance by Allen, President Reagan's national security adviser, of a $1,000 payment from a Japanese magazine that wanted an interview with Nancy Reagan. Allen, who placed the money in a White House safe, claimed he took the money so as not to offend the magazine and had actually intended to return it. Later, it was also disclosed that Allen had accepted three expensive watches from former Japanese business associates. Subsequent Justice Department and White House investigations concluded that Allen had not violated any criminal laws or White House standards of conduct. Nevertheless, Allen resigned his position in late January 1982.[16]

The Smith and Allen affairs, while temporary embarrassments, produced little public concern; neither did periodic reports of questionable conduct by other high-level Reagan appointees. A March 1983 article in the *New York Times* attempted to explain why these early disclosures did little damage to the Reagan presidency. One explanation pointed to the popularity of the president. Another pointed to an expected drop in interest after the Watergate affair. Still another expert believed that the "ethics of the business world have become the ethics of Washington under Mr. Reagan, and to many people, that development is not objectionable."[17]

In spite of these early problems, the White House continued to lobby quietly for amendments to the Ethics Act. A June 1983 article in the *New York Times*, entitled "The Trials of a Top-Level Appointee," implied that the 1978 Ethics Act forced nominees to subject themselves to a microscopic review of their entire life history and then caused them to worry about "conflicts of interest and financial sacrifices, stock divestitures, blind trusts, sharp drop[s] in salary, and finally public probing at Senate confirmation hearings." The article reported that the "Administration [was] quietly considering new legislation to change some of the procedures on financial disclosure."[18]

Common Cause did not let these assertions about the Ethics Act go unchallenged. Frustrated by the lack of public interest in the issue of government ethics, Ann McBride, vice president for program operations, accused the Reagan Administration of being "riddled with ethical insensitivity and scandal since it got there and [of using] the ethics act as a public whipping boy." McBride maintained that all reliable evidence indicated that the Ethics Act had not hurt recruitment.[19]

ETHICAL INSENSITIVITY AND PUBLIC SERVICE

In total numbers, no other recent presidency has had allegations of wrongdoing leveled against so many high-level officials as has the Reagan Presidency. The vast majority of the allegations have charged officials with failing to separate their public lives from continuing private activities and relationships. These alleged examples of ethical misconduct have generally been related to:

1. continuing relationships with former employers;
2. engaging in private business dealings related to the public responsibilities of the official;
3. using public positions to help out a friend or private business associate;
4. misusing government perquisites;
5. receiving gifts, gratuities, or favors from those with a direct stake in government policies, contracts, or programs; and
6. negotiating for future employment while still in the government.

Continuing Relationships and the Former Employer

Congress enacted the prohibition against private supplementation of salaries in an effort to safeguard the loyalty of federal employees and officials. Severance payments have thus come to be regarded as an unethical and possibly illegal way to get around the supplementation prohibition. For instance, Harold E. Shear, who entered government in 1981 to head the Federal Maritime Administration, failed to report on his disclosure statement a $45,000 severance payment from his former employer, a steamship company. A subsequent investigation determined that Shear had inadvertently left the payment off his disclosure statement and that the payment was permissible because it was for past service.[20]

The Boeing severance payment controversy has had much greater long-term significance. When five Boeing officials took high-level positions with the Department of Defense in 1981, these officials allegedly received some $485,000 in severance payments from the company.[21] Such payments, apparently made to ease the transition of these officials into government service, ran counter to interpretations of the supplementation prohibition made by the Justice Department since the early 1960s.

Although the case was uncovered during Reagan's first term, the Justice Department did not take action against the officials until the spring of 1986. Rather than prosecute these officials and Boeing for violating the criminal prohibition against supplementing the salaries of government officials, in July 1986 the Justice Department brought a civil suit against Boeing and the officials to recover the payments under a claim of unjust enrichment. Boeing did not deny making the payments; in fact, Boeing maintained that the payments were made to help their officials go to work for the Defense Department. In other words, the payments were "consistent with long-standing industry practice . . . to encourage qualified employees to accept national-defense positions."[22]

Early in 1987 a Federal District judge ruled that the payments neither violated the statutory supplementation prohibition nor went against public policy since they were made prior to the individuals entering the federal government. The Justice Department did not appeal the decision.

Besides the supplementation issue, broader issues of bias caused by former employment relationships have brought frequent allegations of conflicts of interest. For instance, before James C. Miller became the director of the Office of Management and Budget, he served as chairman of the Federal Trade Commission (FTC). Before taking his FTC position, Miller received some $75,000 in consulting fees from General Motors. When the FTC considered the antitrust implications of a joint venture between GM and Toyota and heard a defects case involving General Motors cars, a number of public interest groups demanded that Miller disqualify himself because of his earlier consulting relationship with GM. When Miller refused, one of these groups brought suit claiming that Miller was violating conflict of interest rules and regulations. Federal District Judge Harold Green ruled that federal conflict of interest laws did not apply to the Miller case because he did not have a present interest in GM.[23]

Actions Involving Personal Financial Interests

As noted, except for a few narrow statutes applicable to specific federal agencies, federal criminal law does not require divestiture as a remedy for conflicts of interest. Whether Executive Order 11222 requires divestiture depends upon interpretation. Disqualification has thus become the most frequently used remedy for self-dealing conflict of interest problems, and the failure to disqualify has caused the greatest number of conflict of interest problems for Reagan Administration officials.

In the spring of 1981, for example, congressional concern increased over consultants and members of federal advisory boards taking part in decisions that might financially benefit them or their private employers.[24] A July 1982 General Accounting Office study of a Pentagon advisory board on defense computer procurement found that members of the board might benefit if the Defense Department adopted the board's recommendations.[25] However, subsequent Justice Department and Defense Department reviews uncovered no criminal conduct or violations of department standards of conduct.[26]

A similar and more heated controversy developed in late 1982 over President Reagan's private-sector survey on cost control, popularly known as the Grace Commission. Critics accused the Grace Commission and the White House of circumventing conflict of interest requirements by recruiting hundreds of private-sector volunteers to serve on various commission task forces. Since the final report of the commission strongly advocated deep cuts in government programs and turning over the operation of many government programs to the private sector, some of the volunteers' companies might have benefited by the adoption and implementation of the Grace Commission recommendations.[27] However, this controversy failed to attract significant national attention or to result in any finding of wrongdoing or impropriety.

Another self-dealing controversy involved an agreement worked out between the Senate and Robert F. Burford, who was confirmed as director of the Interior Department's Bureau of Land Management. During confirmation proceedings, Burford agreed to make "no decision regarding grazing permits," and to comply with Interior Department divestiture requirements. Shortly after entering government Burford transferred two federal grazing permits to his sons. Later, however, congressional critics alleged that Burford had continued to participate in the formulation of policy affecting the management of grazing lands that could increase the value of his Colorado ranch and the grazing permits held by his sons. Burford has steadfastly maintained that there is no actual conflict of interest or even an appearance of one.[28]

When Everett G. Rank, Jr., became head of the Agricultural Stabilization and Conservation Service in 1981, he kept his partnership in a large California farm. As part of the administration's efforts to slow the rapidly escalating farm-support programs, Rank helped to design and subsequently administer the PIK, or payment-in-kind program, which paid farms with surplus commodities in return for production limitation. Rank's farm partnership received almost a million dollars in surplus cotton. Although a subsequent Justice Department investigation found no criminal wrongdoing, the Justice Department cautioned Rank to be more careful in the future.[29] Rank maintained that he would have disqualified himself from the PIK program had he known that his partners had enrolled the farm in it.

By the spring of 1983, the late William Casey, director of the Central Intelligence Agency and one of President Reagan's closest friends, became embroiled in his own conflict of interest controversy. When Casey took the position at the CIA, he did not set up a blind trust. As the law required, Casey agreed to disqualify himself from decisions that might affect his large financial holdings. However, a number of senators argued that the disqualification agreement could not adequately deal with the conflict of interest problems that Casey faced on a day-to-day basis, since Casey had access to vast amounts of secret intelligence and economic data that might prove extremely useful in making investment decisions.

Throughout the early summer, pressure increased on Casey either to divest himself of much of his holdings in the stock market or to set up a blind trust. Though the general counsel of the CIA ruled in July 1983 that no actual or apparent conflict of interest existed between Casey's financial dealings and his access to information about world economic affairs,[30] Casey agreed to set up a blind trust in compliance with the 1978 Ethics Act.[31] The trust subsequently received the approval of the Office of Government Ethics.

Although allegations of official misconduct in the Environmental Protection Agency received the most media attention during Reagan's first term, few involved conflicts of interest. Most of the charges involved the apparent refusal of the Environmental Protection Agency (EPA) to aggressively enforce statutory environmental regulations and the claim that high EPA officials favored the interests of private business rather than the interests of public health and safety.

A part-time EPA consultant, James W. Sanderson, withdrew his name from nomination for the position of assistant administrator for policy in the EPA after it was disclosed that, while working as an EPA consultant, he had represented private companies subject to EPA regulation.[32] He denied any wrongdoing, and the Justice Department did not proceed with legal action against him.

Rita M. Lavelle, head of the EPA's toxic waste cleanup program, was fired and subsequently convicted of lying to Congress and obstructing a congressional inquiry. She received a six-month prison sentence.[33] In another case, Anne M. Burford, administrator of the EPA, resigned after a heated battle with Congress over access to EPA enforcement documents.

A subsequent shake-up in the EPA caused a number of other high-level officials to resign as the result of allegations of wrongdoing. However, only Rita Lavelle was charged with a violation of criminal law. On the whole, the turmoil in EPA did little long-term damage to President Reagan.

The Perquisites of Office

Also throughout the Reagan Administration, a surprisingly large number of officials have been accused of using perquisites of their public offices for private purposes. Section 204 of Executive Order 11222 states that "an employee shall not use Federal property of any kind for other than officially approved activities. He must protect and conserve all Federal property, including equipment and supplies, entrusted or issued to him."[34] Other federal criminal statutes also prohibit the misuse of government property.

Robert P. Nimmo resigned as head of the Veterans Administrations in 1982, "just before a General Accounting Office report criticized him for improper use of chartered military aircraft, first–class airline service and a chauffeured government car."[35] Another resignation came from Edmund S. Savas, who resigned as assistant secretary of housing and urban development in 1983 after allegedly using his staff to type and proofread his privately published book, *Privatizing the Public Sector*. Throughout the controversy, Savas maintained he had done nothing improper.[36] Neither criminal nor administrative action was taken against him.

In still another case, Arthur Hull Hayes, commissioner of the food and drug administration, resigned in 1983 after allegations that he had billed the government for traveling expenses for which private groups had also reimbursed him. Again the Justice Department found no criminal misconduct.[37]

In almost all the cases where high-level officials left the Reagan Administration after allegations of impropriety, it is difficult to determine whether they left voluntarily or were given a "gentle push" by the White House. The White House never publicly criticized any of the officials who left.

THE POLITICS OF SLEAZE

In January 1984, the *National Journal* published the names of forty-eight Reagan officials accused of various types of official and personal misconduct.[38] In February 1984 Democratic presidential candidate Gary Hart used this article to accuse the Reagan White House of "appointing 48 Government officials" who had been involved in "criminal wrongdoing, unethical behavior and abuses of power and privilege."[39]

Then, during the spring of 1984, the Democratic National Committee briefly ran a thirty-second commercial attacking the president for bringing unethical people into government. The commercial pictured Edwin Meese III, William J. Casey, and Richard Allen as examples of unethical Reagan appointees. The commercial ended with the announcer saying, "This is moral leadership? Vote Democratic."[40]

While the Democratic Party tried to turn the sleaze factor into a national campaign issue, print and electronic media outside Washington and New York generally ignored the issue. Tom Wicker, in May 1984, doubted that the Democrats could turn the problem into a major issue because the record "of sleazy financial and political dealings alleged or proven against Reagan Administration officials and nominees [were] most striking for one thing: the ability of the man who brought these people to Washington, and who ultimately is most responsible for his own Administration, to escape blame and to show no shame for their actions."[41]

Tom Wicker was right. The sleaze issue did not catch on. To the contrary, the financial disclosure problems of Democratic vice presidential candidate

Geraldine Ferraro proved more damaging and embarrassing to the Democratic Party than the sleaze issue did to the Republicans.

Reauthorization and a Clean Bill of Health

The ease with which Congress reauthorized the Office of Government Ethics shows that little concern had developed over the integrity issue. When, on November 11, 1983, President Reagan signed into law Public Law 98–150, extending the life of the Office of Government Ethics until September 30, 1988, Congress made very few changes in it.[42] Equally significant, prior to the passage of the reauthorization law, there was very little criticism of the management of the Ethics Office. In fact, there appeared to be general agreement that it had done an excellent job in reversing the decline of the conflict of interest prevention program. Moreover, the Reagan White House did not fight the reauthorization of the independent counsel provisions of the 1978 Ethics in Government Act.

Both the Senate and the House, however, expressed some concern over the independence of the director of the Ethics Office from the White House. They questioned whether the director of this small office would stand up to the White House on conflict of interest issues. In spite of assurances that the White House did not pressure the office to see things its way on conflict of interest matters, Congress established a five-year term for any director of the office nominated or renominated after October 1, 1983.

Early in 1983, J. Jackson Walter, the second director of the office, voluntarily resigned. President Reagan nominated, and the Senate confirmed, David H. Martin as the third director of the office. However, when Congress reauthorized the Office of Government Ethics, the White House did not replace Martin nor renominate him for a full five-year term.

To further increase the power of the Office, Congress gave the director specific authority to request assistance from all executive agencies in carrying out the office's statutory mission. Finally, the reauthorization gave the director the authority to seek assistance from Inspector General offices in federal agencies and departments. In brief, Congress began to develop some concern over the independence of the Ethics Office and its willingness to confront the White House on integrity issues involving high-level officials.

THE INTEGRITY ISSUE HITS CLOSE TO HOME

When William French Smith resigned as attorney general, President Reagan nominated Edwin Meese to take his place. However, during the winter of 1983, reports surfaced that Meese had received substantial financial assistance from friends in California when he moved to Washington in 1981. It was revealed that someone had helped to arrange the sale of Meese's California house, and others had helped Meese to obtain some personal loans. It was also revealed that Meese had failed to report on his public disclosure form that his wife had received a $15,000, no-interest loan.

What led to the appointment of an independent counsel to investigate the Meese case was additional disclosures that some of those who provided financial assistance to Meese then received appointments to federal positions.[43] Critics argued it appeared that Meese might have helped his friends get government jobs in return for financial help. The finding by independent counsel Jacob A. Stein late in 1984 that Meese had not violated any criminal law did not end the controversy.

When Stein found that Meese had not violated any criminal prohibition, President Reagan asked the Senate to confirm Meese as attorney general.[44] However, critics of the nomination maintained that the Senate should not confirm Meese because he had violated White House standards of conduct regulations through conduct that created the appearance of impropriety.[45]

Pressed for a ruling by the Senate Judiciary Committee, in January 1985 David H. Martin notified Committee Chairman Strom Thurmond that "no conflicts of interest existed and that only one of the allegations rose to the level of a violation of the standards of conduct."[46] In this instance, Martin ruled, Meese had not violated White House standards of conduct regulations. Furthermore, Martin maintained that the "standards of conduct for the Executive Office of the President" were "aspirational" in nature.[47] In other words, an appearance of a conflict of interest did not automatically result in the violation of the standards of conduct. This statement produced a storm of controversy and led critics to imply that the White House pressured Martin to make such a ruling.

In his January 31, 1985, testimony before the Judiciary Committee, Martin expanded on his interpretation of the section directing officials and employees to avoid even the appearance of impropriety. Martin explained:

This rule is aspirational in nature. That is, we all try to avoid that, creating an appearance, but as we know in the public sector, that is often difficult to do. Our attitude is, when there is an appearance problem, that the persons involved have done no wrong, have committed no improprieties, and are presumed to have acted ethically. It is an appearance only. However, the job of the Agency ethics official, and those of my staff, is to determine whether or not there is any substance or reality to the appearance.[48]

The Martin interpretation was almost immediately criticized as undercutting the ability of agencies and departments to punish officials and employees for violating their standards of conduct. A leak to the press which claimed Ethics Office lawyers had initially believed Meese had violated standards of conduct regulations added fuel to the fire.[49]

Throughout the controversy during the first half of 1985, Director Martin maintained that legitimate fairness issues existed regarding the application of impropriety standards to federal employees and officials. Simply stated, the standard was so vague that the reasonable public servant had no idea what type of conduct was permissible or impermissible.

In a letter replying to a series of questions from Senator William S. Cohen, David R. Scott, Chief Counsel of the Ethics Office between May 1980 and June 1984, sharply disagreed with Martin's interpretation of the general appearance standard. Scott argued that Section 201(c) "plainly equates an 'appearance of a conflict of interest' with an actual conflict of interest."[50] The violation of either, Scott concluded, could be grounds for disciplinary action, but Scott did not mention any case where the Ethics Office had recommended either to President Carter or to President Reagan disciplinary action based on a violation of the appearance standard.

A subsequent memorandum prepared by the Congressional Research Service of the Library of Congress uncovered a number of cases where agencies and the federal courts had upheld the use of the general appearance standard as grounds for disciplining employees. Again, however, none of these cases involved a Presidential appointee subject to Senate confirmation.[51] The Merit Systems Protection Board also took the position that federal agencies had broad authority to discipline federal employees for conduct that weakened public confidence in the integrity of the federal work force.[52]

Criticism of the Ethics Office continued in April 1985 when the Senate subcommittee on Oversight of Government Management conducted oversight hearings. Again Martin received little support for his position. For instance, the first director of the office, Bernhardt K. Wruble, argued that the "appearance" standard should not be regarded as "aspirational" just because "we find it difficult to enforce in some circumstances." Instead of abandoning the standard, argued Wruble, "we should strengthen it by giving it more concreteness and content.[53] Ann McBride, senior vice president of Common Cause, argued that the Martin interpretation would make ethics enforcement virtually impossible and would be an "open invitation for increased conflicts of interest throughout the government."[54] Through the summer of 1985, the Ethics Office worked on a revisison of the Executive Order to address the concerns of Director Martin. But, no revision of the Order was forthcoming from the White House.[55]

The Meese controversy focused attention on the fact that the Ethics office had refused to publicly criticize high-level officials for conduct that violated or appeared to violate standards of conduct regulations.

Even though the management of agency ethics programs had improved significantly since the 1970s, management problems still remained. A November 1984 Common Cause report entitled *Bureaucratic Orphans: The Administration of Government Ethics Programs as Viewed by Agency Ethics Officials*, was based on survey responses of some fifty designated agency ethics officials and concluded that, although management had improved since the

1970s, serious problems remained. The report argued that the quality of agency programs varied greatly, that too many ethics officers believed their responsibilities were limited to the review of financial disclosure statements, that too little time was spent on ethics training and education, and that ethics officers had low visibility within their organizations.

The survey also uncovered some frustration on the part of designated agency ethics officials with the way Justice handled their referrals. Some of those who responded wanted the Office of Government Ethics to use its influence to persuade Justice to prosecute more officials and former officials under 18 U.S.C. 203–209.

By the close of 1985, the credibility of the Ethics Office had been seriously damaged. However, the criticism did not do much to remodel a system that produced large numbers of allegations of impropriety which rarely resulted in clear decisions of guilt or innocence.

ETHICS AND THE MILITARY INDUSTRIAL COMPLEX

Throughout Reagan's first term, critics of the great increase in military expenditures maintained that much of the money was being wasted because of illegal conduct by defense contractors and poor procurement management by the Department of Defense (DOD). Reports of alleged overcharging by defense contractors and other allegations of misconduct seriously threatened the Reagan buildup program. Again critics pointed to the revolving door as one of the major reasons for poor government supervision of defense contractors, and calls to prohibit certain defense department personnel from taking positions with defense contractors reappeared.

In her July 1985 testimony before the Senate Governmental Affairs Committee, Ann McBride of Common Cause supported such a ban on the grounds that "the problem is not only what people do after they leave government, but what they do while in government in expectation of future employment."[56] McBride reported that in 1983 alone, 2,100 people left DOD "for jobs with defense contractors or moved from jobs with contractors to DOD employment."[57]

In July 1985, President Reagan established a Blue Ribbon Commission on Defense Management to conduct a comprehensive review of all aspects of defense management.[58] At the same time, the Department of Defense and the Justice Department instituted a new program to vigorously prosecute instances of waste, fraud, and abuse in defense procurement.

Symbolic of this new initiative was the indictment, in November 1985, of former Navy Assistant Secretary George A. Sawyer for violating the negotiating-for-employment prohibition of 18 U.S.C. 208. The Justice Department accused Sawyer of negotiating for employment with General Dynamics Corporation at the same time that he had responsibility for Navy shipbuilding contracts.[59] On December 17, 1985, a Federal District Court found Sawyer not guilty.[60] During the same period, Mary Ann Gilleece, the Defense Department's deputy undersecretary for procurement, came under investigation for writing letters to twenty-eight defense contractors to seek clients for a consulting firm she planned to start once she left the government. Gilleece resigned her position on August 20, 1985.[61]

On November 8, 1985, Congress passed the Defense Procurement Improvement Act, which included a provision prohibiting "presidential appointee in federal employment, who acts as a primary negotiator for government contracts," from accepting employment with the contractor with whom he is involved for two years after the involvement ends. Congress understood that the new prohibition would apply to only a handful of Defense Department officials.[62]

In June 1986, President Reagan's Blue Ribbon Commission on Defense Management submitted its final report, *A Quest for Excellence*. Besides recommending sweeping procurement reforms and strict enforcement of existing criminal prohibitions, the commission urged the Department of Defense to devote much more attention to ethics education and enforcement. However, the majority of commission members rejected calls for a new general prohibition on defense department personnel taking positions with defense contractors. One member of the commission, Herbert Stein, argued that Congress should enact a new general prohibition applicable to personnel involved in the acquisition process.[63]

Early in 1987, Congress enacted a sweeping prohibition to prevent Defense Department personnel engaged in procurement activities from taking positions with defense contractors for a two-year period after leaving the federal government. These new restrictions apply to thousands of Defense Department procurement officials.[64]

THE DEBATE JOINED AGAIN: PRESIDENTIAL RECRUITMENT AND ETHICS MANAGEMENT

In February 1984, John Macy, coming out of retirement to work on the National Academy of Public Administration's Presidential Appointee Project, urged candidates for the presidency to tell the country how they planned to select some 3,000 people for top federal policy-making positions. Macy reported that a survey of White House personnel chiefs from the Truman through the Reagan administrations found that most had resorted to "bogsat" ("a bunch of guys sitting around a table") to identify possible nominees.[65] Each time, the "bunch of guys" turned out to be close friends of the president-elect.

Macy argued that this ad hoc method of identifying talent made it extremely difficult for a president to staff his administration. Equally important, Macy argued that in order to increase the pool of qualified individuals willing to serve, Congress needed to "make it easier for able individuals to accept the sacrifices necessary to leave comfortable private life for public service."[66] Congress could help by:

1. severing the link between executive and congressional salaries;
2. simplifying the unnecessarily confusing and restrictive blind-trust laws; and
3. requiring less, not more detailed financial data on disclosure statements.[67]

In November 1985, the Presidential Appointee Project of the National Academy of Public Administration issued its final report, *Leadership in Jeopardy: The Fraying of the Presidential Appointment System*. The report concluded that presidents were finding it increasingly difficult to recruit "the best and the brightest" and that turnover had gone from bad to worse. The report found that besides inadequate compensation and the unwillingness of many to interrupt family and careers, the conflict of interest regulations had been "costly to the relations between the news media and public officials, and costly in financial sacrifices to a number of honest and dedicated public officials."[68]

The report recommended a major reduction in the reporting requirements in order to reduce the complexity of public disclosure requirements. Second, it recommended enacting legislation "permitting presidential appointees to delay the impact of capital gains taxes" which resulted from appointees having to divest themselves of holdings in order to comply with conflict of interest rules and regulations.[69] Third, it recommended prohibiting appointees from discussing future employment with the private sector, but would also offer appointees demonstrating a "genuine financial need up to three months of severance pay to afford them a period of transition out of the federal government."[70]

Another publication of the Presidential Appointee Project, *The Presidential Appointee's Handbook*, provides a step-by-step description of the clearance and confirmation processes for presidential nominees. Prepared with the assistance of the White House Counsel's Office and the Office of Government Ethics, the handbook explains internal White House clearance procedures, public financial disclosure requirements, and the workings of the criminal conflict of interest prohibitions. However, the handbook makes no specific mention of Executive Order 11222 or of the agency standards of conduct.

The handbook simply states that "in practice . . . public officials are wise to avoid participation in matters in which they may appear to have a conflict of interest even if they believe it likely that their participation incurs no technical violation of conflict of interest laws."[71] A nominee reading this passage would have little idea that Executive Order 11222 requires all officials to avoid even the appearance of a conflict of interest.

In spite of the allegations of official misconduct related to conflicts of interest, a significant body of opinion during the Reagan second term still

views conflict of interest regulation as a major obstacle to executive recruitment.

A CRISIS IN PUBLIC SERVICE ETHICS

Early in April 1986, allegations appeared stating that Michael Deaver,
former White House official and close friend of President Reagan, may have
violated postgovernment service lobbying restrictions by contacting the
White House on the behalf of some of his clients. Deaver denied any improper or illegal conduct, and President Reagan publicly defended his former
aide.[72]

In early May 1986, however, the General Accounting Office notified the
Department of Justice that its investigation had determined that Deaver
might have violated criminal postemployment prohibitions. The Office of
Government Ethics subsequently notified the Justice Department of a similar
finding.[73] Acting on a request by Attorney General Meese, on May 30,
1986, a special federal court named ex-United States attorney Whitney
North Seymour as independent counsel to investigate the allegations made
against Deaver.[74] After a ten-month investigation, on March 18, 1987,
Michael Deaver was indicted for five counts of perjury involving his testimony before a House subcommittee and a grand jury. Deaver was not
indicted for a substantive violation of any conflict of interest law.[75] Deaver
failed to get the federal courts to block the indictment on the grounds that
the special prosecutor or independent counsel law was unconstitutional
under the separation-of-powers doctrine.

The Deaver affair revived media and public interest in the public integrity
issue. Haynes Johnson, in a May 14, 1986, *Washington Post* editorial, saw
the Deaver case as symbolic of sinking "standards that govern public service
here in the era of privatization."[76] However, Johnson argued against a rush
to pass new and tighter regulations. "The solution," argued Johnson, "is
simply to observe the letter and the spirit of existing laws and codes and
rigorously enforce them."[77] He sharply criticized the Office of Government
Ethics for not publicly challenging the conduct of top officials.

Finally, Johnson blamed President Reagan for helping to create an "officially sanctioned air of indifference to all questions of ethical conduct and
impropriety"[78] by dismissing most allegations as not justified by the facts.
In sum, Johnson maintained that a president must require his appointees
not only to comply with the letter of the law, but also to avoid any appearance of using public service as a way to increase private business opportunities.

If the Deaver controversy was not enough, on February 3, 1987, after a
formal request by Attorney General Meese, a special three-judge federal
court appointed Washington attorney James C. McKay as independent
counsel to investigate former White House aide Lyn Nofzinger's lobbying

activities after he left the White House in 1982,[79] specifically, lobbying on behalf of Wedtech Corp., a Bronx-based defense contractor.

Then, in early May of 1987, reports appeared alleging that while Edwin Meese, III served as counselor to the president in 1982, he was asked to intervene on behalf of Wedtech in order to assist in overcoming Army resistance to awarding the company defense contracts. A subsequent Justice Department investigation led to James C. McKay's being given authority to investigate whether the attorney general might have violated federal law.[80]

Various explanations have been made to explain why so many Reagan officials have been implicated in official wrongdoing. Defenders of the record of the administration maintain that the 1978 Ethics Act changed the rules and clearance procedures so that it became much more likely for appearance problems to make the national headlines. They maintain that the problem is not that more Reagan appointees are prone to unethical behavior, but that the system has changed to permit greater public scrutiny of the conduct of high-level officials.

Critics of the Reagan record maintain that because the president has steadfastly refused to criticize the conduct of any of his appointees, he has effectively accepted lower standards of conduct on their behalf. In other words, as long as appointees do not violate criminal law, the president will not criticize them or publicly ask for their resignation.

Regardless of the outcome of the various criminal investigations involving Reagan officials, the Reagan years have thrown into question the entire system for regulating conflicts of interest. There is little question that the "sleaze" factor will emerge as an issue in the 1988 presidential campaign. The problem remains whether the "sleaze" debate will result in a constructive review of a system that clearly does not work or will continue to encourage partisan charges and countercharges.

NOTES

1. "Countdown to the White House: The Reagan Transition," Public Broadcasting Service, Wednesday, January 21, 1981.

2. Dick Kirsheten, "Wanted: 275 Reagan Team Players, Empire Builders Need Not Apply," *National Journal*, December 6, 1980, p. 2077; Hedrick Smith, "Reagan Is Behind Schedule On Cabinet," *New York Times*, Saturday, December 6, 1980, p. 20.

3. Interview, Robert Flynn, Director of the Agency Relations Unit, Office of Government Ethics, Washington, D.C., January 1981.

4. Edward T. Pound, "Reagan Team Screens Nominees to Avoid Surprise," *New York Times*, December 8, 1986, pp. iv, 10.

5. Peter Behr and T. R. Reid, "Merrill Lynch's Regan Becomes Added Starter for Treasury Post," *Washington Post*, December 5, 1980, p. A4.

6. Hedrick Smith, "Reagan Administration Pressing for Fast Start on 4-Year Course," *New York Times*, January 23, 1981, p. A15.

7. National Academy of Public Administration, *Leadership in Jeopardy: The Fraying of the Presidential Appointments System*: The Final Report of the Presidential Appointee Project, November 1985, p. 11.

8. Ibid., p. 8.

9. 5 C.F.R. 604(c), expedited procedure in the case of individuals appointed by the president and subject to confirmation by the Senate.

10. National Academy of Public Administration, p. 13.

11. 5 C.F.R. 734.401, Qualified Blind and Diversified Trusts.

12. Bob Woodward, "Payments Like Smith's Disapproved in Past," *Washington Post*, May 20, 1982, p. A6.

13. David S. Broder, "A Conservatism of Convenience," *Washington Post*, May 19, 1982, p. A23.

14. Richard Cohen, "Propriety," May 18, 1982, p. B1.

15. Joseph Kraft, "A Matter of Attitude," *Washington Post*, May 20, 1982, p. 31.

16. *Washington Post*, November 14, 1981, sec. I, p. 4.

17. John Herbers, "Is Post-Watergate Government Morality Slipping?" *New York Times*, March 29, 1983, p. I18.

18. Stuart Taylor, "The Trials of a Top-Level Appointee," *New York Times*, June 16, 1983, sec. II, p. 12.

19. Ibid.

20. *Washington Post*, April 27, 1986, p. A12.

21. Caryle Murphy, "U.S. Sues Boeing Co. Over Severance Pay," *Washington Post*, July 23, 1986, p. A7.

22. *Washington Post*, August 22, 1986, p. C9; see also *Washington Post*, February 18, 1987, p. F30.

23. *Center For Auto Safety* v. *Federal Trade Commission*, 586 F. Supp., p. 1245 (1984).

24. *Consultant Reform and Disclosure Act of 1981*, Hearing, 97th Cong., 1st Sess. on S. 719, Sept. 18, 1981 (Washington, D.C.: U.S. Government Printing Office), Subcommittee on Federal Expenditure, Research and Rules, Committee on Governmental Affairs.

25. *Washington Post*, July 22, 1982, p. A14.

26. *Washington Post*, December 11, 1982, p. A4.

27. *President's Private Sector Survey on Cost Control*, report of the General Accounting Office and hearing, 97th Congress, 2d Sess., Sept. 15 and 21, 1982 (Washington, D.C.: G.P.O., 1982); Robert M. Cohen, "Reagan's Cost Control 'Bloodhounds' Are Hounded by Charges of Conflicts," *National Journal*, January 15, 1983, pp. 122–24.

28. *Washington Post*, April 27, 1986, p. A12.

29. *Washington Post*, November 3, 1983, p. A19.

30. *Washington Post*, July 16, 1983, p. A9.

31. *Washington Post*, July 26, 1983, p. A2.

32. Philip Shabecoff, "Dismissed Official Faults E.P.A. Chief," *New York Times*, February 24, 1983, p. B14.

33. *Washington Post*, July 26, 1986, p. A2.

34. Executive Order 11222; Prescribing Standards of Ethical Conduct for Government Employees, Section 204, p. 2.

35. *Washington Post*, July 26, 1986, p. A2.

36. *See Washington Post*, January 12, 1986, p. A3; January 22, 1986, p. A2; January 29, 1986, p. A2; July 8, 1986, p. A1; July 18, 1986, p. A11.

37. *Washington Post*, April 30, 1986, p. A16; *Washington Post*, July 29, 1986, p. A3.

38. *National Journal*, January 14, 1984, pp. A92–93.

39. *New York Times*, February 3, 1984, sec. I, p. 14.

40. *New York Times*, July 4, 1984, sec. I, p. 11.

41. *New York Times*, May 29, 1984, p. A19.

42. Public Law 97–409.

43. *Washington Post*, March 28, 1984, p. A1.

44. *Report of Independent Counsel Concerning Edwin Meese III*, before Senior Circuit Judge Robb, Washington, D.C., Division for the Purpose of Appointing Independent Counsels, U.S. Court of Appeals for the District of Columbia, Circuit. Also see *Washington Post*, September 21, 1984, p. A1.

45. Common Cause, *The Case againt Edwin Meese III for Attorney General: A Review of the Independent Counsel's Report*, Washington, D.C.: Common Cause, 1984.

46. Letter, David H. Martin, Director, to Honorable Strom Thurmond, United States Senate, January 28, 1985.

47. From testimony of David H. Martin, Esq., Director, Office of Government Ethics, before the Senate Committee on the Judiciary at the nomination hearings of Edwin Meese III, January 31, 1985, *Oversight of the Office of Government Ethics*, p. 149.

48. *Oversight of the Office of Government Ethics*, Hearing before the Subcommittee on Oversight of Government Management, Committee on Governmental Affairs, 99th Cong., April 24, 1985, p. 149.

49. Ronald Brownstein, "Agency Ethics Officers Fear Meese Ruling Could Weaken Conflict Laws," *National Journal*, March 23, 1985, p. 631.

50. *Oversight of the Office of Government Ethics*, p. 142.

51. Ibid., p. 175.

52. Ronald Brownstein, "Agency Ethics Officers Fear Meese Ruling Could Weaken Conflict Laws," *National Journal*, March 23, 1985, p. 642.

53. *Oversight of the Office of Government Ethics*, p. 49.

54. Ibid., p. 70.

55. This author served as a consultant on the revision of the executive-branch standards of conduct.

56. *Oversight of the Office of Government Ethics*, p. 25.

57. Ibid., pp. 25–26.

58. Executive Order 12526 (July 15, 1985).

59. *Washington Post*, November 1, 1985, p. A1.

60. *Washington Post*, December 18, 1985, p. A1.

61. *Washington Post*, August 20, 1985, p. A5.

62. Public Law 99–145, Title IX, 99 Stat. 682. For Legislative History see 1985 CIS Annual Legislative Histories, Washington, Congressional Information Service.

63. The President's Blue Ribbon Commission on Defense Management, *A Quest for Excellence: Final Report to the President* (Washington, D.C.: President's Blue Ribbon Commission on Defense Management, June 1986), p. 106.

64. 10 U.S.C. 2397b. *See also* P.C. 99–500, P.C. 99–591, and P.C. 99–661, Title IV of the National Defense Authorization Act for Fiscal Year 1987, 1986, *CISI Index of Legislative Histories* 765.

65. *New York Times*, February 9, 1984, sec. I, p. 31.

66. Ibid.

67. Ibid.

68. National Academy of Public Administration, *Leadership in Jeopardy: The Fraying of the Presidential Appointment System*: Final Report of the Presidential Appointee Project (Washington, D.C.: November 1985), p. 13.

69. Ibid., p. 15.

70. Ibid., p. 16.

71. The Presidential Appointee Project of the National Academy of Public Administration, *The Presidential Appointee's Handbook*, Washington: National Academy of Public Administration, 1985, p. 17.

72. *Washington Post*, April 1, 1986, p. A1: *Washington Post*, April 10, 1986, p. A34.

73. *Washington Post*, May 10, 1986, p. A1.

74. *Washington Post*, May 30, 1986, p. A1.

75. *Washington Post*, March 19, 1986, p. A1.

76. "Private Trust, Public Trust," *Washington Post*, May 14, 1986, p. A2.

77. Ibid., p. A2.

78. Ibid.

79. *Washington Post*, February 3, 1987, p. A5.

80. George Lardner, Jr. and Mary Thorton, "Biaggi, Others Are Said To Face Indictment Today: Latest Criminal Case in Wedtech Affair," *Washington Post*, June 3, 1987, p. A3.

X

Epilogue

As in earlier administrations, during the Reagan Administration, the issue of public service ethics has become the focus of the news media, political candidates, and a concerned citizenry. A perjury case involving Michael Deaver, President Reagan's former chief of staff; a criminal lobbying case involving Lyn Nofziger, a former top political aide; questions about financial compliance by Attorney General Edwin Meese; and the whole business of the Iran-Contra affair, where profits from sales of arms to the Iranians were used to support Nicaraguan rebels, have fueled a debate over ethics that began before the Civil War.

Because Americans are more comfortable ignoring history, we respond to the scandals of each administration with a sense of outrage and a demand for action. However, before we begin agitating for quick remedies for deep-seated ills, it might be wiser to look at the present in the broader context of the past. The purpose of this study has been to trace the history of the complex system for dealing with conflict of interest in the executive branch as a basis for understanding the present and anticipating the future.

The issue of ethics in government today is not drastically different from what it was in earlier administrations. However, the picture of former high-level federal officials turning to lobbying for a ready source of income, and other questionable forms of official conduct, have increased public cynicism over the ability of American society to keep government clean.

Without the risk of making a premature historical judgment, I can make these generalizations. First, during the Reagan Administration, political polarization over the issue of integrity in government has sharpened. Liberals continue to attack the president for letting private-interest groups set government policy and dictate the operation of key programs. On the other hand, conservatives continue to denounce provisions of the ethics law as intentionally designed to embarrass presidential appointees who came into government to implement the Reagan revolution. Such polarization will make it difficult to build a consensus on how to maintain integrity in the public service.

Second, extended media exposure and private-life muckraking have cooled the enthusiasm of many prospective government servants. The sleaze factor will make it more difficult to recruit top-flight executive talent for policy-making positions in presidential administrations. The cost of national public service in the fishbowl atmosphere of Washington, D.C., may be too high for sought-after candidates and their families.

Third, the integrity problems of the Reagan years will surely promote a prolonged debate over where we go from here in the management of government ethics.

THE POLITICS OF INTEGRITY

The May 25, 1987, edition of *Time Magazine* pointed to the misconduct allegations leveled against more than one hundred high-level Reagan officials as evidence that the administration had apparently "suffered a breakdown of the immune system [and opened] the way to all kinds of ethical and moral infections."[1] The article made the point that almost every one of the Reagan officials implicated in wrongdoing maintained that they had done nothing illegal or unethical.

On December 17, 1987, a federal grand jury found Michael Deaver guilty of three counts of perjury regarding his lobbying activities after leaving the Reagan White House.[2] A day after the verdict, independent counsel Whitney North Seymour publicly lashed out against "to much 'loose money' " in Washington and about too little concern about ethics in government."[3] Seymour declared that the Ethics in Government Act had done little to limit behind-the-scenes lobbying by former high-level officials because it contained too many loopholes. Almost eight years after the passage of the 1978 Ethics Act, the Deaver conviction is the first jury conviction obtained by an independent counsel appointed to investigate allegations of criminal conduct by senior government officials.

Still, confusion over ethics regulations persists. On December 15, 1987, Ronald Reagan signed the independent counsel reauthorization into law despite his "very strong doubts about its constitutionality."[4] President Reagan argued that his veto of the law would have eroded public confidence in government. As the Reagan presidency draws to a close, the country seems no closer to solving the problems of conflicts of interest in government than it was when Congress enacted the Ethics in Government Act.

From the beginning of the Reagan Administration, the White House and Reagan nominees and appointees have taken a legalistic view of conflict of interest regulation and public service ethics. Despite the fact that Executive Order 11222 directed both political appointees and career officials to avoid even the appearance of impropriety, the Reagan White House has refused to publicly criticize a presidential appointee for violating the order. Since the media and most members of Congress know very little about the scope of the order, the strategy of simply ignoring it has worked throughout most of the Reagan Administration. Only possible violations of criminal law have warranted close administration attention.

The Reagan Administration has viewed the Ethics in Government Act of 1978 as liberal legislation designed to make it difficult for a conservative Republican president to recruit and retain supporters to lobby for and implement his programs. However, the Reagan White House soon realized that Congress would not repeal any provisions of the Ethics Act and that a significant watering down of Executive Order 11222 could reinforce the charge that the administration did not care about integrity in government. The sleaze factor, the administration maintains, is a political issue, and has nothing to do with the types of individuals recruited or the quality of leadership by the president. The Reagan White House has taken a position remarkably similar to that of the Eisenhower White House when it was confronted with charges of impropriety which had been leveled against many of its officials.

Critics of the Reagan Administration typically explain this attitude toward public service ethics as the result of overconfidence brought about by two landslide election victories and the recruitment of key officials with a disdain for government. However, this explanation is too simplistic when one looks at the evolution of conflict of interest regulation. The debate centers on sharp differences of opinion on how to keep both elected and nonelected officials accountable to the electorate as discretionary government increases. It reflects wide differences on the legislative and administrative steps Congress and a president should take to safeguard against even the appearance of financial interest in decision making.

Since the end of the Second World War, liberals have generally argued that, with the emphasis on the accumulation of wealth in our society, Congress and the president must take a strong stand to let appointed and career officials and employees know that personal financial interests must not play a role in any official action. Conservatives, on the other hand, argue that ethical rules and regulations can go only so far before they deter those individuals needed to make government run efficiently and effectively. Liberals, the conservatives argue, have pushed morality for political purposes rather than for better ethics in government.

In early 1985, during Senate confirmation proceedings, attorney general designate Edwin Meese pledged "to avoid any circumstance that could be misunderstood or misconstrued in any way," including taking "extraordinary steps in terms of [his] financial affairs." By the spring of 1987, the attorney general came under strong criticism for apparently failing to live up to his promise.

On April 30, 1987, Senator Carl Levin, Democrat from Michigan, asked David Martin, the director of the Office of Government Ethics, to investigate the failure of the attorney general to list on his annual financial disclosure statements transactions related to the management of a "limited blind partnership" Meese and his wife had entered into in May of 1985. The partnership drew national attention because it was managed by San Francisco businessman and former Wedtech Corp. official W. Franklin Chinn. On an initial investment of $50,662, Meese and his wife earned $35,000 over a two-year period.[5]

The attorney general's financial disclosure statement reported the investment as managed by Financial Management, Inc. (a limited blind partnership) and also accurately reported income from the partnership. The Office of Government Ethics had not approved the partnership as a blind trust, however. Without approval of the Ethics Office, the financial interests acquired by the partnership were the financial interests of the attorney general even though he had no knowledge of the investments made by Mr. Chinn. This meant that federal law prohibited Meese from taking action with respect to any matter involving any of the investments made by the blind partnership. Although a subsequent disclosure by the attorney general revealed that none of the transactions involved a matter dealt with him personally, critics of Meese maintained that he had violated the Ethics Act.[6]

On May 11, 1987, David H. Martin, the director of the Office of Government Ethics, informed Senator Levin that the Ethics Office had not approved the limited blind partnership as a blind trust, and that the law prohibited such an arrangement from obtaining approval. In early July 1987, when Senator Levin released this letter, the attorney general placed the blame for the confusion on the Office of Government Ethics because of its failure to notify him that the partnership did not qualify as a blind trust.[7] Fred Wertheimer, president of Common Cause, laid the blame on the attorney general on the grounds that the attorney general, if anyone, should know what the law regulates.[8] Wertheimer also urged appropriate government officials "to determine what sanctions should be imposed for Mr. Meese's violations."[9]

A persistent critic of the Reagan Administration's record on integrity and the management of the Office of Government Ethics, Senator Levin held a hearing on July 9, 1987 to investigate the attorney general's blind partnership arrangement. Senator Levin sharply criticized the Office of Government Ethics for not questioning the blind partnership arrangement, and criticized Mr. Meese for not realizing that the Ethics Act did not permit the "blinding" of such an arrangement without Ethics Office approval. The attorney general continued to maintain that he had not realized his error. After the hearing, Meese accused Senator Levin of engaging in partisan politics by attempting to portray the blind partnership arrangement as an effort to conceal dealings with a former Wedtech official.

David Martin resigned his position as director of the Office of Government Ethics in late August 1987, to go into private law practice.[10]

Public Service and Life Beyond the Beltway

Following the Second World War, debate over conflict of interest and other integrity issues has complicated recruitment for high-level political and career government positions. Publicity surrounding the problems of Reagan Administration officials will make it more difficult for future presidents to convince the country's executive talent to make the sacrifices associated with high-level federal service. Future presidents may then have to rely heavily on the increasing ranks of policy experts and consultants already living and working in the Washington, D.C., metropolitan area. These professionals typically have few relocation costs and tend to have a higher tolerance for the restrictions placed on their public and private conduct. However, increased reliance on the bureaucracy-in-waiting would have significant drawbacks: It would lessen the input of individuals who are not part of the Washington establishment and who might have a better understanding of the problems of the country as a whole. Significantly, the relationship between conflict of interest regulation and executive recruitment involves the problem of diversity of appointments rather than the problem of unfilled positions.

During the early 1950s, Senator Paul Douglas came to recognize that the modern administrative state multiplied opportunities for conflicts of interest on the part of nonelected government officials. More important, he also recognized that in an era of increased discretionary government, the success or failure of a policy or program often hinged on whether the legislative branch, the media, and the American public trusted the individual official responsible for advocating or implementing the policy. A major consequence of discretionary government had to be greater concern with the ethical behavior of public officials.

The importance of trust in public officials, as Senator Douglas observed, was illustrated during the recent Iran-Contra hearings. Before the majority of the American public accepted the explanation of Oliver North for his participation in the arm sales to Iran and in the diversion of profits to the Nicaraguan Contras, Colonel North had to explain why he had used travelers checks purchased with Contra funds for personal purposes and why he had accepted a security system from a private source when regulations prohibited the acceptance of gifts from individuals having dealings with the United States Government. North explained that he had used the travelers checks to reimburse himself for out-of-pocket expenses related to aiding the Contras, and that he had accepted the security system because of the government's refusal to protect his family after terrorist threats. Oliver North, in other words, had to convince Americans that he had not gained personally from his activities.

High-level presidential appointments often underestimate the effect of minor appearance problems on the credibility of an official. Moreover, it is often even more difficult for these officials to understand the need to avoid appearance problems in order to protect the credibility of discretionary decision making. When the Bureau of Internal Revenue scandal erupted during the final years of the Truman Administration, Congress and key Truman advisers realized that, without quick action to clean up the mess, large numbers of taxpayers might write off the tax system as corrupt and further increase the already serious tax evasion problem.

Most government agencies rely on voluntary compliance with the rules and regulations essential to operating government programs. If the public loses trust in its nonelected or elected officials, voluntary compliance with these rules on the part of thousands of federal workers will suffer. To this extent, conflict of interest regulation serves a vital symbolic role: it demonstrates to the public that public service requires officials to remain beyond reproach, not just within the letter of the law.

However, conflict of interest regulation should not be used to exclude competent people from entering government on the claim of bias or predisposition. As explained by J. Jackson Walter, the director of the Office of Government Ethics from 1979 to 1983, "Whether [one's] previous career will permit objective and impartial performance in government office is a decision to be made in the first instance by the president, who is the appointing authority, and subsequently by the Senate, which is the confirming body."[11]

Moving into the Glass House

Since the early 1960s, the White House counsel's office has spent increasingly large amounts of time reviewing the backgrounds of nominees and appointees for conflict of interest problems and negotiating solutions. With the passage of the Ethics in Government Act in 1978, the Office of Government Ethics assumed an important clearance responsibility, but for reasons of time and policy, the emphasis on public trust and decision making has varied from one administration to the next. Many officials come to view the complex conflict of interest regulations as potential land mines hindering their ability to do their jobs, and work under the constant fear that they might unintentionally violate some regulation and find themselves on the front page of the *Washington Post* for an alleged violation.

While not stating it publicly, many political appointees believe that the appearance standard creates too much pressure and opens them to unjustified partisan attacks. To avoid an appearance of a conflict of interest, they are forced to examine and possibly alter all types of relationships they have developed over a lifetime. In brief, conflict of interest regulation lacks the institutional support of many officials responsible for setting the ethical tone of their government organizations.

During the Kennedy and Johnson administrations, John Macy worked to build the administrative ethics program in the belief that it would eliminate much of the confusion surrounding conflict of interest rules and regulations. Over time, he hoped, both career and political officials would come to rely on their designated agency ethics officials to guide them around potential problems. With detailed agency standards of conduct, he believed, employees and officials would know what was permitted and what was not. Clarifying the rules would remove one of the objections to entering government service. However, Macy greatly underestimated the organizational resistance to making ethics management a high-priority item.

Bipartisanship and Public Service Ethics

Republican Administrations, the record shows, have regarded conflict of interest regulations as more burdensome on Republican appointees than on their Democratic counterparts. The Eisenhower, Nixon, and Reagan administrations actively recruited large numbers of individuals from business and industry on the theory that only executives who had to meet a payroll would have a good grasp of running an organization efficiently. In contrast, Democratic presidents Truman, Kennedy, Johnson, and Carter relied much more heavily on federal career officials, state and local officials, and university faculty to fill key positions. The media thus judge a new Republican administration in terms of how many successful private-sector supporters accept top positions. A Democratic president is not expected to recruit many corporate leaders to direct federal programs.

Republican administrations, consequently, expect liberals to challenge their appointees on the grounds that private-sector businessmen will use their positions to help their former employers or industries to gain special treatment. Democratic administrations, in contrast, expect conservatives to challenge Democratic appointees on the grounds that they will use their positions to impose stronger government regulation of business and industry. These opposing methods of staffing executive federal positions are reflected in attitudes about conflict of interest regulation. With the exception of Harry Truman, every post–Second World War Democratic president has strongly endorsed tighter conflict of interest regulations. In contrast, few Republican administrations have taken any conflict of interest initiatives.

Throughout most of this century, Democrats have campaigned on the platform that Republicans use their economic power to get candidates elected and later to tempt nonelected decision makers. Throughout most of this century, Republicans have campaigned on the platform that Democrats can run a government only by taxing and spending, whereas in fact government can be run efficiently only by those with practical business experience. Consequently, the morality-in-government issue, so often used by the Democrats, is to the Republicans a red herring to divert attention from the real issue—efficiency in government.

If conflict of interest regulation is ever going to be effective, it must be divorced from partisan politics. Until a consensus on conflict of interest policy is reached, these disputes will continue to hamper presidential administrations and to further polarize views on the usefulness of conflict of interest regulations. Until that consensus includes both criminal and noncriminal regulations and makes a legitimate effort to reduce the burden of conflict of interest regulations on executive recruitment, the issue of ethics in government will remain unresolved.

A NATIONAL COMMISSION ON PUBLIC INTEGRITY

Congress and President Carter believed that the Ethics in Government Act would restore public confidence in the objectivity of investigations involving allegations of wrongdoing on the part of high-level government officials. It has not done so. Because of lack of trust in the impartiality of the Department of Justice, the Office of Government Ethics, and investigations by individual agencies and departments, almost every allegation of impropriety results in a call for the appointment of an independent counsel. The Ethics Act, however, prohibits the attorney general from asking a special federal court to appoint an independent counsel unless there is reason to believe that an official has violated a criminal law. As noted, however, many abuses of public office do not involve criminal wrongdoing. The Ethics Act did not solve the credibility crisis because noncriminal conduct damages public trust as much as criminal conduct.

What steps can be taken? The suggestion made in December of 1960 by Professor Abram Chayes is worth reconsidering. Professor Chayes urged President-elect Kennedy to appoint a "panel of well-known legal figures outside the government" to review the financial affairs of appointees and nominees for potential conflict of interest problems. Chayes believed that an outside panel would have a great deal more credibility than an internal White House review. However, the Kennedy White House decided to keep conflict of interest reviews within the walls of the White House.

After almost thirty years, perhaps the time has come to build on the recommendations of Professor Chayes by considering the establishment of an entirely independent National Commission on Public Integrity to take over authority for conflict of interest clearance activities and to take responsibility for investigating all forms of alleged misconduct by high-level executive-branch officials. This commission could take over the public integrity responsibilities of the Department of Justice, the Office of Government Ethics, and the White House Counsel's Office with respect to high-level officials. If a preliminary investigation by the commission revealed possible criminal wrongdoing, the law could require the commission to request the appointment of an independent counsel. At the same time, the law could require the commission to issue public reports on whether the official had violated any other rule or regulation, or acted in any inappropriate manner.

Under the law, the commission could have the authority to pursue disciplinary action against any official found to have violated a law, rule, or regulation. This action might include fines, restitution, demotion, or removal from the federal government.

The Commission and the Presidential Transition

Besides giving this commission broad investigatory and prosecutorial powers, Congress could give it broad authority to help resolve potential conflict of interest problems and ease recruitment. First, to speed up the clearance and confirmation process, Congress could permit the nominees for president to submit the names of possible appointments for preliminary background checks. At the request of the nominee, the commission could have the authority to work with possible nominees on transition-related problems.

After the election, and prior to sending the name of a nominee to Congress, federal law could require the nominee to enter into a contract with the commission detailing steps taken or steps that the nominee will take to deal with actual or apparent conflict of interest problems. In return for a candidate taking these steps, the commission could have the authority to provide supplemental transition assistance. For instance, because of the extremely high cost of housing in the metropolitan Washington, D.C., area the commission could have the authority to grant very low-interest mortgate loans up to a specified amount. Officials would have to repay the loan when they left the designated position or the federal government.

Current federal law, as noted, does not generally require the divestiture of financial interests. It does require the official not to take action on a matter that might affect a financial interest of the official or the official's family. Congress should amend federal law to sharply limit the use of disqualification agreements as a remedy for potential conflict of interest problems. In return, Congress should give the commission the authority to grant capital-gains tax exemptions for individuals directed to divest themselves of certain financial interests.

To assure that each designated nominee or appointee avoids conflict of interest and other misconduct problems during his or her period of service, the commission could assign a staff member to act as the official's designated ethics officer. On a periodic basis, the commission ethics officers could hold orientation sessions with nominees and appointees to assure that no confusion existed regarding the application of appropriate rules and regulations. Federal law could also require nominees or appointees to contact their ethics officers prior to negotiating for employment with any entity outside the federal government.

Finally, the commission could have the authority to grant severance payments, not to exceed one year's salary, to those officials who agreed not to lobby any federal agency or department regarding any matter for a period of four years after leaving government service.

To guarantee the independence of the commission, the president could nominate five individuals to lifetime terms. Confirmed by the Senate, commission members could have the authority to hire and fire all staff necessary to accomplish its mission. Moreover, the law could appropriate funds for the operation of the commission on a ten-year basis.

A National Commission on Public Integrity is one approach to a problem of long concern. Unfortunately, the likelihood of Congress and a president approving such a commission is slight. Few presidents want to place in the hands of an independent commission the power to review the qualifications of high-level appointees. The Department of Justice would vigorously oppose the concept of placing criminal conduct issues under the jurisdiction of the commission, just as it historically has opposed the appointment of an independent counsel as reflecting badly on the objectivity of the Justice Department. Other groups would strongly oppose any move to supplement the salaries of high-level officials or grant them tax exemptions on the grounds that they already receive high enough salaries and should be willing to sacrifice to serve their country.

Since such a commission would certainly grow to have tremendous power and influence, there is always the risk of centralizing this type of authority. If anything has been learned from the history of the evolution of conflict of interest regulation, no way has yet been found to resolve controversies over the integrity of high-level national officials without automatically making the controversies part of much larger partisan political battles.

Whether such a commission is feasible or desirable may be as arguable today as it was in the 1960s, yet the solution raises a point that needs to be heard. It might put an end to the constant debate over imposing newer and tighter regulations and turn our attention to making existing laws work. In the Deaver lobbying case, for example, Morton Halperin argued in a *New York Times* interview, that "strengthening the law" was not the answer. Unless the government can identify some pattern of harm, he argued, then longer-term and broader restrictions will abridge the First Amendment rights of former officials. They in effect make a condition for government employment a surrendering of First Amendment rights." The point here is that we need a workable mechanism to enforce the law.[12]

Conflict of Interest Regulation and the Politics of Polarization

Throughout American history, public integrity issues have had major political overtones. But the focus on conflicts of interest since the end of the Second World War has profoundly changed the public integrity landscape. While the Reagan revolution slowed the growth of the non-military side of federal government, it did not reduce the power of elected and nonelected federal officials to shape the development and implementation of public policy.

It is the exercise of discretion that creates the opportunity for officials to use their public positions to further their own financial interests. Because so many decisions with national implications are made behind closed doors, the appearance of self-interest can effectively destroy public confidence in the fairness and impartiality of government decision making.

The American public wants to believe that there are individuals who still view public service as a public trust rather than as a road to personal fortune. Sometimes the public expects its public servants to adhere to standards of conduct not demanded of anyone else. Regardless, a significant number of public officials will not be able to live up to the expectations of the American public. When it occurs, this failure to respect the theory of public trust must be dealt with. As yet, no one has come up with a fool-proof method of predicting which public servants will put self interest ahead of public interest.

The challenge is to find a way to enforce high standards and to make our public servants accountable without making every violation of the public trust a partisan issue. An even greater challenge will be to attract to public service qualified individuals, regardless of their positions on the issues of the day and regardless of their backgrounds, who understand the trust that must go with public service.

At a time when America is celebrating the Constitution and honoring its writers, it is fitting to recall the words of James Madison:

It may be a reflection on human nature, that such devices should be necessary to control the abuse of government. But what is government itself, but the greatest of all reflections on human nature? If men were angels, no government would be necessary. If angels were to govern men, neither external nor internal controls on government would be necessary. In framing a government which is to be administered by men over men, the great difficulty lies in this: you must first enable the government to control the governed; and in the next place oblige it to control itself.

The Federalist, No. 51

NOTES

1. *Time* Magazine, May 25, 1987, p. 17.
2. Bill McAllister, "Deaver Found Guilty Of Lying About Lobbying," *Washecington Post*, December 17, 1987, A1.

3. Bill McAllister, "Seymour: 'Loose Money,' Lax Ethics Plague Capital," *Washington Post*, December 18, 1987, Al.

4. George Lardner, "Counsel Act Is Signed By Reagan," *Washington Post*, December 16, 1987, Al.

5. George Lardner Jr., "Meese Financial Partner Hired in 1985 as Wedtech Consultant," *Washington Post*, April 17, 1987, p. A4. A4. *See also* David A. Wise, "Meese Stock Fund Manager Traded Mostly in New Issues Sold In 1 Day," *Washington Post*, July 8, 1987, p. A3.

6. George Lardner, Jr. and Mary Thorton, "Partnership Omitted on '85 List By Meese," *Washington Post*, July 3, 1987, p. A3.

7. Letter to Honorable Carl Levin, Chairman, Subcommittee on Oversight of Government Management, Committee on Governmental Affairs, United States Senate, Washington, May 11, 1987.

8. Common Cause, Letter to the Honorable Carl Levin, July 9, 1987; released at Levin Hearing, Office of Government Ethics, Review of the Attorney General's Financial Disclosure, July 9, 1987.

9. Press Release, Common Cause, July 9, 1987; released at Levin Hearing.

10. Update, "A 'Watch Dog' Bows Out," *Newsweek*, August 31, 1987, A6. Martin announced he would advise state and local governments on how to apply current ethics standards.

11. J. Jackson Walter, "The Ethics in Government Act, Conflict of Interest Laws and Presidential Recruiting," *Public Administration Review*, November–December 1981, p. 663.

12. *New York Times*, August 2, 1987, p. E5.

Selected Bibliography

Adams, Bruce and Kathryn Kavannagh-Baran. *Promises and Performance: Carter Builds a New Administration*. Lexington, Mass.: Lexington Books, 1981.

Association of the Bar of the City of New York. *Conflict of Interest and Federal Service*. Cambridge, Mass.: Harvard University Press, 1960.

Barry, Kevin J. and Richard R. Kelly. "Avoidance of Post-employment Conflicts of Interest for the Federal Employee." *Federal Bar News & Journal* 33 (December 1986): 410–17.

Bernstein, Marver H. *The Job of the Federal Executive*. Washington, D.C.: The Brookings Institution, 1959.

Bertozzi, Mark. "The Federal Special Prosecutor: Too Special?" *Federal Bar News & Journal* 29 (May 1982): 222–30.

Broder, David S. "A Conservatism of Convenience." *Washington Post* (May 19, 1982): A23.

Brownstein, Ronald. "Agency Ethics Officers Fear Meese Ruling Could Weaken Conflict Laws." *National Journal* 17 (March 23, 1985): 639–42.

Brownstein, Ronald, and Nina Easton. *Reagan's Top 100 Officials*. Washington, D.C.: Presidential Accountability Project, 1982.

Carlson, Margaret. "Going Blind for the Public Trust: Is the Price Too High?" *Washington Dossier* 9 (June 1983): 37, 39–42.

Carson, John J. *Executives for Federal Service: A Program for Action in Time of Crisis*. New York: Columbia University, 1952.

Cohen, Francis T. *Federal Employees in War and Peace*. Washington, D.C.: The Brookings Institution, 1949.

Cohen, Richard. "Propriety." *Washington Post*, (May 18, 1982): B1.

Cohen, Robert M. "Reagan's Cost Control 'Bloodhounds' Are Hounded by Charges of Conflicts." *National Journal* (January 15, 1983): 122–24.

Common Cause. *The Senate Rubberstamp Machine: A Common Cause Study of the U.S. Senate's Confirmation Process*. Washington, D.C.: Common Cause, 1977.

————. *Serving Two Masters: A Common Cause Study of Conflicts of Interest in the Executive Branch*. Washington, D.C.: Common Cause, 1977.

————. *Bureaucratic Orphans: The Administration of Government Ethics Programs as Viewed by Agency Ethics Officials*. Washington, D.C.: Common Cause, November 1984.

————. *The Case against Edwin Meese III for Attorney General: a Review of the Independent Counsel's Report*. Washington, D.C.: Common Cause, 1984.

Cooper, Ann. "Carter Signs Government-wide Ethics Bill." *Congressional Quarterly Weekly* (October 28, 1978): 3121–24.

Cowen, Wilson, Philip Nichols, Jr., and Marion T. Bennett. *The United States Court of Claims: A History, Part II*. Washington, D.C.: The Committee on the Bicentennial of the Independence and the Constitution of the Judicial Conference of the United States, 1978.

Cross, Mercer. "Carter's Guidelines: New, Stringent Rules." *Congressional Quarterly Weekly* (January 8, 1977): 52–58.

Cuff, Robert D. *The War Industries Board: Business-Government Relations during World War I*. Baltimore, Md.: Johns Hopkins, 1973.

Cutler, Lloyd N. J. "Conflicts of Interest." *Emory Law Journal* 30 (Fall 1981): 1015–34.

David, Paul T., and Ross Pollack. *Executives for Government: Central Issues of Federal Personnel Administration*. Washington, D.C.: The Brookings Institution, 1957.

Davis, Ross D. "The Federal Conflict of Interest Laws." *Columbia Law Review* 54 (June 1954): 893–915.

Douglas, Paul Howard. *Ethics in Government*. Cambridge, Mass.: Harvard University Press, 1952.

Eisler, Kim I. "Deaver Faces Client Exodus." *Legal Times* 9 (August 18, 1986): 1, 5.

Emmerich, Herbert. "A Scandal in Utopia." *Public Administration Review* 12 (Winter 1952): 1–9.

"Ethics in Washington." *Washington Post* (April 27, 1986): A1, A11–13; (April 28, 1986): A1, A10-A11.

Fitzhugh, Josh. "Money and the Revolving Door." *National Law Journal* 1 (March 19, 1979): 16–17.

Frahm, Christine Mosie. "The Corporate 'Termination Bonus' for Executives Entering Public Service: Proper Government Recruiting or Conflict of Interest?" *Southern California Law Review* 49 (May 1976): 827–79.

Frier, Donald A. *Conflict of Interest in the Eisenhower Administration*. Ames: Iowa State University Press, 1969.

Graham, George A. *Morality in American Politics*. New York: Random House, 1952.

Green, Mark. "Reagan's Regulatory Rule: Don't Just Do Something—Stand There." *Village Voice* 28 (March 15, 1983): 1, 9–11.

Hamby, Alonzo L. *Beyond the New Deal: Harry S Truman and American Liberalism*. New York: Columbia University Press, 1973.

Harris, Joseph P. *The Advice and Consent of the Senate*. Berkeley: University of California, 1953.

Harvard Business School Club of Washington, D.C. *Businessmen in Government: An Appraisal of Experience*. Washington, D.C.: 1959.

Heclo, Hugh. *A Government of Strangers: Executive Politics in Washington.* Washington, D.C.: The Brookings Institution, 1977.

Heller, Francis H., ed. *The Truman White House: The Administration of the Presidency: 1945–1953.* Lawrence, Kans.: The Regents Press of Kansas, 1980.

Herbers, John. "Is Post-Watergate Government Morality Slipping?" *New York Times* (March 29, 1983): A18.

Herring, Edward P. *Public Administration and the Public Interest.* New York: Russell and Russell, 1967.

Hershman, Arlende J. "They Put Their Trust in Blind Trusts." *Dun's Business Month* 119 (May 1982): 42–45, 48–49.

Hoogenboom, Ari. "Did Gilded Age Scandals Bring Reform?" In *Before Watergate*, edited by Ari Hoogenboom, New York: Columbia Univ. Press, 1978.

———, ed. *Before Watergate.* New York: Columbia University Press, 1978.

Huntley, Steve, Kathryn Johnson, and Patricia A. Avery. " 'Revolving Door' Furor." *U.S. News and World Report* (May 12, 1986): 27–29.

Jack, Louis Bernard. "Constitutional Aspects of Financial Disclosure under the Ethics in Government Act." *Catholic University Law Review* 30 (Summer 1981): 583–603.

Jenkins, John A. "The Revolving Door between Government and Law Firms." *Washington Monthly* 8 (January 1977): 36–44.

Johnson, Hayes. "Private Trust, Public Trust." *Washington Post* (May 14, 1986): A2.

Kinsley, Michael. "The Conflict-of-Interest Craze." *Washington Monthly* 10 (November 1978): 39–47.

Kittle, Robert A. "Furor over Pentagon's Revolving Door." *U.S. News and World Report* 98 (April 29, 1985): 27–30.

Kraft, Joseph. "A Matter of Attitude." *Washington Post* (May 20, 1982): 31.

Lankford, John. *Congress and the Foundations in the Twentieth Century.* River, Wisc.: Wisconsin State University Press, 1964.

Lanouttee, William J. "The Revolving Door—It's Tricky To Stop It." *National Journal* 9 (November 1977): 1796–1803.

Loth, David. *Public Plunder: A History of Graft in America.* Westport, Conn.: Greenwood Press, 1966.

Mackenzie, Calvin G. *The Politics of Presidential Appointment.* New York: Free Press, 1980.

Macy, John W., Bruce Adams, and J. Jackson Walter. *America's Unelected Government: Appointing the President's Team.* Cambridge, Mass.: Ballinger, 1983.

Mann, Dean E. *The Assistant Secretaries: Problems and Processes of Appointment.* Washington, D.C.: The Brookings Institution, 1965.

Manning, Bayless. *Federal Conflict of Interest Law.* Cambridge, Mass.: Harvard University Press, 1964.

———. "The Purity Potlatch: An Essay on Conflict of Interest, American Government, and Moral Escalation." *The Federal Bar Journal* 24 (Spring 1964): 239–56.

Monypenny, Philip. "A Code of Ethics as Means of Controlling Administrative Conduct." *Public Administration Review* 13 (Summer 1953): 184–87.

———. "The Control of Ethical Standards in the Public Service." *Annals* 297 (January 1955): 98–104.

Mosher, C. Frederick. *Democracy and the Public Service*. New York: Oxford University Press, 1982.
———. *The GAO: The Quest for Accountability in American Government*. Boulder, Colo.: Westview Press, 1979.
National Academy of Public Administration, Presidential Appointee Project. *Leadership in Jeopardy: The Fraying of the Presidential Appointment System, The Final Report*. Washington, D.C.: The Academy, 1985.
———. *The Presidential Appointee's Handbook*. Washington, D.C.: The Academy, 1985.
Neely, Alfred S. *Ethics-in-Government Laws: Are They too "Ethical"?* Washington, D.C.: American Enterprise Institute for Public Policy Research, 1984.
Newland, Chester A. "Federal Employee Conduct and Financial Disclosure." *Record of the Association of the Bar of the City of New York* 22 (March 1967): 158–80.
Perkins, Roswell B. "The Federal Conflict of Interest Law." *Harvard Law Review* 76 (April 1963): 1113–69.
Phillips, Cabell. *The Truman Presidency*. New York: The Macmillan Company, 1966.
Pound, Edward T. "Reagan Team Screens Nomineees to Avoid Surprise." *New York Times* (December 8, 1980): 10.
President's Blue Ribbon Commission on Defense Management. *A Quest for Excellence: Final Report to the President*. Washington, D.C.: June 1986.
Rapp, David. "Deaver Lobbying Probe Spurs New Legislation." *Congressional Quarterly Weekly Report* 44 (May 17, 1986): 1130–32.
Reagan, Michael. "Serving Two Masters: Problems in the Employment of Dollar-a-Year and Without Compensation Personnel." Ph.D. diss., Princeton University, 1959.
Reich, David. "Ethics." *Civil Service Journal* 16 (January 14, 1984): 92–93.
Richardson, Elmo. *The Presidency of Dwight D. Eisenhower*. Lawrence, Kans.: The Regents Press, 1976.
Riehle, Thomas. "Scandals, Etc. from A to Z." *National Journal* 16 (January 14, 1984): 92–93.
Smith, Hedrick. "Carter Aide Finds Conflict of Interest Rules Hard to Draw." *New York Times* (December 2, 1976): 50.
———. "Reagan Is Behind Schedule On Cabinet." *New York Times* (December 6, 1980): 20.
———. "Reagan Administration Pressing for Fast Start on 4-Year Course." *New York Times* (January 23, 1981): A15.
Solow, Herbert. "Conflicts of Interest: a Legal Nightmare." *Fortune* (January 1961): 97–99.
Stanley, David T., Dean E. Mann, and Jameson W. Doig. *Men Who Govern: A Biographical Profile of Federal Political Executives*. Washington, D.C.: The Brookings Institution, 1967.
Taylor, Stuart. "The Trials of a Top-Level Appointee." *New York Times* (June 16, 1983): II, 12.
Tell, Lawrence J. "Blind Trusts: Meet the Man Who Invests Ronald Reagan's Money." *Barron's* 64 (August 20, 1984): 6, 7, 31–35.
Thompson, Dennis F. "The Possibility of Administrative Ethics." *Public Administration Review* 45 (September-October 1985): 555–61.

Tolchin, Martin. "The Arbiter of Ethics, Perception and Reality." *New York Times* (May 15, 1986): B14.

U.S. General Accounting Office. *Framework for Assessing Job Vulnerability to Ethical Problems*, Washington, D.C.: General Accounting Office, 1981.

U.S. General Accounting Office. *No Strong Indication That Restrictions on Executive Branch Lobbying Should Be Expanded*. Washington, D.C.: General Accounting Office, 1984.

U.S. General Accounting Office. *DOD Revolving Door: Many Former Personnel Not Reporting Defense-Related Employment*. Report to the Chairman, Committee on Governmental Affairs, U.S. Senate, March 1986.

U.S. General Accounting Office. *Guidance on Employee Ethics and Conduct*. Office of General Counsel, U.S. General Accounting Office, Washington, D.C., 1986.

Van Woodward, Comer, ed. *Responses of the Presidents to Charges of Misconduct*. New York: Delacorte Press Company, 1974.

Walter, J. Jackson. "The Ethics in Government Act, Conflict of Interest Laws and Presidential Recruiting." *Public Administration Review* 41 (November-December 1981): 659–65.

White, Leonard D. *The Federalists*. New York: The Free Press, 1965.

———. *The Jacksonians*. New York: The Free Press, 1965.

———. *The Jeffersonians: A Study in Administrative History 1801–1829*. New York: The Free Press, 1965.

———. *The Republican Era: 1869–1901*. New York: The Free Press, 1965.

Wiecek, William M. "The Origin of the United States Court of Claims." *Administrative Law Review* 387 (1967): 330.

Wildavsky, Aaron. *Dixon-Yates: A Study in Power Politics*. Westport, Conn.: Greenwood Press, 1976.

Wise, David. "Why the President's Men Stumble." *New York Times Magazine* (July 18, 1982): 14–17, 44, 46.

Woodward, Bob. "Payments Like Smith's Disapproved in Past." *Washington Post* (May 20, 1982): A6.

Index

About the Author

ROBERT N. ROBERTS is Assistant Professor of Political Science at James Madison University. He has contributed chapters to *Public Personnel Policy* and *Centenary Issues of the Pendleton Act* and articles to *Education for Public Service, Review of Public Personnel Administration,* and *Public Administration Review.*